PITMAN'S
BOOK OF
SYNONYMS AND
ANTONYMS

PITMAN'S
BOOK OF
SYNONYMS AND ANTONYMS

LONDON
SIR ISAAC PITMAN & SONS, LTD.
1937

SIR ISAAC PITMAN & SONS, Ltd.
PITMAN HOUSE, PARKER STREET, KINGSWAY, LONDON, W.C.2
THE PITMAN PRESS, BATH
PITMAN HOUSE, LITTLE COLLINS STREET, MELBOURNE

ASSOCIATED COMPANIES
PITMAN PUBLISHING CORPORATION
2 WEST 45TH STREET, NEW YORK
205 WEST MONROE STREET, CHICAGO

SIR ISAAC PITMAN & SONS (CANADA), Ltd.
(INCORPORATING THE COMMERCIAL TEXT BOOK COMPANY)
PITMAN HOUSE, 381–383 CHURCH STREET, TORONTO

PREFACE

THE English language, derived as it is from many different sources, is peculiarly rich in synonymous words—words, that is to say, which, conveying more or less exactly the same meaning, can be substituted for a given word. In this way the speaker, or the writer, has at his command a variety of equivalent terms to relieve the monotony of a restricted vocabulary. It must be remembered, however, that, except in rare instances, no two words are exactly synonymous, for, through its use in so many contexts, a word acquires a diversity of meanings, while its synonym has also taken on its own different shades of meaning ; and the greatest care has to be taken in choosing a synonym that most clearly expresses the sense of the word for which it is to be substituted, and is suitable to the context in which it will appear. An example from the book will show what is meant—

> CHARGE. Care, custody, trust ; order, injunction, command, instruction, address ; allegation, impeachment, indictment ; attack, assault ; cost, expense ; heraldic bearing.

Here we have sixteen words, all synonymous with the initial word " Charge," but not synonymous, for the most part, with one another. Thus, " custody," " command," " impeachment," " attack," and " cost " may each be substituted for " charge," but not for one another. Therefore, the differences of meaning must be noted in the choice of a synonym, and those differences, where they exist, are marked by the use of semi-colons, which must not be disregarded.

v

PREFACE

A characteristic feature of this book is the supply of antonyms, that is, of words opposite in sense to the initial word. These are, in the same way, and with like differences, synonymous among themselves. Thus the list of synonymous words is considerably extended, and light is thrown on the meanings of the initial words by the antonyms, which, where they exist and are supplied here, show what the other words do not mean.

It will thus be evident that this book, though it should greatly help the student, will not relieve him of the necessity for thinking. Rather, it should compel him to think, in order that his choice of words may the most felicitously express his mind.

SYNONYMS
AND ANTONYMS

Aban'don. Leave, relinquish, forsake ; resign, cede.

ANT. *Stay with, retain.*

Aban'doned (*adj.*). Dissolute, depraved, profligate, immoral.

ANT. *W e l l - p r i n c i p l e d, moral.*

Abase'. Humiliate, bring down, humble, disgrace.

ANT. *Exalt, uplift, honour.*

Abash'. Confound, confuse, disconcert, shame.

ANT. *Encourage.*

Abate'. Diminish, lessen, reduce, subside, decline.

ANT. *Raise, increase, rise.*

Abate'ment. Diminution, decrease, discount, allowance.

ANT. *Increase, rise.*

Abbre'viate. Shorten, reduce, condense.

ANT. *Lengthen, expand.*

Abet'. Help, assist, encourage.

ANT. *Hinder, discourage.*

Abhor'. Detest, hate, loathe, abominate.

ANT. *Like, approve.*

Abhor'rence. Loathing, detestation, repugnance.

ANT. *Liking, approval.*

Abide'. See LAST and REMAIN.

Abi'ding (*adj.*). Lasting, continuing, permanent.

ANT. *Passing, fleeting.*

Abil'ity. Cleverness, aptitude, skill, talent, facility.

ANT. *Disability, feebleness, ignorance.*

Ab'ject Mean, degraded, grovelling, servile.

ANT. *Proud, independent.*

Abjure'. Forswear, disclaim, disavow, repudiate.

ANT. *Avow, accept, claim.*

Abnor'mal. Irregular, unusual, unnatural.

ANT. *Normal, usual, regular.*

Abode'. Dwelling, domicile, house, home, habitation.

Abom'inable. See EXECRABLE.

Abom'inate. See ABHOR.

Aborig'inal. Native, indigenous, autochthonous.

ANT. *Immigrant, imported.*

Abort'ive. Futile, fruitless, unsuccessful.

ANT. *Effective, well-timed, successful.*

About'. Near, around ; concerning, respecting, with reference to ; approximately, nearly.

ANT. *Far from.*

Abridge'. Shorten, condense ; curtail, lessen.

ANT. *Lengthen, expand, extend, enlarge.*

Abridg'ment. Compendium, shortening, epitome, summary, abstract.

ANT. *Enlargement, fuller statement ; extension.*

Ab'rogate. See ANNUL.

Abrupt'. Steep, precipitous ; sudden, hasty, curt.

ANT. *Gently s l o p i n g, gentle.*

Abscond'. Decamp, run off, bolt.

ANT. *Remain, stay.*

Ab'sent (*adj.*). Away, not

1

present, gone ; inattentive, pre-occupied.

ANT. *Present, on the spot.*

Ab'solute. Unconditioned, independent, unlimited, supreme, despotic.

ANT. *Limited, constitutional, mild.*

Absolve'. See ACQUIT.

Absorb'. Swallow up, imbibe, drink in ; engross.

ANT. *Disgorge.*

Abstain'. See FORBEAR.

Ab'stract. See ABRIDGMENT.

Abstruse'. Hidden, recondite, obscure, occult, deep.

ANT. *Open, simple.*

Absurd'. Silly, foolish, ridiculous, inane, irrational.

ANT. *Rational, sane.*

Absurd'ity. See FOOLERY and FLUMMERY.

Abund'ant. Plentiful, plenteous, ample, rich, copious, exuberant.

ANT. *Meagre, inadequate, poor.*

Abuse' (*vb.*). Use ill, maltreat, injure ; revile, upbraid.

ANT. *Use well, praise.*

Abuse' (*n.*). Ill-usage, insolent language, vituperation, invective.

ANT. *Use ; approval, commendation.*

Accede'. Consent, assent, comply ; enter upon (an office).

ANT. *Refuse ; resign, quit*

Accel'erate. Quicken, hasten, expedite, forward.

ANT. *Retard, reduce speed.*

Access'ion. Addition, enlargement, extension ; a thing added, entrance on (an office).

ANT. *Diminution, loss.*

Ac'cident. Chance, casualty, mishap ; non-essential property.

ANT. *Expected event; design ; substance.*

Accident'al. See CASUAL.

Accliv'ity. Ascent, rising ground.

ANT. *Declivity, downward slope, decline.*

Accom'modate. Suit, fit, reconcile ; oblige, supply with.

ANT. *Disoblige, refuse.*

Accom'plish. Finish, execute, fulfil, achieve, do.

ANT. *Fail, leave undone.*

Accord'. Harmony, agreement.

ANT. *Discord, disagreement.*

Accord' (*vb.*). Harmonize, agree; allow, vouchsafe.

ANT. *Be discordant ; refuse.*

Accost'. See HAIL and GREET.

Account'. Reckoning, narration, story.

Account' (*vb.*). Consider, regard, reckon, estimate.

ANT. *Disregard, ignore.*

Accout'rement. Equipment, dress, outfit.

Accred'ited. Authorized, delegated, entrusted.

ANT. *Unauthorized, discredited.*

Accu'mulate. Pile up, amass, collect, store.

ANT. *Squander, waste.*

Accusa'tion. See IMPUTATION.

Ac'curate. Exact, careful, precise, true.

ANT. *Inaccurate, inexact, careless.*

Accuse'. See IMPEACH.

Accus'tom. See INURE.

Accust'omed. See HABITUAL.

Acerb'ity. Bitterness, harshness, asperity, acrimony.

ANT. *Sweetness, mildness.*

Achieve'. See ACCOMPLISH.

Achieve'ment. See EXPLOIT.

Acknowl'edge. Allow, admit, own, recognize.

ANT. *Disavow, deny, disown.*

Ac'me. See HEIGHT.

Acquaint'. See APPRISE.

Acquaint'ance. Knowledge, cognizance ; a person known, but not intimately.

ANT. *Ignorance ; an intimate friend, an intimate.*

Acquiesce'. See ACCEDE.

Acquire'. Gain, attain, obtain.
ANT. *Miss, lose.*

Acquit'. Absolve, release, clear, exonerate.
ANT. *Condemn, sentence.*

Acrimo'nious. See PUNGENT.

Ac'rimony. See ACERBITY.

Act'ive. Busy, alert, nimble, brisk, eager.
ANT. *Inactive, inert, lazy.*

Act'uate. Instigate, impel, cause to operate.
ANT. *Arrest, stop.*

Acute'. Sharp, penetrating ; shrewd, intelligent.
ANT. *Dull, blunt ; stupid.*

Acute'ness See GUMPTION.

Ad'age. Saw, maxim, proverb.

Adapt'. See ACCOMMODATE.

Addict'ed. Devoted, accustomed to, given up to.
ANT. *Free, unaddicted.*

Address'. Appeal, petition ; discourse, speech, direction ; ability, adroitness.

Adept'. Skilful, expert.
ANT. *Clumsy, inexpert.*

Ad'equate. Equal, sufficient, effectual.
ANT. *Inadequate, insufficient, unequal, ineffectual.*

Adhere'. Stick, abide by, cling.
ANT. *Come undone, break from.*

Adhe'rent. See FOLLOWER.

Adhe'sion. Attachment, union, support.
ANT. *Detachment.*

Adieu'. See FAREWELL.

Adja'cent. Close to, near, contiguous.
ANT. *Remote, distant.*

Adjourn'. Put off, postpone, delay, defer.
ANT. *Hurry on, advance.*

Ad'junct. Appendage, addition.

Adjust'. Fit, regulate ; settle, put right.
ANT. *Upset, disorder.*

Admin'ister. Direct, superintend, execute, supply.
ANT. *Neglect, withhold.*

Admira'tion. See ESTIMATION.

Admire'. Wonder at, esteem, respect.
ANT. *Despise, dislike.*

Admiss'ion. Access, entrance ; concession, allowance.
ANT. *Exclusion ; denial.*

Admon'ish. Caution, rebuke, warn, chide.
ANT. *Praise, commend.*

Adopt'. Appropriate, choose, take, assume.
ANT. *Reject, drop.*

Adora'tion. Worship, reverence, love.
ANT. *Irreverence, contempt.*

Adorn. See EMBELLISH.

Adroit'. Clever, dexterous, skilful, expert.
ANT. *Clumsy, unskilled, inexpert.*

Advance'. Bring (or move) forward, promote ; allege, adduce.
ANT. *Hinder, retard ; deny.*

Advant'age. Gain, profit, benefit ; superiority.
ANT. *Loss, injury, failure.*

Advantage'ous. See PROFITABLE.

Advent'ure. See ENTERPRISE.

Advent'urous. Daring, enterprising, bold, rash.
ANT. *Timid, cautious.*

Ad'versary. See ENEMY.

Ad'verse. Opposed to, inimical, hostile ; unwilling ; unfortunate.
ANT. *Friendly, favourable ; fortunate.*

Advers'ity. Misfortune, distress, calamity, hardship.
ANT. *Prosperity, good fortune.*

Advert'. Refer to, notice.
ANT. *Omit.*

Ad'vertise. Apprise, announce, notify, publish, herald.
ANT. *Conceal, suppress.*

Advice'. Caution, warning ; notice, intelligence.

Advise'. Give advice ; inform ; confer, consult with.

Ad'vocate. Defend, support, favour, countenance.

ANT. *Oppose, disapprove, discountenance.*

Aff'able. Courteous, civil, accessible, polite.

ANT. *Surly, uncivil, impolite, unapproachable.*

Affect'. Influence, act upon, move ; pretend, assume.

Affecta'tion. Pretence, mannerism, conceited air.

ANT. *Simplicity, naturalness.*

Affect'ed. See JAUNTY.

Affect'ing. See IMPRESSIVE.

Affec'tion. Feeling, love, fondness ; inclination.

ANT. *Dislike, disinclination.*

Affin'ity. Alliance, kinship ; sympathy with.

ANT. *Antipathy.*

Affirm'. Asseverate, assert, maintain, declare.

ANT. *Deny, disclaim.*

Afflic'tion. Trouble, distress, calamity, sorrow, grief.

ANT. *Comfort, ease, wellbeing.*

Af'fluence. Wealth, opulence, riches.

ANT. *Poverty, indigence, need.*

Affray. Fight, contest, brawl, feud.

Affright'. Terrify, alarm, confound, intimidate, dismay.

ANT. *Encourage.*

Affront'. Insult, outrage, offence, indignity.

ANT. *Compliment.*

Age'. Time, era, epoch, decline of life.

ANT. *Youth.*

A'gent. Factor, intermediary ; a natural force. See also REPRESENTATIVE.

Ag'gravate. Heighten, intensify, make worse.

ANT. *Diminish, lighten.*

Aghast'. Appalled, awestruck.

ANT. *Calm, unperturbed.*

Ag'ile. See ACTIVE.

Ag'itate. See FLUSTER.

Agita'tion. Shaking, violent movement ; emotion, disturbance, excitement.

ANT. *Stillness ; calmness.*

Ag'onize. See EXCRUCIATE.

Agree'. See ACCEDE and ACQUIESCE.

Agree'able. See AMIABLE and DELECTABLE.

Aid. Help, succour, further, assist, promote.

ANT. *Hinder, oppose.*

Akin'. See RELATED.

Alac'rity. Activity, alertness, briskness, readiness, promptitude.

ANT. *Inactivity, inertness.*

Alarm'. See AFFRIGHT.

Alarm' (*n.*). See FEAR.

Alert'. See ACTIVE.

A'lien. See EXOTIC.

A'lienate. Estrange ; transfer.

ANT. *Reconcile ; recover.*

Allay'. Calm, soothe, assuage, tranquillize, alleviate, quiet.

ANT. *Excite, disturb.*

Allege'. See AFFIRM.

Alle'giance. See FEALTY.

Alli'ance. Union, confederacy, league, combination.

ANT. *Separation, opposition.*

Allot'. Apportion, share, appropriate.

Allow'. Permit, suffer, concede ; admit.

ANT. *Forbid, deny.*

Allude'. Hint, imply, intimate.

ANT. *State plainly.*

Allure'. Entice, attract, inveigle, ensnare.

ANT. *Repel.*

Alterca'tion. Quarrel, dispute, wrangle.

ANT. *Agreement.*

Alt'itude. Height, elevation.

ANT. *Depth.*

Altogeth'er. Entirely, completely, in all.

ANT. *Partly.*

Amass'. See ACCUMULATE.

Ama'zing. Astonishing, wonderful, surprising, stupendous.

ANT. *Usual, natural.*

Ambig'uous. Doubtful, equivocal, uncertain.
ANT. *Clear, simple, obvious, intelligible.*

Ame'liorate. Improve, better, amend.
ANT. *Worsen, cause to deteriorate, spoil.*

Ame'nable. Responsible, accountable ; tractable, responsive.
ANT. *Exempt ; surly.*

Amend'. See AMELIORATE.

Amends.' Compensation, reparation, satisfaction.
ANT. *Injury.*

A'miable. Lovable, charming, engaging, winning.
ANT. *Unlovable, unattractive.*

Am'icable. Friendly, cordial, sociable.
ANT. *Unfriendly, unsociable, cold.*

Amp'le. Large, spacious, wide ; abundant.
ANT. *Contracted, narrow ; scanty.*

Amuse'ment. See ENTERTAINMENT.

Anal'ogy. Resemblance ; comparison, similitude, parallelism.
ANT. *Difference, dissimilarity.*

An'cestry. See RACE.

An'cient. Old, aged, antique, primitive, primeval.

An'ger. Wrath, ire, indignation, fury, choler, animosity.
ANT. *Calmness, forbearance.*

An'ger (*vb.*). See ENRAGE.

An'guish. Pain, agony, suffering, woe.
ANT. *Ease, comfort.*

An'imate. See ENCOURAGE.

Animos'ity. See ANGER.

An'nals. Archives, records, chronicles.

Annex'. Join, add, append ; appropriate.
ANT. *Disjoin, detach.*

Anni'hilate. Annul, destroy, extirpate, abolish, ruin.

ANT. *Restore, preserve, spare.*

Announce'. See ADVERTISE.

Announce'ment. See REPORT.

Annoy'. Vex, worry, irritate, molest, trouble, harass, infest.
ANT. *Leave alone, please.*

Annul'. Cancel, invalidate, quash, rescind, abrogate.
ANT. *Ratify, confirm, restore.*

Anom'alous. See ABNORMAL.

An'swerable. See AMENABLE.

Antagonist'ic. Opposed, hostile, adverse, inimical.
ANT. *Friendly, sympathetic.*

Ante'rior. Preceding, previous, prior, foregoing.
ANT. *Posterior, later.*

Antic'ipate. Forestall, forecast, prejudge, foresee.
ANT. *Be behindhand, miss.*

Antip'athy. Dislike, hostility, aversion.
ANT. *Sympathy, liking.*

Antique'. See ANCIENT.

Antith'esis. Opposition, contrast.
ANT. *Identity, likeness.*

Apathet'ic. Inert, unfeeling, indifferent, impassive, listless.
ANT. *Feeling, interested, active.*

Apoc'ryphal. Hidden, unauthentic, uncanonical.
ANT. *Canonical, certain.*

Apost'ate. See RECREANT.

Appal'. See AFFRIGHT.

Appa'rent. Clear, distinct, evident, visible ; seeming, specious.
ANT. *Hazy, obscure ; real, genuine.*

Appeal'. Call on, invoke, entreat.

Appease'. Assuage, pacify, quiet, soothe.
ANT. *Vex, provoke.*

Appella'tion. Title, style, name, designation.

Applaud'. Cheer, approve, extol, praise, laud.
ANT. *Cry down, hiss.*

Appoint'. Prescribe, ordain,

5

designate, settle ; equip, furnish.

Appor'tion. See ALLOT.

Ap'posite. Pertinent, relevant, apt.

ANT. *Inapposite, irrelevant.*

Appraise'. Price, estimate.

Appre'ciate. Estimate, value, recognize, acknowledge ; rise in value.

ANT. *Depreciate.*

Apprehend'. Grasp, seize, arrest; perceive ; fear.

ANT. *Miss, relax, let go ; misunderstand, misapprehend; be unconcerned.*

Apprise'. Inform, notify, acquaint.

ANT. *Keep secret.*

Approba'tion. Approval, sanction, authority ; praise, commendation.

ANT. *Disapproval ; censure.*

Appro'priate (*vb.*). Take for oneself, assume, allot, usurp.

ANT. *Give away.*

Appro'priate (*adj.*). Fitting, suitable, meet, relevant.

ANT. *Unfitting, unsuitable, irrelevant.*

Appro'val. See APPROBATION.

ANT. *Disapproval.*

Apt'. See APPROPRIATE (*adj.*).

Ar'bitrary. Tyrannical, absolute, imperious, dictatorial, intolerant.

ANT. *Reasonable, constitutional, mild.*

Ar'bitrator. See REFEREE.

Archa'ic. Ancient, antiquated, old-fashioned.

ANT. *Modern, new-fangled, recent.*

Ar'chives. Record office ; records. See also ANNALS.

Ar'dent. Fiery, heated, hot, impassioned, eager, intense.

ANT. *Calm, cool.*

Ar'duous. Difficult, laborious, trying.

ANT. *Easy, light.*

Arg'ue. Debate, dispute, contend ; prove.

ANT. *Agree   disprove.*

Ar'id. See DRY.

Ar'my. See HOST.

Arouse'. Waken, stir, incite, stimulate ; animate.

ANT. *Leave alone, calm ; depress.*

Arraign'. See INDICT.

Arrange'. See ADJUST.

Array' (*vb.*). Arrange, dispose, marshal ; equip, dress.

ANT. *Disorder ; strip.*

Array' (*n.*). Disposition, arrangement ; equipment, dress.

ANT. *Disorder.*

Arrest'. Seize, apprehend ; attract, stop.

ANT. *Let slip, loose.*

Ar'rogance. See HAUGHTINESS.

Ar'rogant. Imperious, indolent, haughty, overbearing, lordly.

ANT. *Humble, condescending, tolerant.*

Art'. Skill, dexterity, profession ; cunning, deceit.

ANT. *Clumsiness.*

Artifi'cial. Factitious, not natural ; affected.

ANT. *Natural ; simple.*

Art'less. Simple, natural, ingenuous.

ANT. *Artful, disingenuous.*

Ascend'ancy. Superiority, mastery ; sway, upper hand.

ANT. *Inferiority, subjection.*

Ascertain'. Learn, discover, determine.

ANT. *Be ignorant, fail to perceive.*

Ascribe'. Impute, attribute, charge.

Ask'. See BESEECH.

As'pect. Air, look, mien, appearance.

Asper'ity. Harshness, roughness, severity.

ANT. *Smoothness, mildness.*

Asperse'. Slander, traduce, calumniate, vilify.

ANT. *Defend, praise, commend.*

Aspira'tion. Longing, yearning, ambition.

ANT. *Indifference, apathy.*

6

Assail'. Attack, assault, invade, charge.

ANT. *Defend.*

Assem'ble. Gather together, collect, meet together.

ANT. *Scatter, break up, disperse.*

Ass'ent. See ACQUIESCE.

Assert'. See AFFIRM.

Assid'uous. See INDEFATIGABLE.

Ass'ign. See ALLOT.

Assist'. Be present at, take part in. See also AID.

ANT. *Be absent from.*

Assist'ant. Helper, associate, attendant, ally.

ANT. *Principal, chief.*

Asso'ciate. See ASSISTANT.

Associa'tion. Alliance, combination, company, union; group.

ANT. *Disunion, dissolution.*

Assuage'. See ALLAY.

Assume'. Undertake, take on, usurp; take for granted.

ANT. *Lay down, decline; reason.*

Assu'rance. Confidence, certainty, conviction; impudence, effrontery.

ANT. *Mistrust, uncertainty; modesty.*

Aston'ish. See AMAZE.

Astute'. Cunning, crafty, sharp.

ANT. *Simple, stupid.*

Asy'lum. See HARBOUR.

Athletic. Muscular, brawny, vigorous, active.

ANT. *Unathletic, weak, flabby.*

Atone'ment. Reconciliation, propitiation, amends.

Atro'cious. Monstrous, heinous, infamous, flagrant, flagitious.

ANT. *Mild, decent.*

Atroc'ity. See ENORMITY.

Attack'. See ASSAIL.

Attain'. Reach, obtain, achieve, win.

ANT. *Miss, fall short of.*

Attempt'. Try, endeavour, essay, strive.

ANT. *Desist, shirk.*

Attempt' (*n.*). See ESSAY.

Attend'. Listen, hearken; accompany, wait on, escort.

ANT. *Be inattentive; lead, conduct.*

Attent'ive. Heedful, mindful, watchful, civil.

ANT. *Inattentive, heedless, uncivil.*

Attest'. See AFFIRM.

Attire'. Dress, garments, clothing, apparel, garb, habiliments.

ANT. *Nakedness.*

Attract'. Draw. See also ALLURE.

ANT. *Repel.*

Attract'ive. Alluring, charming, enticing, agreeable, captivating.

ANT. *Unattractive, unpleasing, disagreeable.*

Attrib'ute. Impute, charge. See also ALLOT.

Att'ribute (*n.*). Equality, property, characteristic.

Auda'cious. Bold, daring, impudent, presumptuous.

ANT. *Timid, shrinking.*

Audac'ity. See EFFRONTERY.

Augment'. Increase, enlarge, extend, swell.

ANT. *Decrease, lessen.*

Au'gur. See BETOKEN.

August'. Majestic, dignified, princely, stately, imposing.

ANT. *Humble, lowly; undignified, unimpressive.*

Auspic'ious. Lucky, fortunate, favourable, well-omened, propitious.

ANT. *Unlucky, ill-omened, unpropitious, unfavourable, inauspicious.*

Austere'. Harsh, severe, rigorous, stern, strict.

ANT. *Mild, gentle.*

Authen'tic. True, certain, genuine, veritable.

ANT. *Unauthentic, spurious.*

Author'ity. Government, rule, sway, command; permission, sanction, licence.

Au'thorize. Sanction, commission, empower, warrant.
ANT. *Discountenance, disapprove, forbid.*

Auxil'iary. Helping, subsidiary, ancillary.
ANT. *Chief.*

Avail'able. Accessible, obtainable, useful, advantageous.
ANT. *Inaccessible, not for use, unobtainable.*

Av'arice. Greed, covetousness, cupidity.
ANT. *Generosity.*

Avaricious. See GRASPING.

Avenge'. Retaliate, requite, punish, vindicate.
ANT. *Forgive, overlook.*

Aver'. See AFFIRM.

Averse'. Disinclined, unwilling, loth.
ANT. *Ready, willing, favourable.*

Aver'sion. Hostility, unwillingness, distaste, dislike, hatred.
ANT. *Willingness, readiness, liking.*

Avid'ity. See GREEDINESS.

Avoca'tion. Recreation, employment of leisure.
ANT. *Vocation, business.*

Avoid'. Shun, flee, escape, elude; refrain from, forbear.
ANT. *Follow, meet, confront.*

Avow'. See AFFIRM.

Await'. See EXPECT.

Award'. Adjudge, decree, assign.

Aware'. Conscious, mindful of, apprised of.
ANT. *Unaware, ignorant of.*

Awe'. Dread, fear, veneration.
ANT. *Contempt, irreverence.*

Aw'ful. Venerable, solemn, dreadful, shocking.
ANT. *Secular, unimpressive, pleasant.*

Awk'ward. Clumsy, unhandy, ungainly ; clownish, rude.
ANT. *Handy, clever ; graceful ; refined.*

Ax'iom. Established proposition ; maxim, aphorism.

Awry'. Crooked, twisted, contorted.
ANT. *Straight.*

B

Bab'ble. Prate, prattle, chatter.
ANT. *Discourse gravely.*

Bacch'anal. Reveller, drunkard, carouser.

Back'bite. Slander, calumniate, defame, malign.
ANT. *Defend, praise.*

Bad'. Evil, wicked. Also see ABANDONED.
ANT. *Good, upright, moral.*

Baf'fle. Balk, defeat, elude ; puzzle, confuse.

Bait'. Lure, snare, enticement.

Bal'ance. Poise, counterpoise, compensate ; equalize, settle.

Bale'ful. Harmful, noxious, sad, calamitous.
ANT. *Harmless, cheerful.*

Balk'. See BAFFLE.

Balm'y. Fragrant, odorous, ambrosial ; soothing, genial.

ANT. *Not sweet ; rough, ungenial.*

Bane'ful. Injurious, noxious, hurtful, pestilential.
ANT. *Beneficial, harmless.*

Banqu'et. Feast, entertainment, dinner.

Bant'er. Jeering, mockery, rallying, twitting, raillery.
ANT. *Serious talk.*

Bar'. Rail, stave ; hindrance, obstruction ; tribunal ; body of lawyers, barristers (collectively).
ANT. *Opening, free passage ; bench.*

Bar'barous. Uncivilized, wild, savage ; cruel, inhuman, rude.
ANT. *Civilized, gentle, refined.*

Bar'gain. Agreement, stipulation, deal, negotiation, transaction.

Bar'ter. Exchange, deal, traffic.

Base' (*adj.*). Low, mean, ignoble, servile, vile ; counterfeit.
ANT. *Exalted, noble ; genuine.*

Base' (*n.*). Foundation, ground, groundwork ; chief ingredient.
ANT. *Superstructure; mixture.*

Bashful. See COY.

Ba'sis. See BASE.

Batt'er. Strike, smite, shatter, destroy.

Baub'le. Gewgaw, gimcrack, trinket, plaything.

Beak'. Bill, mandible ; prow, stem, bow.
ANT. *Tail ; stern.*

Bear'. Carry, transport, support ; endure, suffer ; produce, give birth to.
ANT. *Drop, let down ; shrink from.*

Beat'. Strike, buffet, thump, hammer ; conquer, defeat, surpass.

Beau'tiful. Comely, charming, lovely, fair, handsome.
ANT. *Ugly, uncomely.*

Becom'ing. Befitting, suitable, decent, neat.
ANT. *Unbecoming.*

Befriend'. Help, aid, succour, patronize.
ANT. *Refuse to help.*

Begin'ning. Origin, source, inception, commencement.
ANT. *Ending, termination, cessation.*

Begrudge'. See GRUDGE.

Beguile'. Deceive, ensnare, cheat ; amuse, divert.
ANT. *Enlighten, treat honestly ; displease.*

Behest'. Command, order, charge, injunction.

Behind'hand. Slow, tardy, dilatory, late.
ANT. *Beforehand, prompt.*

Behold'. See, observe, regard.

Behove'. Befit, beseem, become.
ANT. *Be unbecoming.*

Belief'. Faith, trust, confidence, assent, creed.
ANT. *Unbelief, distrust, mistrust, denial.*

Belong'. Appertain, be owned by, relate to, concern.

Benef'icent. Kindly, bountiful, generous, liberal.
ANT. *Maleficent, unkind, ungenerous.*

Ben'efit. See ADVANTAGE.

Benev'olence. See HUMANITY.

Benev'olent. Benign, charitable. See also BENEFICENT.
ANT. *Malevolent, uncharitable.*

Benign. See BENEVOLENT.

Bent' (*n.*). Tendency, bias, prepossession, leaning, predilection.

Beseech'. Ask, beg, pray, entreat.

Beset'. Surround, environ, encompass, besiege.

Bestow'. See IMPART.

Beto'ken. Denote, mark ; portend, indicate.

Betray'. Disclose, divulge ; deceive, give away treacherously.
ANT. *Conceal ; defend, be loyal.*

Bewail'. See LAMENT.

Bewild'er. Puzzle, perplex, confuse, mystify.
ANT. *Enlighten, illuminate.*

Bewitch'. Enchant, captivate, entrance.
ANT. *Repel, disgust.*

Bi'as. See BENT.

Bid'. Charge, command, enjoin, ask, invite ; offer a price.
ANT. *Obey ; respond.*

Big'. Large, great, massive, huge ; pregnant.
ANT. *Small, little ; empty.*

Big'oted. See FANATICAL.

Bill'. Note, reckoning, measure (law). See also BEAK.

Bind'. See LINK.

Bind'ing. Compulsory, obligatory, stringent ; astringent.
ANT. *Voluntary ; laxative.*

Bit'. See FRAGMENT.

Bit'ter. Acrid, acid ; sharp, severe ; harsh, cruel ; poignant.

    ANT. *Sweet ; mild ; sad, sorrowful.*

Bizarre'. See GROTESQUE.

Black'. Ebon, dark, swarthy ; gloomy, dull, dismal ; wicked, evil.

    ANT. *White, pale ; bright, cheerful ; good.*

Blame'. Censure, reprehend, accuse, upbraid.

    ANT. *Excuse, pardon.*

Blame' (*n.*). See APPROBATION.

Blame'less. See INNOCENT.

Bland'. Mild, courteous, soft, gentle. See also BENIGN.

    ANT. *Rough, d i s c o u r t-eous.*

Bland'ishment. Flattery, cajolery, fawning, coaxing.

    ANT. *Bluntness, plain speaking, disrespect.*

Blas'phemy. Profanity, swearing, impiety.

    ANT. *Reverence.*

Blast'. Wind, gale, storm, squall ; blare, clang ; explosion.

Bla'tant. Noisy, vociferous, clamorous.

    ANT. *Quiet, gentle.*

Bleak'. Cold, chilly, raw ; bare, cheerless.

    ANT. *Warm, sunny ; comfortable.*

Blem'ish. Flaw, speck, spot, fault ; disgrace.

    ANT. *Merit, good point.*

Blend'. Mix, mingle, compound, amalgamate ; coalesce.

    ANT. *Dissolve.*

Bless'. Gladden ; consecrate, sanctify ; give thanks, praise.

    ANT. *Curse, desecrate.*

Blight'. Wither, shrivel, blast, mildew ; ruin.

    ANT. *Revive, restore.*

Bliss'. Happiness, felicity, joy, delight, rapture.

    ANT. *Unhappiness, infelicity, misery.*

Blithe'. Happy, merry, joyous, gay, gladsome.

    ANT. *Sad, sorrowful, dispirited.*

Bloom'. Freshness, efflorescence, flush.

    ANT. *Decay, withered state.*

Blot'. Spoil, bespatter ; disgrace.

    ANT. *Improve, embellish.*

Blot' (*n.*). See BLEMISH.

Blow'. Stroke, hit, knock ; disaster, calamity.

    ANT. *Good luck, good fortune.*

Bluff'. Abrupt, blustering, brusque, rough.

    ANT. *Cool, polite.*

Blund'er. Error, mistake, oversight, slip.

    ANT. *Accuracy, correctness.*

Blunt'. Edgeless, pointless, bluff, coarse.

    ANT. *Sharp, pointed.*

Blust'ering. See BLUFF.

Boast'. Vaunt, brag, vapour, glory, swagger.

    ANT. *Be modest.*

Bog'gle. Falter, doubt, waver, hesitate.

    ANT. *Be certain, act promptly.*

Boist'erous. Noisy, stormy, violent, clamorous.

    ANT. *Quiet, peaceful, calm.*

Bold'. Daring, courageous, intrepid ; imprudent, saucy, immodest.

    ANT. *Cowardly, timid ; respectful, modest.*

Bomb'ast. Fustian, rhodomontade, rant.

    ANT. *Sober speech.*

Bond'. See LINK.

Bond'age. Captivity, servitude, thraldom, restraint, subjection.

    ANT. *Freedom, liberty.*

Bonn'y. Comely, fair, pretty, buxom, gay.

    ANT. *Uncomely, ugly.*

Book'ish. Learned, studious, literary.

    ANT. *Unlearned, illiterate.*

10

Boor'ish. Rude, surly, uncivilized, rustic.

ANT. *Cultivated, civilized.*

Boot'y. Plunder, pillage, loot.

Bore'. Pierce, penetrate, drill ; weary, tire.

ANT. *Cheer, amuse.*

Both'er. Worry, trouble, annoyance.

ANT. *Comfort, relief.*

Bound'. See LIMIT.

Bount'eous. See BENEFICENT.

Bount'eousness. See GENEROSITY.

Bourn'. Boundary, limit, goal.

Brace'. See INVIGORATE.

Brava'do. See BOAST.

Brave'. See BOLD.

Bra'very. See COURAGE.

Brawl'. Fight, squabble, uproar, altercation.

ANT. *Harmony, amity.*

Brawn'y. See ATHLETIC.

ANT. *Weak, flabby.*

Bray'. Pulverize, bruise, triturate.

Breach'. Rift, rent, hiatus, cleft, gap, chasm ; infraction, violation.

ANT. *Unbroken surface ; repair.*

Break'. Rend, tear, sever, crack, fracture, demolish, smash, destroy ; violate, infringe.

ANT. *Mend, join, repair.*

Breed'. See ENGENDER.

Breeze'. See GUST.

Brev'ity. Shortness ; conciseness, terseness, succinctness.

ANT. *Length, longwindedness, circumlocution.*

Bright'. Shining, splendid, glittering ; clear, cheerful, intelligent ; auspicious, propitious.

ANT. *Dull, dingy, dark, cheerless ; stupid ; unlucky.*

Bril'liancy. See RADIANCE.

Bril'liant. See BRIGHT.

Brisk'. See AGILE.

Britt'le. Breakable, fragile, frangible.

Broach'. Tap, open, start, utter.

ANT. *Close, stop.*

Broil'. See AFFRAY and BRAWL.

Bruise'. See BREAK.

Bru'tal. Beastlike, animal, savage, cruel, rough. Also see BARBAROUS.

ANT. *Human, kindly, gentle.*

Build. Rear, erect, form, construct, raise.

ANT. *Destroy, raze, demolish.*

Bulk'. Size, volume, mass, gross ; majority, chief part.

ANT. *Minority.*

Bul'wark. See RAMPART.

Bull'y. See HECTOR.

Bull'ying. See BLUFF.

Bung'ler. Fumbler, botcher, lubber, awkward fellow.

ANT. *Expert.*

Burlesque'. Comical, farcical ; caricaturing.

ANT. *Serious.*

Burn'ing. See ARDENT.

Burst'. Break, shiver, split, explode.

ANT. *Join together.*

Bus'iness. Engagement, calling, vocation, affairs, matter, concern.

ANT. *Idleness, being unoccupied, leisure.*

Butt'ress. Prop, shore, stay, support.

ANT. *Undermine, let down.*

Bux'om. Brisk, lively, jolly, blithe ; plump.

ANT. *Dull, unhappy ; lean.*

Buy'. See PURCHASE.

By'stander. Looker-on, onlooker, spectator, beholder.

ANT. *Performer, actor.*

11

C

Cabal'. Party, faction, clique, coterie ; plot, intrigue.

Cadav'erous. Wan, pale, ghastly, pallid.
ANT. *Healthy-looking.*

Cait'iff. Villain, scoundrel, rascal, miscreant.
ANT. *Gentleman.*

Cajole'. Wheedle, coax, inveigle, entice, flatter.
ANT. *Repel, treat roughly.*

Cajo'lery. See FLATTERY.

Calam'ity. See ADVERSITY.

Cal'culate. Estimate, count, reckon, compute, guess.

Cal'lous. Hard, indifferent, cold-blooded.
ANT. *Soft, tender, considerate.*

Calm'. See ALLAY.

Calum'niate. See ASPERSE.

Cal'umny. Aspersion, defamation, slander, detraction.
ANT. *Praise, commendation.*

Can'cel. See ANNUL.

Cand'id. Fair, impartial, just ; frank, ingenuous, straightforward.
ANT. *Unfair, partial ; disingenuous.*

Can'on. Rule, statute, formula, roll, the Sacred Scriptures ; a cathedral dignitary so named.

Cant'. Humbug, slang, pretence, hypocrisy.
ANT. *Honesty, sincerity, genuineness.*

Can'vass. Investigate, scrutinize, inspect ; solicit, bespeak.
ANT. *Leave alone ; refuse.*

Capa'cious. See AMPLE.

Capa'city. Magnitude, volume, dimensions ; ability, efficiency ; sphere, position, province.
ANT. *Incapacity.*

Cap'ital. Chief, principal, pre-eminent ; excellent, first-rate.
ANT. *Lowest ; third-rate.*

Caprice'. Freak, whim, fancy, vagary.
ANT. *Steadfastness.*

Capri'cious. See CHANGEABLE.

Cap'tious. Critical, fault-finding, touchy, peevish, cavilling.
ANT. *Fair, tolerant, indulgent.*

Captiv'ity. See BONDAGE.

Cap'tivated. See ENAMOURED.

Card'inal. Chief, principal, primary, main.
ANT. *Subordinate.*

Care'. Concern, anxiety, trouble, attention, circumspection, regard ; charge, direction, management.
ANT. *Lightheartedness, carelessness.*

Care'ful. Heedful, anxious, solicitous, circumspect, thrifty, wary, discreet.
ANT. *Heedless, careless ; extravagant, indiscreet.*

Caress'. Fondle, hug, embrace, pet.
ANT. *Repel, discourage.*

Car'go. See FREIGHT.

Caricature'. See BURLESQUE.

Carn'age. Bloodshed, massacre, butchery, slaughter.

Carn'al. Fleshly, sensual, animal, lascivious.
ANT. *Spiritual, regenerate.*

Carp'. See CAVIL.

Car'riage. Conveyance, transportation ; vehicle ; demeanour, bearing.

Car'ry. See BEAR.

Case'. Event, circumstance ; plight, situation, lawsuit, action.

Cast'. See FLING.

Cast'igate. Chastise, flog, punish, correct.
ANT. *Commend, praise.*

Castiga'tion. See PUNISHMENT.

Cas'ual. Accidental, fortuitous, uncertain, occasional.
ANT. *Designed, calculated.*

Catas'trophe. See ADVERSITY.

Cat'alogue. List, index, roll, register, record.

Catch'. Grasp, capture, arrest, snatch, apprehend, grasp meaning.

ANT. *Miss, let loose ; misapprehend.*

Categor'ical. Positive, explicit, direct, emphatic.

ANT. *Uncertain, unexplicit.*

Cath'olic. Universal, whole ; wide, tolerant.

ANT. *Limited, exclusive, Protestant.*

Cause'. Bring about, make, originate, induce, occasion, create.

ANT. *Result, be consequent.*

Caust'ic. Burning, corrosive ; pungent, sarcastic, severe, biting.

ANT. *Harmless ; mild, kindly.*

Cau'tion. Forethought, care, circumspection ; advice, counsel, warning.

ANT. *Carelessness, thoughtlessness.*

Cav'il. Carp, censure, criticize severely.

ANT. *Favour, approve.*

Cav'ity. Hole, hollow, chasm, opening, aperture.

ANT. *Solid surface.*

Cease'. Leave off, stop, desist, refrain, discontinue.

ANT. *Begin, continue.*

Cede'. Give up, surrender, relinquish, yield.

ANT. *Hold, refuse.*

Cel'ebrated. Famous, notable, renowned, glorious, eminent.

ANT. *Unknown, inglorious, undistinguished.*

Celer'ity. Speed, swiftness, velocity, quickness, rapidity.

ANT. *Slowness, tardiness.*

Cement'. Weld, solder, join, unite, bind.

ANT. *Disjoin, unsolder.*

Cen'sure. Blame, condemn, reprove, reprimand.

ANT. *Praise, commend.*

Ceremo'nious. Formal, solemn, punctilious, courtly.

ANT. *Unceremonious, informal, undignified.*

Cer'tain. Ascertained, actual, true, trustworthy, positive, assured ; some, specified.

ANT. *Uncertain, doubtful, untrustworthy.*

Cer'tify. See AFFIRM.

Cessa'tion. Ending, pause, ceasing, rest, intermission, discontinuance.

ANT. *Beginning, continuance.*

Chafe'. See FRET.

Chaf'fer. See HAGGLE.

Chagrin'. Disappointment ; mortification, dissatisfaction.

ANT. *Satisfaction, pleasure.*

Chal'lenge. Defy, dare, provoke ; require, claim ; question, dispute.

ANT. *Propitiate ; agree.*

Chance'. See ACCIDENT.

Change'. Vary, alter, modify ; veer, turn.

ANT. *Be constant, remain fixed.*

Change'able. Variable, fitful, shifting, fickle, inconstant, unsettled, wavering.

ANT. *Steady, unchanging, constant, reliable.*

Char'acter. Letter, emblem, type ; disposition, temperament, quality, nature.

Char'acterize. Distinguish, describe, mark, designate.

Charge (*vb.*). See BLAME.

Charge'. Care, custody, trust ; order, injunction, command, instruction, address ; allegation, impeachment, indictment ; attack, assault ; cost, expense ; heraldic bearing.

ANT. *Neglect ; defence ; retreat.*

Char'itable. See BENEVOLENT and BENEFICENT.

Char'ity. See LOVE and HUMANITY.

Char'latan. See IMPOSTOR.

Charm'. See BEWITCH.

Cha'ry. Cautious, wary, scrupulous, careful, thrifty.
ANT. *Reckless, incautious, wasteful.*

Chasm'. See BREACH.

Chaste'. Pure, continent, undefiled, immaculate ; elegant, refined.
ANT. *Impure, unchaste, inelegant, unrefined.*

Chast'en. See CASTIGATE.

Chastise'. See CASTIGATE.

Chast'isement. See PUNISHMENT.

Chat'ter. See BABBLE.

Cheat'. Dupe, defraud, gull, beguile, swindle, outwit.
ANT. *Treat fairly, be honest.*

Check'. Curb, bridle, hinder, restrain ; reprimand ; tick off, note.
ANT. *Loose, free.*

Cheer'. Gladden, encourage, refresh, elate ; solace, comfort ; applaud.
ANT. *Depress, dishearten ; hiss down.*

Cheer'ful. Lively, cheery, gay, blithe, happy, contented ; pleasant.
ANT. *Cheerless, gloomy, discontented ; disagreeable.*

Cher'ish. Nourish, foster ; entertain, harbour, encourage.
ANT. *Neglect ; repel.*

Chide'. See ADMONISH.

Chief'. Principal, leading. See also CARDINAL.
ANT. *Minor, unimportant.*

Child'ish. Puerile, infantine, juvenile, boyish ; silly, weak.
ANT. *Grown up ; grave, sensible.*

Chimer'ical. Fanciful, fantastic, visionary, illusory, imaginary.
ANT. *Real, well-founded, credible.*

Chiv'alrous. Knightly, heroic, brave, gallant, courteous, generous.
ANT. *Cowardly, ungallant, uncourtly, ungenerous.*

Chiv'alry. See GALLANTRY.

Choice'. Selection, preference, option, alternative.

Chol'er. See ANGER.

Chol'eric. Angry, passionate, irascible, testy, hasty.
ANT. *Good-tempered, calm.*

Chop'. See HEW.

Chron'icle. See ANNALS.

Churl'ish. Rude, sullen, uncivil. See also BOORISH.
ANT. *Civil, cheerful, obliging.*

Circu'itous. Roundabout, devious, tortuous, winding.
ANT. *Straightforward, direct.*

Cir'culate. Spread, disseminate, diffuse, propagate.
ANT. *Suppress.*

Cir'cumscribe. Surround, bound, encircle, limit, restrict, confine.

Cir'cumspect. Cautious, wary, prudent, careful.
ANT. *Incautious, heedless, imprudent, indiscreet.*

Cir'cumstance. Fact, event, incident, situation.

Circumvent'. Overreach, outwit, stop, ensnare.

Cite'. Summon, mention, name ; adduce, quote.

Civ'il. Political ; intestine ; polite, affable.
ANT. *Military ; foreign ; rude.*

Claim'. Demand, require, exact, challenge.
ANT. *Renounce, forgo.*

Clam'our. Outcry, din, uproar, shouting, hubbub.
ANT. *Silence, peace.*

Clandes'tine. Secret, underhand, sly.
ANT. *Open, above board.*

Clasp'. Fasten, connect ; embrace, grasp, clutch.
ANT. *Loose.*

Class'. See GENUS.

Class'ify. Arrange, rank, systematize, assort.
ANT. *Disarrange muddle.*

Clause'. Passage, paragraph; article, proviso.

Clean' *(adj.).* See PURE.

Clean' *(vb.).* See PURIFY.

Cleanse'. See PURIFY.

Clear'. Pellucid, transparent, evident, fair, fresh; entire, perfect; innocent.

ANT. *Obscure; guilty.*

Clem'ency. Gentleness, mildness, indulgence, mercy, leniency.

ANT. *Harshness, severity, intolerance.*

Clev'er. See GIFTED.

Clev'erness. See ABILITY.

Cling'. See ADHERE.

Clique'. See CABAL.

Close'. Shut; conclude, finish, complete.

ANT. *Open; begin.*

Clothes'. Dress, apparel, garments, attire, raiment.

ANT. *Nakedness.*

Clown'. Jester, droll. See also BOORISH and CHURLISH.

Cloy'. See GLUT.

Clum'sy. See AWKWARD.

Clust'er. See GENUS and GROUP.

Clutch'. See CLASP.

Coalesce'. Mingle, join, cohere, blend.

ANT. *Remain separate, be in solution.*

Coali'tion. Alliance, confederacy, league, combination.

ANT. *Disunion, separation.*

Coarse'. Rough, gross, thick; rude, indelicate, vulgar.

ANT. *Thin, fine; refined.*

Coax'. See CAJOLE.

Cod'dle. Pet, nurse, caress, humour.

ANT. *Repel, treat roughly.*

Coerce'. Compel, force, repress, subdue.

ANT. *Persuade, lead, free.*

Coe'val. Contemporary, contemporaneous, synchronous.

ANT. *Anterior, posterior.*

Co'gent. Forcible, compelling, convincing, effective.

ANT. *Feeble, unconvincing.*

Cog'itate. Meditate, ponder, reflect, muse, think.

Cog'nate. See RELATED.

Cohere'. See COALESCE.

Coincide'. See AGREE and AC-QUIESCE.

Collat'eral. Indirect, not lineal; confirmatory.

ANT. *Lineal, direct.*

Col'league. Assistant, helper, coadjutor, partner.

ANT. *Opponent.*

Collect'. See ASSEMBLE.

Collect'ed *(adj.).* Cool, calm, self-possessed, placid.

ANT. *Perturbed, unrestrained.*

Col'loquy. Conference, conversation, tête-à-tête.

ANT. *Soliloquy.*

Coloss'al. Gigantic, huge, enormous, vast.

ANT. *Diminutive, small, puny.*

Col'our. Hue, tint, shade, dye, complexion; appearance, pretext.

ANT. *Pallor, colourlessness.*

Com'bat. Struggle, fight, battle, encounter.

ANT. *Peace.*

Come'ly. Good-looking, fair, pretty. See also BECOMING.

ANT. *Uncomely, ugly.*

Com'fort. Solace, consolation, encouragement; ease, satisfaction, enjoyment.

ANT. *Irritation, discouragement; discomfort.*

Com'fortable. Pleasant, agreeable, commodious; snug, cosy.

ANT. *Uncomfortable, inconvenient, cheerless.*

Com'ic. Comical, droll, ludicrous, laughable, funny, amusing.

ANT. *Tragic, dull, serious.*

Command'. See BID and GOVERN.

Command' *(n.).* See INJUNCTION.

Commence'. See BEGIN.

Commend'. Commit, hand over, recommend, praise, applaud, approve.

ANT. *Censure, disapprove.*

Commens'urate. See EQUIVA-
LENT.

Com'ment. Note, annotation,
observation, criticism.

Com'merce. Trade, traffic, dealing ; intercourse, communication.

Commis'erate. Pity, compassionate, sympathize, condole
with.

Commiss'ion. Charge, warrant,
mandate, function ; fee, allowance, brokerage; body of
delegates or commissioners ;
perpetration.

Commo'dious. Convenient,
roomy, spacious, fit.
ANT. *Inconvenient, cramped,
incommodious.*

Com'mon. General, popular ;
ordinary, usual ; low, mean,
vulgar ; frequent.
ANT. *Particular, individual ;
unusual ; refined ; infrequent,
rare.*

Com'monplace. See HACK-
NEYED.

Commu'nicate. Take part in,
impart, tell, reveal, publish.
ANT. *Refuse to share in,
conceal, keep silent.*

Commu'nion. Intercourse, con-
verse, fellowship, agreement ;
Eucharist, Mass.
ANT. *Non-communion, dis-
agreement.*

Com'pact. Agreement, contract, covenant, bargain.
ANT. *Disagreement, quarrel.*

Com'pany. Associates, society,
group ; corporation.
ANT. *Solitude.*

Compare'. Parallel, liken, col-
late.
ANT. *Contrast.*

Com'pass. Surround, encircle.
See also ACCOMPLISH.
ANT. *Exclude ; lose.*

Compassion. Pity, sympathy,
commiseration, mercy, hu-
manity.
ANT. *Ruthlessness, anti-
pathy.*

Compat'ible. Suitable, accordant, consonant, consistent.
ANT. *Incompatible, disso-
nant.*

Compel'. See ENFORCE.

Com'pensate. Reward, recompense, repay. See also
BALANCE.

Com'petent. Able, fitted, sufficient ; clever, qualified.
ANT. *Incompetent, unqualified.*

Compla'cent. See AFFABLE.

Complain'. See GRUMBLE.

Complaint'. Charge, lament,
murmuring ; sickness, illness.
ANT. *Cheerful cry ; health.*

Complai'sant. See AFFABLE.

Complete'. Finish, perfect, fulfil,
consummate, end.
ANT. *Begin, attempt.*

Complex'ion. See ASPECT.

Com'pliment. Commendation,
flattery, praise, favour.
ANT. *Disapproval, disfa-
vour.*

Comply'. See ACCEDE.

Compose'. Constitute, form,
make ; settle, adjust ; soothe,
calm.
ANT. *Unsettle, discompose,
excite.*

Compound'. (*vb.*) Mix, combine,
blend, settle, adjust, compromise.
ANT. *Separate, dissolve,
leave unsettled.*

Com'pound (*n.*). Mixture, combination, medley.
ANT. *Solution.*

Compo'sure. See EQUANIMITY.

Comprehend'. Comprise, embrace, include ; grasp, perceive, understand.
ANT. *Exclude ; misunder-
stand, fail to perceive.*

Comprehens'ible. See INTELLI-
GIBLE.

Comprehen'sive. Inclusive, extensive, broad.
ANT. *Exclusive, narrow.*

Compress'. Squeeze, press ;
condense, contract.
ANT. *Loosen, widen.*

Comprise'. Embrace, include, comprehend.

ANT. *Exclude.*

Com'promise. Settle, compound; implicate.

ANT. *Leave unsettled; excuse.*

Compul'sion. Force, coercion, pressure.

ANT. *Freedom, liberty.*

Compul'sory. See INVOLUNTARY.

Compunc'tion. Remorse, regret, sting of conscience.

ANT. *Impenitence, recklessness.*

Compute'. See CALCULATE.

Conceal'. Hide, cover, shelter, dissemble, disguise.

ANT. *Reveal, disclose, uncover.*

Concede'. See ALLOW.

Conceive'. See COMPREHEND.

Concern'. Care, anxiety, solicitude; affair, matter, importance, weight; business, establishment.

ANT. *Indifference, unimportance.*

Concert'. Contrive, plot, devise.

Concil'iate. Reconcile, appease, pacify, win over.

ANT. *Repel, anger, annoy.*

Concise'. Short, brief, terse, summary, succinct, pithy.

ANT. *Diffuse, lengthy, long-winded.*

Conclude'. See CLOSE.

Conclu'sion. End, termination, close; inference, deduction.

ANT. *Beginning, commencement.*

Con'cord. Agreement, harmony, accord, unison.

ANT. *Disagreement, discord.*

Con'course. Assembly, gathering, crowd, throng.

ANT. *Solitude.*

Concur'. See ACCEDE.

Condemn'. Blame, censure, reproach, upbraid; sentence, convict.

ANT. *Praise, approve; pardon, acquit.*

Condense'. Compress, consolidate; abridge; epitomize; thicken, harden.

ANT. *Loosen, disintegrate, dissolve; lengthen, expand; soften.*

Condescen'sion. Submission, humiliation; deference, courtesy, favour, civility.

ANT. *Arrogance; discourtesy, incivility.*

Condi'tion. Circumstances, case, situation, plight, state; stipulation, terms, provision.

Condole'. See COMMISERATE.

Conduct' (*vb.*). See GUIDE.

Con'duct. Behaviour, demeanour, bearing, management, guidance, escort.

Confed'eracy. See ALLIANCE.

Confer'. Give, bestow: consult, discuss, deliberate.

ANT. *Refuse.*

Confess'. Admit, grant, allow; reveal, avow, acknowledge.

ANT. *Disallow, deny, conceal, disavow.*

Con'fidence. Assurance, trust, belief; boldness, self-reliance.

ANT. *Distrust, disbelief; fear, doubt.*

Confirm'. Strengthen, establish, settle; verify, corroborate; ratify, bind.

ANT. *Weaken, unsettle; disprove; loose, dissolve.*

Con'flict. See COMBAT.

Conflict'ing. Discordant, disagreeing, contrary.

ANT. *Agreeing, consistent.*

Confound'. Mix, confuse; embarrass, perplex, astonish; defeat, overthrow.

ANT. *Distinguish; enlighten; maintain.*

Confront'. See COMBAT.

Confuse'. Mix, mingle; disorder, disarrange; perplex, obscure; abash, disconcert.

ANT. *Distinguish; order, arrange; illuminate; encourage.*

Confute'. Disprove, refute, oppugn.

ANT. *Prove, support.*

17

Congrat'ulate. Felicitate, compliment, salute.
ANT. *Condole.*

Con'gregate. See ASSEMBLE.

Con'gruous. Fit, appropriate, concordant, consistent.
ANT. *Unfit, unseemly, discordant.*

Conjec'ture. Hypothesis, supposition, surmise, guess.
ANT. *Certainty.*

Conjure'. Adjure, implore, beseech, supplicate.
ANT. *Command.*

Connect'. Bind, join, unite, couple, link.
ANT. *Unbind, loosen, disconnect, disjoin, uncouple.*

Connive'. Wink at, overlook, disregard.
ANT. *Oppose, refuse to take part in.*

Con'quest. Victory, triumph, mastery; subjection.
ANT. *Defeat ; domination.*

Conscien'tious. Scrupulous, high-principled, exact, honourable.
ANT. *Unscrupulous, unprincipled, dishonourable.*

Con'secrate. Sanctify, dedicate, hallow, devote.
ANT. *Desecrate.*

Consent'. See ACCEDE.

Con'sequence. Effect, result, issue, outcome ; weight, importance.
ANT. *Cause, antecedents ; unimportance.*

Consid'er. See COGITATE.

Consid'erate. Thoughtful ; unselfish, forbearing.
ANT. *Thoughtless ; selfish.*

Consign'. Commit, deliver, deposit.
ANT. *Withhold, withdraw.*

Consist'ent. Congruous, conscientious. See COMPATIBLE.
ANT. *Inconsistent.*

Console'. See COMMISERATE.

Con'sonant. See CONGRUOUS.

Conspic'uous. Noticeable, remarkable, famous ; manifest.

ANT. *Insignificant, unknown ; obscure.*

Conspir'acy. Plot, combination, intrigue, league.

Conspire'. Combine, co-operate ; hatch treason, plot, intrigue.
ANT. *Hold aloof.*

Con'stancy. Firmness, stability, steadiness, steadfastness ; persistence, regularity.
ANT. *Instability, unsteadiness ; irregularity.*

Con'stitute. Make, form, compose ; appoint, empower.

Constitu'tional. Fundamental ; lawful, legitimate.
ANT. *Unconstitutional, illegitimate.*

Constrain'. See COERCE.

Construct'. See BUILD.

Construc'tion. Building, erection, formation, structure ; form, shape ; rendering, interpretation.
ANT. *Destruction.*

Con'strue. Analyse, interpret, translate, explain ; understand, take to mean.

Consult'. See CONFER.

Consume'. Destroy, exhaust, devour, spend, squander.
ANT. *Preserve, save.*

Consum'mate (*adj.*). Complete, perfect, finished, arrant.
ANT. *Incomplete, imperfect, worst.*

Con'summate (*vb.*). Finish, perfect, conclude, achieve.
ANT. *Begin, attempt.*

Contain'. See COMPREHEND.

Contam'inate. Pollute, defile, infect, taint.
ANT. *Purify.*

Contemn'. Despise, scorn, disregard.
ANT. *Admire, regard, honour.*

Con'template. Observe, consider, ponder, nurse, meditate ; intend, purpose, plan.

Contempt'ible. Despicable, mean, paltry, worthless, pitiful.
ANT. *Honourable, worthy, great.*

Contempt'uous. Scornful, disdainful, supercilious, haughty.
 Ant. *Approving, laudatory, condescending.*
Contend'. Strive, struggle, compete, vie ; maintain, affirm.
 Ant. *Give in, yield.*
Content'ed. Satisfied, pleased, placid. See also Calm.
 Ant. *Discontented, displeased.*
Conten'tious. Disputatious, quarrelsome, captious, litigious.
 Ant. *Peaceful, placid, yielding.*
Con'test. See Affray.
Contig'uous. Adjoining, adjacent, beside, neighbouring.
 Ant. *Separate, remote, apart.*
Contin'gency. See Accident.
Contin'ual. Constant, everlasting, uninterrupted, unceasing.
 Ant. *Short-lived, limited.*
Contin'ue. See Last.
Contin'uous. Connected, prolonged, extended.
 Ant. *Unconnected, shortened, broken, severed.*
Contort'ed. Twisted, wrenched, bent, writhing.
 Ant. *Straight, unbent.*
Contract'. See Abbreviate.
Con'tract (*n.*). See Compact.
Contradict'. See Gainsay.
Con'trary. See Adverse.
Contravene'. Contradict ; interfere, oppose, counteract.
 Ant. *Stand aside, assist.*
Contrib'ute. Furnish, supply, subscribe ; conduce, tend.
 Ant. *Withhold.*
Con'trite. Penitent, sorry, repentant, humble.
 Ant. *Impenitent, obstinate.*
Contri'vance. Formation, fabrication, invention, design, scheme.
Control'. See Check.
Con'troversy. See Altercation.
Controvert'. See Gainsay.
Con'tumely. Insult, opprobrium, indignity.
 Ant. *Courtesy, respect.*

Convene'. See Assemble.
Conve'nient. See Commodious.
Conversa'tion. Intercourse, discourse, dialogue, talk, chat.
 Ant. *Silence.*
Convert'. Turn, change, alter, appropriate ; convince.
 Ant. *Leave unchanged ; fail to convince.*
Con'vert. Proselyte, neophyte, catechumen.
Convey'. Carry, bear, support, transfer ; demise, devolve.
 Ant. *Drop.*
Convict'. Detect, convince, confute.
 Ant. *Charge, accuse.*
Con'vict. Felon, culprit, criminal.
 Ant. *Innocent person.*
Conviv'ial. Festive, social, joyous, merry, hilarious.
 Ant. *Sad, unsociable.*
Convoke'. See Assemble.
Convulse'. Shake, agitate, shatter, perturb.
 Ant. *Steady, soothe.*
Convul'sion. Spasm, cramp. See also Agitation.
Cool'. Coldish ; calm ; dispassionate ; impudent.
 Ant. *Warm ; impassioned, excited ; respectful.*
Coop'. Confine, cage, cramp, immure.
 Ant. *Enlarge, set free.*
Co-op'erate. See Aid.
Co'pious. See Abundant.
Copy' (*vb.*). Imitate, follow, transcribe.
 Ant. *Originate.*
Copy (*n.*). See Example.
Cor'dial. Warm-hearted, friendly, agreeable, hearty ; restorative.
 Ant. *Cold, frigid ; depressing.*
Corol'lary. Inference, induction, consequence.
 Ant. *Proposition.*
Corpo'real. Bodily, physical, substantial.

ANT. *Spiritual, non-material.*

Corp'ulent. Stout, fat, portly, obese, fleshy.

ANT. *Thin, lean.*

Correct'. Accurate, right, faultless, upright, strict.

ANT. *Inaccurate, careless, loose.*

Correspond'. Agree, fit, harmonize, tally, match ; write.

ANT. *Disagree, be unlike.*

Correspond'ence. Writing, communication. See also AGREEMENT.

Corrob'orate. Strengthen, establish, confirm, support.

ANT. *Weaken, disprove.*

Corro'sive. Corroding, caustic, acrid.

ANT. *Harmless.*

Corrupt' (*vb.*). See DEBASE.

Corrupt'. Debased, defiled, tainted ; impure, depraved ; venal.

ANT. *Incorrupt, incorruptible, pure ; honest.*

Cor'uscate. Flash, gleam, glitter, scintillate.

ANT. *Flame, burn steadily.*

Cory'phaeus. Leader, conductor, *chef d'orchestre.*

ANT. *Follower.*

Cost'. Price, charge, amount.

Cost'ly. Dear, expensive, high-priced.

ANT. *Cheap, low-priced, inexpensive.*

Cost'ume. See ATTIRE.

Coun'cil. Meeting, gathering, congress, conclave, diet.

Coun'sel. Deliberation, forethought ; advice, suggestion ; barrister, advocate.

ANT. *Client.*

Count'. See ESTIMATE.

Coun'tenance. See ASPECT.

Coun'tenance (*vb.*). Favour, sanction, approve.

ANT. *Discountenance, disapprove, forbid.*

Coun'terfeit. Forged, false, suppositions, sham.

ANT. *Real, genuine.*

Coun'terpart. Match, fellow, duplicate.

ANT. *Contrast, antithesis.*

Coup'le. Join, unite, buckle.

ANT. *Uncouple, disjoin.*

Cour'age. Bravery, intrepidity, valour, heroism, daring, prowess.

ANT. *Cowardice, timidity.*

Coura'geous. See BOLD.

Course'. Passage, progress, direction. See also ADVANCE.

Court'. Woo, flatter, make love, solicit.

ANT. *Ignore, repel, shun.*

Court'eous. See AFFABLE and CIVIL.

Court'esy. Politeness, urbanity, civility, respect.

ANT. *Discourtesy, incivility, rudeness.*

Court'ly. See AFFABLE and CIVIL.

Cov'enant. See COMPACT.

Cov'er. See CONCEAL.

Cov'ert. Hidden, secret, private, disguised, clandestine.

ANT. *Open, undisguised, overt.*

Cov'et. Long for, desire, lust after, aspire to.

ANT. *Disdain.*

Cov'etous. See GRASPING.

Cow'ard. Craven, dastard, poltroon.

ANT. *Hero, warrior.*

Cow'er. Shrink, crouch, stoop, squat.

ANT. *Face, stand upright.*

Coy'. Modest, bashful, shy, reserved.

ANT. *Unblushing, forward.*

Coz'en. See CHEAT.

Craft'. Skill, art, dexterity : guile, cunning ; trade, occupation.

ANT. *Clumsiness, simplicity, ingenuousness.*

Craft'y. Cunning, artful, wily, sly, insidious, astute.

ANT. *Ingenuous, honest, direct.*

Crave'. Ask, beg, seek, petition.

ANT. *Refuse, be indifferent to.*

Cra'ven. See COWARD.

Crawl'. See CREEP.

Cra'zy. Shattered, broken, weak ; insane, deranged, mad, silly.

ANT. *Strong, unbroken ; sane, sensible.*

Create'. See CAUSE.

Cre'dence. Belief, faith, trust, confidence ; a side table (ecclesiastical).

ANT. *Doubt, distrust.*

Creden'tial. Voucher, testimonial, warrant, certificate.

Cred'ible. Believable, true, probable.

ANT. *Incredible, unbelievable.*

Cred'it. Belief, trust, faith ; reputation, estimation ; merit, praise ; allowance.

ANT. *Discredit, distrust ; debit.*

Cred'itable. Praiseworthy, honourable, respectable.

ANT. *Discreditable, dishonourable.*

Credu'lity. See GULLIBILITY.

Cred'ulous. Gullible, simple.

ANT. *Critical, sharp, sceptical.*

Creep'. Crawl, cringe.

ANT. *Walk upright.*

Crest'. Plume, tuft, comb ; head, summit.

Crev'ice. Cleft, fissure, rift, interstice.

Crime'. Offence, fault, misdeed ; felony, sin, iniquity.

ANT. *Innocence, guiltlessness.*

Crim'inal. Malefactor, culprit, delinquent ; felon, convict.

ANT. *Innocent person, well-doer.*

Cringe'. See COWER.

Crip'ple. Lame, disable, cramp, weaken.

ANT. *Help, strengthen, free.*

Cri'sis. Turning-point ; emergency, conjuncture ; strait.

Crit'ical. Dangerous, hazardous;

delicate, fastidious, carping ; momentous.

ANT. *Safe ; undiscriminating ; tolerant ; unimportant.*

Crite'rion. Test, touchstone, standard, proof.

Crit'icism. Stricture, animadversion, notice, review, analysis.

ANT. *Approval, indulgence.*

Cross'. Intersecting, transverse ; peevish, ill-tempered, crusty, pettish.

ANT. *Straight, vertical ; good-tempered, contented.*

Crowd'. Throng, multitude, mob, mass.

Cru'cial. Testing, severe, trying, decisive.

ANT. *Indecisive.*

Crude.' Raw, uncooked, unripe ; undigested; unfinished; coarse.

ANT. *Cooked, digested ; ripe : perfect ; refined.*

Cru'el. Savage, fierce, barbarous, harsh, pitiless ; hard, bitter.

ANT. *Gentle, civilized, pitiful ; mild, easy.*

Cru'elty. See FEROCITY.

Crust'. Incrustation, coating ; shell, surface ; piece of bread.

ANT. *Inside, interior ; crumb.*

Cud'gel. Club, stick, bludgeon.

Cuff'. Knock, beat, buffet, slap.

Culmina'tion. Summit, zenith, top, crown.

ANT. *Bottom, base.*

Cul'pable. Blameworthy, guilty, faulty, censurable.

ANT. *Blameless, innocent.*

Culp'rit. See CRIMINAL.

Cul'ture. Husbandry, farming ; refinement, civilization ; improvement.

ANT. *Neglect, rudeness, ignorance, unenlightenment.*

Cun'ning. See CRAFTY.

Cupid'ity. Covetousness, avarice, greediness.

ANT. *Unselfishness.*

Curb'. See CHECK.

Cure'. Remedy, healing, specific ; recovery ; charge of souls (ecclesiastical).

ANT. *Illness, malady.*

Curios'ity. Inquisitiveness ; interest ; oddity, novelty, rarity.

ANT. *Indifference, incuriousness ; familiar object.*

Cu'rious. Inquisitive, prying ; rare, strange, queer.

ANT. *Uninquisitive, incurious ; ordinary.*

Cur'rency. Publicity ; circulation ; money.

ANT. *Concealment, suppression.*

Curse'. Malediction, execration, ban, excommunication ; bane, plague.

ANT. *Blessing, absolution.*

Curs'ory. Transient, rapid, summary ; superficial.

ANT. *Constant ; leisurely ; thorough.*

Curtail'. See ABRIDGE.

Cus'tody. Guardianship, ward, charge ; confinement, imprisonment.

ANT. *Freedom, release.*

Cus'tom. Usage, habit, fashion, manner ; patronage, support ; tax, duty.

Cus'tomary. Usual, wonted, ordinary, familiar, habitual.

ANT. *Unusual, unwonted, unfamiliar.*

Cyn'ical. Snarling, captious, sarcastic, morose.

ANT. *Benignant, generous uncritical, cheery.*

D

Daft'. Silly, idiotic, witless.

ANT. *Sane, wise.*

Daint'y. Delicious, palatable ; nice ; delicate, neat.

ANT. *Unpalatable ; uncritical ; inelegant.*

Dam'age. Injury, hurt ; loss, harm, mischief.

ANT. *Reparation ; gain.*

Dance'. See HOP.

Dand'le. See CARESS.

Dan'ger. Peril, hazard, risk, jeopardy.

ANT. *Safety, security.*

Dan'gerous. See HAZARDOUS.

Dare'. Venture, hazard ; challenge, defy.

ANT. *Shirk, dread.*

Dark'. Black, dusky, sable ; shady ; obscure, abstruse ; dismal ; benighted, ignorant ; vile, foul.

ANT. *Light, unshaded ; clear ; cheerful, bright ; intelligent, well-informed ; clean.*

Dark'ness. See GLOOM.

Dart'. Hurl, cast, throw, emit ; rush, fly.

Dash'. Hurl, cast ; smash, destroy ; abash, disappoint ; rush, haste.

ANT. *Retain ; encourage; stand still.*

Dast'ard. See COWARD.

Daunt'. Dismay, terrify, intimidate, scare.

ANT. *Encourage, cheer.*

Dawn'. Break, appear, gleam, rise ; begin, open.

ANT. *Sink, disappear, set ; end.*

Dead'. Deceased, departed, defunct, lifeless ; dull, cold, torpid.

ANT. *Living, alive ; lively, animated.*

Dead'ly. Fatal, lethal, destructive, noxious.

ANT. *Harmless, innocuous.*

Deaf'. Without hearing, averse, inexorable.

ANT. *Willing, placable.*

Dear'. Costly, precious ; beloved, cherished.

ANT. *Cheap, low-priced; hateful, disliked.*

Dearth'. Scarcity, lack, want, famine.

ANT. *Plenty.*

Debar'. Hinder, prevent, exclude, shut out.

ANT. *Facilitate, admit.*

Debase'. Degrade, humiliate ; corrupt, pollute.

ANT. *Exalt ; purify.*

Debate'. See ARGUE.

Debauch'ery. Dissipation, intemperance, licentiousness.

ANT. *Temperance, purity.*

Debil'ity. Weakness, infirmity, feebleness.

ANT. *Strength, health.*

Debt'. Liability, obligation ; trespass, transgression, sin.

ANT. *Credit.*

Decay'. Decline, waste, wither, fade.

ANT. *Grow, increase, flourish.*

Decayed'. See CORRUPT.

Decease'. Death, dissolution, demise.

ANT. *Birth.*

Deceased'. See DEAD.

Deceit'. See FRAUD.

Deceive'. See CHEAT.

De'cent. See BECOMING.

ANT. *Indecent.*

Decep'tive. See FALLACIOUS.

Decide'. Determine, conclude ; adjudge, resolve, purpose.

ANT. *Begin ; defer judgment, hesitate.*

Deci'pher. Unfold, interpret, solve, explain.

Decis'ion. Settlement, conclusion, judgment ; firmness, resolution.

ANT. *Indecision, irresoluteness.*

Declaim'. Harangue, recite, speak out.

ANT. *Be silent.*

Declare'. See AFFIRM.

Decline'. Lean, droop. See also DECAY.

ANT. *Stand upright.*

Decliv'ity. Slope, incline, descent.

ANT. *Acclivity, ascent.*

Dec'orate. Adorn, embellish, ornament, beautify.

ANT. *Spoil, mar.*

Deco'rum. Propriety, decency, gravity, staidness.

ANT. *Impropriety, levity, lack of dignity.*

Decrease'. Lessen, diminish, reduce, abate.

ANT. *Enlarge, increase, raise.*

Decree'. Law, edict, ordinance, mandate.

Decry'. Cry down, disparage, denounce. See also ABASE.

ANT. *Praise, applaud.*

Ded'icate. See CONSECRATE.

Deed'. Act, achievement, exploit ; document, instrument.

Deem'. Consider, judge, think, believe.

ANT. *Doubt.*

Deep'. Profound, intense ; recondite, abstruse ; cunning.

ANT. *Shallow ; simple.*

Deface'. Disfigure, damage, injure, spoil.

ANT. *Improve, preserve.*

Defama'tion. See CALUMNY.

Default'er. Delinquent, peculator.

Defeat'. See CONQUEST.

Defect'. See BLEMISH.

Defec'tion. Desertion, abandonment.

ANT. *Loyalty, adherence.*

Defective. See IMPERFECT.

Defend'. See GUARD.

Defend'. Guard, protect, shield ; maintain, vindicate.

ANT. *Desert, leave unprotected ; repudiate ; accuse.*

Defer'. See ADJOURN.

Def'erence. Respect, reverence, honour, homage.

ANT. *Disrespect, rudeness.*

Defi'cient. Lacking, inadequate, wanting.

ANT. *Sufficient, adequate.*

Defile'. Corrupt, soil, stain, contaminate.

ANT. *Cleanse, purify.*

Define'. Limit, bound, determine, specify ; explain.

ANT. *Enlarge ; leave uncertain.*

Def'inite. Fixed, determined, precise, clear.

ANT. *Indefinite, uncertain, vague, dim.*

Defin'itive. Positive, express ; final, conclusive.

ANT. *Inconclusive, vague.*

Deform'ity. Malformation, ugliness, disfigurement, monstrosity.

ANT. *Shapeliness.*

Defraud'. See CHEAT.

Defray'. Discharge, liquidate, settle.

ANT. *Be in debt.*

Defunct'. See DEAD.

Degen'erate. See CORRUPT.

Degra'ded. See CORRUPT and BASE (*adj.*).

Degree'. Step, stage ; class, rank ; limit, space, interval.

ANT. *Leap, bound.*

Deign'. Deem worthy, condescend ; grant. See also ACCORD.

ANT. *Disdain, refuse.*

Deject'ed. Cast down, depressed, downhearted, crushed.

ANT. *Uplifted, heartened, in good spirits.*

Dejec'tion. See HEAVINESS.

Delay'. Procrastinate. See also ADJOURN.

ANT. *Hasten.*

Delect'able. Delightful, charming, pleasant.

ANT. *Unpleasant, disagreeable.*

Del'egate. Commission, depute, authorize, entrust, transfer.

ANT. *Retain, withhold.*

Delete'rious. Harmful, noxious, penurious, deadly.

ANT. *Innocuous, harmless.*

Delib'erate. See COGITATE.

Delib'erate (*adj.*). Circumspect, cautious, careful, slow.

ANT. *Thoughtless, hasty, ill-considered.*

Del'icacy. Refinement, nicety ; slenderness, weakness ;

scrupulosity, considerateness ; purity.

ANT. *Rudeness, strength ; inconsiderateness, indelicacy.*

Delight'. Pleasure, happiness, joy, rapture.

ANT. *Displeasure, disappointment, dislike.*

Delin'eate. Depict, draw, sketch, portray.

Delin'quent. See CRIMINAL and DEFAULTER.

Deliv'er. Give up, liberate, release, surrender ; utter, pronounce.

ANT. *Hold, imprison.*

Del'uge. See FLOOD.

Delu'sion. Illusion, fancy ; error ; imposture, artifice.

ANT. *Reality.*

Demand'. See CLAIM.

Demean'. Behave, bear oneself.

Demean'our. Behaviour, conduct, bearing.

Dement'ed. See CRAZY and INSANE.

Demise'. Conveyance, alienation (legal) ; see also DECEASE.

Demol'ish. See ANNIHILATE.

Dem'onstrate. Prove, indicate, show, establish.

ANT. *Disprove, weaken.*

Demur'. Stop, pause, hesitate ; object.

ANT. *Act promptly ; agree.*

Demure'. See COY.

Denom'ination. Name, appellation, designation ; sect, school.

Denote'. Signify, betoken, typify.

Denounce'. Accuse, arraign, condemn, inveigh.

ANT. *Defend.*

Deny'. Contradict, gainsay, disavow ; withhold.

ANT. *Affirm ; grant, accept*

Depart'ment. Portion, section, sphere, office.

ANT. *Whole.*

Depart'ure. Removal, withdrawal.

ANT. *Arrival.*

Depend'ent (*n.*). Retainer, client.

ANT. *Patron, lord.*

Depict'. See DELINEATE.

Deplore'. Mourn, lament, bewail ; regret.

ANT. *Rejoice over.*

Deport'ment. See DEMEANOUR.

Depose'. Dethrone, degrade, cashier ; testify.

ANT. *Enthrone, exalt.*

Depraved'. See CORRUPT and BASE.

Depre'ciate. Fall in value. See also DECRY.

ANT. *Appreciate.*

Depressed'. See DEJECTED.

Deprive'. Bereave, despoil, strip, dispossess.

ANT. *Supply, furnish.*

Depute'. See DELEGATE.

Derelic'tion. Relinquishment, abandonment, neglect.

ANT. *Fulfilment.*

Deride'. Ridicule, mock, taunt, flout. See also JEER.

ANT. *Praise, sympathize with.*

Deriva'tion. Origin, source, descent ; etymology.

Der'ogate. See DEPRECIATE.

Descant'. Discourse, expatiate, enlarge.

ANT. *Say nothing.*

Descend'. Fall, come down, sink, alight, be derived.

ANT. *Ascend, rise, mount.*

Describe'. Relate, recount. See also DELINEATE.

Des'ecrate. Profane, pollute.

ANT. *Consecrate, purify.*

Desert'. See ABANDON.

Des'ert (*n.*). Wilderness, wild, waste.

ANT. *Cultivated country, inhabited region.*

Desert' (*n.*). Merit, worth.

ANT. *Demerit.*

Deserve'. Merit, earn, justify.

ANT. *Be unworthy.*

Design'. Sketch, outline, plan ; purpose, intention ; meaning.

Des'ignate. Name, nominate, appoint.

Desire'. See CRAVE and COVET.

Desist'. Leave off, stop, forbear.

ANT. *Continue, go on.*

Des'olate. Deserted, lonely, ruined, devastated ; wretched. See also DISCONSOLATE.

ANT. *Populous, inhabited; untouched ; cheerful.*

Despair'. Hopelessness, despondency, dejection.

ANT. *Hope, confidence, cheerfulness.*

Des'picable. Contemptible, shameful, mean, worthless.

ANT. *Honourable, commendable.*

Despise'. See CONTEMN.

Despond'. Despair, lose hope.

ANT. *Hope, look up.*

Despond'ency. See HEAVINESS and DESPAIR.

Des'pot. Tyrant, lord, oppressor, autocrat.

ANT. *Constitutional ruler, protector.*

Despot'ic. Unconstitutional, arbitrary, tyrannical.

ANT. *Constitutional, reasonable, mild.*

Dest'iny. Destination, lot, fortune, fate.

Des'titute. Wanting ; needy ; poor, indigent, necessitous.

ANT. *Well-provided, well off.*

Destroy'. See ANNIHILATE.

Destruc'tion. Demolition, ruin, extinction, ravage, ruin.

ANT. *Construction, rebuilding, revival.*

Des'ultory. Rambling, discursive, casual, spasmodic.

ANT. *Steady, straightforward.*

Detail'. Particularize, enumerate, specify, detach for special service.

ANT. *Generalize.*

Detain'. Hold, stop. See ARREST.

ANT. *Let go, dismiss.*

Detect'. Discover, expose, descry, unmask.

ANT. *Miss, conceal.*

Deter'. Discourage, frighten, prevent, hinder.

Ant. *Encourage, egg on.*

Dete'riorate. Lower, impair, spoil ; grow worse, degenerate.

Ant. *Ameliorate, improve.*

Determina'tion. Decision, resolve ; firmness, resoluteness ; ending.

Ant. *Hesitation, indecision, irresoluteness ; beginning.*

Detest'. See Abhor.

Detest'able. See Execrable.

Detesta'tion. See Enmity

Dethrone'. See Depose.

Detract'. See Decry.

Det'riment. See Damage.

Detriment'al. See Deleterious.

Dev'astate. Ravage, lay waste, destroy.

Ant. *Repair, cultivate.*

Devasta'tion. See Havoc.

Devel'op. Expand, cultivate, exhibit ; grow.

Ant. *Neglect ; conceal ; decline.*

De'viate. Wander, digress, diverge.

Ant. *Go straight.*

Device'. See Contrivance.

Dev'il. Fiend, Satan.

De'vious. Wandering, roving, rambling, out of the way.

Ant. *Straight.*

Devoid'. Empty, vacant ; unprovided with.

Ant. *Full, well supplied.*

Devolve'. See Delegate, Deliver.

Devote'. Consecrate, dedicate ; apply ; destine.

Ant. *Take back, withhold.*

Devour'. Swallow, gorge ; ravage, destroy, consume.

Ant. *Disgorge ; spare.*

Devout'. Religious, pious, reverent ; devoted.

Ant. *Irreligious, irreverent; indifferent.*

Dexter'ity. Skill, adroitness, facility.

Ant. *Clumsiness,*

Diabol'ical. See Hellish.

Diaph'anous. Transparent, clear.

Ant. *Thick, non-transparent, opaque.*

Di'atribe. Disquisition ; philippic, tirade.

Dictate'. Command, order, enjoin, direct, prompt.

Ant. *Obey.*

Dictato'rial. See Arbitrary and Absolute.

Di'et. Victuals, fare, regimen ; council, congress.

Dif'ferent. Unlike, diverse, various.

Ant. *Identical, same.*

Dif'ficult. Arduous, laborious, hard ; unaccommodating.

Ant. *Easy ; accommodating.*

Dif'fident. Hesitating, doubtful, distrusting, bashful.

Ant. *Confident, trusting ; bold.*

Diffuse'. Loose, verbose, prolix, discursive.

Ant. *Terse, laconic.*

Dig'. Delve, excavate, penetrate.

Digest'. Assimilate, arrange ; systematize, classify ; ponder. See Consider.

Ant. *Confuse, disorder.*

Di'gest. See Abridgment.

Dig'nified. Exalted, noble, stately.

Ant. *Undignified, ungraceful, awkward.*

Digress'ion. See Excursion.

Digress'ive. See Devious.

Dilapida'ted. Ruined, wasted, demolished.

Ant. *In repair, restored.*

Dilate'. Expand, widen, distend ; discourse, descant.

Ant. *Contract, narrow ; be silent.*

Dil'atory. Slow, tardy, slack.

Ant. *Quick, prompt.*

Dil'igence. Industry, care, perseverance, assiduousness.

Ant. *Laziness, slackness, idleness.*

Dim'. See Gloomy.

Dimen′sion. Size, measurement, bulk, magnitude.

Dimin′ish. Lessen, decrease, reduce ; impair.

    ANT. *Increase, enlarge ; strengthen.*

Din′. See CLAMOUR.

Dip′. See IMMERSE.

Dire′. Terrible, horrible, awful, fearful.

    ANT. *Harmless.*

Direct′. Aim, point, turn, guide, lead ; order, address.

    ANT. *Follow ; obey.*

Direct′ *(adj.).* Straight, straightforward ; plain, open ; immediate.

    ANT. *Crooked ; vague ; indirect.*

Disabil′ity. Disqualification, unfitness, incapacity.

    ANT. *Qualification, aptitude, capability.*

Disadvantage. See ADVANTAGE.

Disaffect′ed. Alienated, estranged ; disloyal.

    ANT. *Friendly ; loyal.*

Disagree′able. Unpleasant, displeasing, offensive, distasteful.

    ANT. *Pleasant, agreeable, unoffending.*

Disallow′. See ALLOW and DENY.

Disappoint′. Tantalize, frustrate, balk, foil.

    ANT. *Satisfy, please.*

Disapprove′. Condemn, disallow, reject.

    ANT. *Approve, adopt.*

Disas′ter. See ADVERSITY.

Disavow′. See DENY.

Disburd′en. Unload, relieve, disencumber.

    ANT. *Load, encumber.*

Discern′. Perceive, descry, behold ; distinguish, recognize, judge.

    ANT. *Misunderstand, confuse.*

Discern′ment. Judgment, sagacity, astuteness, perception.

    ANT. *Stupidity.*

Disci′ple. Follower, learner, scholar.

    ANT. *Master, teacher, leader.*

Dis′cipline. Control, government, order ; correction ; drill.

    ANT. *Indiscipline, unruliness.*

Disclaim′. See AVOW.

Disclose′. Uncover, reveal ; divulge, make known.

    ANT. *Cover, hide, conceal ; keep secret.*

Discom′fort. See ANNOY.

Discon′solate. Sad, cheerless, forlorn, miserable.

    ANT. *Happy, cheerful.*

Discontent′ed. See CONTENTED.

Dis′cord. See CONCORD.

Dis′count. Allowance, rebate, drawback, reduction.

    ANT. *Interest, addition.*

Discour′age. Dispirit, depress, cast down ; disfavour, discountenance.

    ANT. *Encourage, hearten ; favour, approve.*

Discov′er. Manifest, reveal ; find, espy.

    ANT. *Conceal ; fail to see.*

Discred′it. Disbelieve, doubt ; disgrace, dishonour.

    ANT. *Credit, believe ; honour.*

Discred′it *(n.).* Disbelief, doubt ; disgrace.

    ANT. *Credit, trust ; honour.*

Discreet′. See CIRCUMSPECT.

Discrim′inate. See DISCERN.

Discrimina′tion. See DISCERNMENT.

Discur′sive. Rambling, digressive, erratic.

    ANT. *Coherent, straightforward.*

Discuss′. See ARGUE.

Disdain′. See CONTEMN ; also DEIGN.

Disease′. Disorder, malady, complaint, sickness, infirmity.

    ANT. *Health.*

Disgrace′. Dishonour, discredit, shame, opprobrium, disfavour.

    ANT. *Credit, repute, favour.*

27

Disguise'. See CONCEAL.

Disgust'. See ABHORRENCE.

Disinclina'tion. See AVERSION.

Disinclined'. See AVERSE.

Disint'erested. Fair, impartial, unbiased ; generous.
ANT. *Biased, partial ; ungenerous.*

Dislike'. See AVERSION.

Dis'mal. See CHEERFUL.

Dismay'. See AFFRIGHT.

Dismiss'. Send away, discharge, cashier ; reject.
ANT. *Summon, retain ; approve.*

Disor'der. See DISCIPLINE and DISEASE.

Disord'erly. Unruly, undisciplined, turbulent, noisy.
ANT. *Disciplined, quiet, orderly.*

Disor'ganize. Derange, disorder, disarrange, break up.
ANT. *Arrange, set in order.*

Disown'. Disclaim, deny, renounce.
ANT. *Acknowledge, accept.*

Dispar'age. See DECRY and ABASE.

Dispass'ionate. See COOL.

Disperse'. See ASSEMBLE.

Display'. Spread out, exhibit, show.
ANT. *Hide, conceal.*

Dispose'. Arrange, adjust, order ; incline.

Dispute'. See ARGUE.

Dispute'. See ALTERCATION.

Disquisi'tion. Discourse, treatise, dissertation.

Disregard'. Overlook, neglect, slight. See also CONTEMN.
ANT. *Notice, favour.*

Disrep'utable. Disgraceful, discreditable, infamous, vile, base.
ANT. *Reputable, creditable, honourable.*

Dissem'ble. See CONCEAL.

Dissem'inate. Spread, scatter, circulate, propagate.
ANT. *Withhold, withdraw.*

Disserta'tion. See DISQUISITION.

Dissim'ilar. See DIVERSE.

Dissimula'tion. Hypocrisy, duplicity, deceit.
ANT. *Sincerity, truthfulness, frankness.*

Dis'solute. See CORRUPT.

Dissolve'. Break up, melt, liquefy ; destroy, ruin ; fade away ; perish.
ANT. *Solidify ; restore ; revive.*

Distaste'. See ABHORRENCE.

Distinct'. Different, separate ; definite ; distinguishable ; clear.
ANT. *Similar, conjoint ; vague, indefinite ; dim.*

Disting'uish. See DISCERN.

Disting'uished. See DIGNIFIED and CELEBRATED.

Distort'ed. See CONTORTED.

Distract'. See BEWILDER.

Distress'. See AFFLICTION.

Distress'. Grieve, pain, harass.
ANT. *Comfort, encourage.*

Distrib'ute. See ALLOT.

Disturb'. Agitate, shake ; perplex, trouble ; interrupt.
ANT. *Steady, hold still ; enlighten, cheer.*

Divar'icate. Diverge, fork, branch off.
ANT. *Keep straight on.*

Diverge'. See DIVARICATE.

Diverse'. Dissimilar, unlike, various.
ANT. *Similar, alike.*

Diver'sion. See GAME.

Divert'. Turn aside, deflect ; amuse, please, entertain.
ANT. *Straighten ; displease.*

Divide'. Sever, sunder, part. See also ALLOT.
ANT. *Join, unite.*

Divine'. Godlike, heavenly, superhuman, supernatural.
ANT. *Human, earthly, natural.*

Divine' (*vb.*). Predict, foretell, prognosticate ; surmise, guess.

Divulge'. See DISCLOSE.

Do'. See ACCOMPLISH.

Do'cile. Amenable, teachable, tractable.

ANT. *Intractable, disobedient.*

Doct'rine. Precept, principle, teaching, tenet.

Dogmat'ic. Authoritative, categorical, positive ; peremptory ; magisterial.

ANT. *Undogmatic ; vague ; conciliatory.*

Dole'ful. See CHEERFUL.

Dol'orous. See CHEERFUL.

Dolt'. Blockhead, ignoramus, dullard, simpleton.

ANT. *Genius.*

Dom'icile. Dwelling, house, residence.

Dom'inant. Ascendant, prevailing, governing.

ANT. *Subordinate, inferior.*

Doom'. Condemnation, judgment, sentence ; destiny, fate.

ANT. *Acquittal.*

Do'tage. Senility, imbecility, second childhood.

ANT. *Youthfulness, vigour ; infancy.*

Doubt'. Hesitation, distrust, scruple ; uncertainty.

ANT. *Belief, certainty.*

Dought'y. Brave, valiant, courageous.

ANT. *Timid, cowardly.*

Down'right. Simple, sincere, blunt, honest.

ANT. *Crooked, insincere, shifty.*

Draft'. Drawing, selection ; bill of exchange, cheque, sketch, outline, rough copy, abstract.

ANT. *Complete statement, entire MS.*

Drag'. See DRAW.

Draw'. Haul, drag, attract ; derive ; sketch, delineate.

ANT. *Push, repel.*

Dread'. See FEAR.

Dread'ful. Awful, appalling, horrible, terrible, frightful.

ANT. *Harmless, pleasing.*

Drear'y. See CHEERFUL.

Dregs'. Lees, refuse, sediment, grounds.

Drench'. Saturate, soak, wet.

ANT. *Dry.*

Dress'. See ATTIRE.

Drift'. Heap, mass ; bearing, direction ; aim, purport, meaning.

Drink'. See ABSORB.

Drive'. Propel, impel ; push ; urge ; compel ; rush.

ANT. *Arrest, stop ; pull, check ; move slowly.*

Droll'. Amusing, funny, whimsical, diverting, ludicrous.

ANT. *Serious, dull.*

Droop'. See DECAY and DECLINE.

Drown'. Sink, submerge, flood ; overpower, overcome.

ANT. *Float, rise ; leave dry ; blend with.*

Drows'y. Sleepy, somnolent, comatose, lethargic.

ANT. *Awake, alert.*

Drunk'. Intoxicated, inebriated, tipsy, fuddled.

ANT. *Sober, clear-headed.*

Dry'. Arid, parched, thirsty ; plain, dull.

ANT. *Moist, well-watered ; uninteresting.*

Du'bious. See AMBIGUOUS.

Duct'ile. Pliant, flexible.

ANT. *Stiff, solid.*

Due'. Owing ; fit, right, fair, just.

ANT. *Undue, unfit, unjust.*

Dull'. See DOLT, CHEERFUL, DISMAL.

Dupe'. See CHEAT.

Duplic'ity. See DISSIMULATION.

Du'rable. Lasting, abiding, firm, constant.

ANT. *Perishable, weak, not lasting.*

Du'tiful. Duteous, obedient, respectful, docile.

ANT. *Undutiful, disobedient, disrespectful.*

Dwell'. Reside, abide, live, stay, continue.

ANT. *Travel, move on.*

Dwind'le. Decrease, grow less, shrink.

ANT. *Increase, grow, expand.*

E

Eag'er. See ACTIVE.

Earl'y. Betimes, not late, opportune.

ANT. *Late, behind time.*

Earn'. Gain, get, reap, deserve.

ANT. *Forfeit, lose, not merit.*

Earn'est. Eager, ardent, intent ; serious, resolved.

ANT. *Slack, apathetic ; trifling, hesitating.*

Earth'ly. Terrestrial ; sordid, carnal, fleshly.

ANT. *Celestial, heavenly ; spiritual.*

Ease'. See COMFORT.

Eas'y. Not difficult ; graceful ; moderate, gentle. See also COMFORTABLE.

ANT. *Difficult, hard ; ungraceful ; severe.*

Eat'able. Edible, esculent, harmless.

ANT. *Uneatable ; noxious.*

Ebb'. Flow back, fall, sink, wane.

ANT. *Flow, rise.*

Eccen'tric. Irregular, anomalous, odd, singular.

ANT. *Regular ; natural.*

Eclat'. Renown, applause, brilliancy.

ANT. *Disapproval, ignominy.*

Eclipse'. Overshadow, dim, obscure, veil.

ANT. *Reveal, illumine.*

Econ'omize. Husband, retrench, save.

ANT. *Squander, spend, be lavish.*

Econ'omy. Good husbandry, management, saving, parsimony, thrift.

ANT. *Bad management, wastefulness, extravagance.*

Ec'stasy. Rapture, transport, trance.

ANT. *Calmness, self-possession.*

Edd'y. Whirlpool, vortex.

ANT. *Flow.*

Edge'. Brink, margin, border; sharpness.

ANT. *Inner part ; bluntness.*

Ed'ible. See EATABLE.

E'dict. Proclamation, law, statute, decree.

Ed'ify. Build, construct ; teach ; improve.

ANT. *Pull down, destroy ; corrupt.*

Ed'ucate. Instruct, teach, train.

ANT. *Neglect.*

Efface'. Blot out, obliterate, destroy. See also ANNIHILATE.

ANT. *Reveal ; restore.*

Effect'. See ACCOMPLISH.

Effect'. See CONSEQUENCE.

Effect'ive. Efficient, efficacious, powerful.

ANT. *Ineffective ; weak.*

Effect'ual. See EFFECTIVE and ADEQUATE.

Effem'inate. Woman-like, unmanly, weak.

ANT. *Manly, strong.*

Effete'. Barren ; worn out, exhausted, decayed.

ANT. *Fruitful ; fresh, vigorous.*

Ef'ficacy. Force, energy, virtue, potency, competency.

ANT. *Weakness, impotence.*

Effi'cient. See EFFECTIVE and also ABILITY.

Eff'ort. Endeavour, attempt, struggle, essay.

ANT. *Apathy.*

Effront'ery. Audacity, impudence, presumption, insolence.

ANT. *Respectfulness.*

Egotist'ic. Self-conceited, self-centred, self-important.

ANT. *Altruistic.*

Egre'gious. Conspicuous ; extraordinary ; monstrous, outrageous.

ANT. *Ordinary, commonplace.*

Eject'. Emit, throw out, dismiss ; dispossess.

ANT. *Keep in, retain, restrain, authorize possession.*

Elab′orate. Laboured, studied, carefully wrought, perfected.

ANT. *Carelessly wrought, imperfect, unfinished.*

Elapse′. Pass, glide, go by.

ANT. *Stand still, remain.*

Ela′ted. Exhilarated, elevated, existed.

ANT. *Depressed ; cool.*

Elect′. Choose, select, pick out.

Elect′rify. Thrill, amaze, startle, astonish.

ANT. *Calm.*

El′egant. Graceful, refined, tasteful. See also BECOMING and BEAUTIFUL.

ANT. *Ungraceful, inelegant, unrefined.*

El′egy. Lament, dirge, threnody.

ANT. *Triumphal song.*

Elemen′tary. Uncompounded, simple ; primary, introductory.

ANT. *Compound ; advanced.*

El′evated. See ELATED.

Eleva′tion. Erection ; exaltation ; uplifting, improvement ; loftiness.

ANT. *Pulling down ; depression, spoiling ; lowness.*

Elic′it. Draw out, extract, evoke, obtain.

El′igible. Fit to be chosen, qualified, suitable.

ANT. *Ineligible, unfit, unqualified.*

Elim′inate. See EJECT.

Elope′. Run away, abscond, decamp.

ANT. *Remain.*

El′oquence. Oratory, rhetoric ; gifted speech.

ANT. *Poor speaking.*

Elu′cidate. Illuminate, make clear, explain, interpret.

ANT. *Darken, obscure, make unintelligible.*

Elude′. See AVOID.

Ema′ciated. See GAUNT.

Em′anate. Flow, proceed, issue, spring.

Eman′cipate. Free, deliver, enfranchise, liberate.

ANT. *Enslave, bind, disfranchise.*

Embar′rass. Entangle, incommode, hamper, confuse, distress.

ANT. *Help, enable.*

Embel′lish. Adorn, beautify, ornament, grace.

ANT. *Spoil, mar.*

Embez′zle. Steal, filch, purloin, peculate.

ANT. *Be honest.*

Em′blem. Figure, type, badge, mark.

Embod′y. Incorporate, include, comprise.

ANT. *Exclude.*

Embold′en. See CHEER.

Embrace′. See CLASP, HUG, and EMBODY.

Emenda′tion. Correction, rectification, improvement.

ANT. *Error, blunder, misprint.*

Emerge′. Issue forth, spring out ; come into sight, appear.

ANT. *Submerge, sink in ; disappear.*

Emer′gency. See CRISIS.

Em′inence. Prominence, height; fame, celebrity, distinction.

ANT. *Depth, obscurity.*

Em′inent. See CELEBRATED.

Emit′. See EJECT ; also EXHALE.

Emol′ument. Gain, reward, pay, remuneration.

ANT. *Loss.*

Emo′tion. See AGITATION.

Emphat′ic. Impressive, forceful, significant, decided.

ANT. *Unemphatic, unimpressive, weak, undecided.*

Empir′ic. Experimental.

ANT. *Theoretic.*

Employ′. Hire, engage ; use, apply ; busy.

ANT. *Dismiss ; disuse, withhold ; idle.*

Employ′ment. Work, occupation, vocation.

ANT. *Idleness, worklessness.*

Empow'er See AUTHORIZE.

Empt'y. Void, vacant ; destitute ; senseless, silly.

ANT. *Full, replete ; sensible.*

Em'ulate. Vie with, compete, rival.

Emula'tion. Competition, rivalry, contention.

Ena'ble. See AUTHORIZE.

Enact'ment. See DECREE.

Enam'oured. See BEWITCH.

Enchant'. See BEWITCH.

Enchant'ment. Incantation, witchcraft, delight, fascination.

ANT. *Disenchantment, disappointment.*

Encir'cle. Encompass, inclose, environ. See also EMBRACE.

ANT. *Exclude, shut out.*

Enclose'. See ENCIRCLE.

Enco'mium. Eulogy, praise, laudation.

ANT. *Dispraise, blame, censure.*

Encom'pass. See ENCIRCLE.

Encount'er. See COMBAT.

Encour'age. See CHEER.

Encroach'. Intrude, trench, trespass, invade.

ANT. *Keep away from, respect privacy.*

Encum'ber. See EMBARRASS.

End'. Termination, close, finish, remnant ; issue ; aim, purpose.

ANT. *Beginning, start, whole.*

Endan'ger. Imperil, jeopardize, hazard, risk.

ANT. *Secure, make safe.*

Endeav'our. See ATTEMPT.

End'less. Boundless, interminable, unceasing, perpetual, continual.

ANT. *Terminable, bounded, limited, ceasing.*

Endorse'. Back, approve, sanction, ratify.

ANT. *Disapprove, oppose.*

Endow'. Dower, furnish, endue, enrich, invest.

ANT. *Deprive, withhold, impoverish.*

Endu'rance. Continuance ; fortitude, patience, submission.

ANT. *Cessation ; impatience ; resistance.*

Endure'. Continue, last ; bear, suffer.

En'emy. Adversary, foe, opponent, antagonist.

ANT. *Friend, supporter, backer.*

Energet'ic. Active, forceful, vigorous, effective, nervous.

ANT. *Inactive, weak, ineffective, nerveless.*

En'ergy. Force, activity, vigour, strenuousness.

ANT. *Inactivity, weakness, apathy.*

En'ervated. Enfeebled, unnerved, debilitated, unstrung.

ANT. *Strengthened, nerved.*

Enfee'bled. See ENERVATED.

Enforce'. Compel, constrain, oblige ; execute.

ANT. *Lead, persuade ; repeal.*

Enfranch'ize. Liberate, set free, give the vote to.

ANT. *Disfranchize.*

Engage'. Pledge, bind ; employ, hire ; busy, engross ; fight with ; undertake.

Engage'ment. Employment ; promise, contract ; combat.

ANT. *Unemployment.*

Engen'der. Generate, breed ; cause.

Engross'. Absorb, occupy. See also ENGAGE.

Enhance'. Increase, heighten, improve.

ANT. *Mar, spoil, diminish.*

Enjoin'. Order, prescribe, urge.

ANT. *Obey, submit.*

Enjoy'. Like, relish ; possess.

ANT. *Dislike ; be without.*

Enjoy'ment. See GRATIFICATION.

Enlarge'. Set free, liberate. See also AUGMENT.

ANT. *Imprison, incarcerate.*

Enlight'en. Illuminate, inform, edify, instruct.

ANT. *Darken, make ignorant.*

Enlist'. Enrol, register ; engage.
    ANT. *Decline service.*

Enli'ven. Quicken, make lively. See also AROUSE and CHEER.
    ANT. *Depress, cast gloom.*

En'mity. Hostility, hate, animosity. See also ANGER.
    ANT. *Friendship, friendliness.*

Enno'ble. Elevate, make noble, dignify.
    ANT. *Degrade.*

Enor'mity. Outrage, atrocity, villainy.

Enor'mous. See COLOSSAL.

Enough'. Sufficient, adequate, abundant.
    ANT. *Insufficient, inadequate, scant, scanty.*

Enrage'. Irritate, provoke, exasperate, infuriate, madden, anger, incense.
    ANT. *Soothe, calm.*

Enrap'tured. See BEWITCH.

Enrich'. See ENDOW and EMBELLISH.

Enrol'. See ENLIST.

Ensconce'. Shelter, cover, hide, screen.

Enshrine'. See CONSECRATE.

En'sign. Banner, standard, colours, badge.

Ensnare'. See ALLURE.

Ensue'. Succeed, follow, result.
    ANT. *Go before, cause.*

Entan'gle. Ravel, involve, implicate, perplex, confuse.
    ANT. *Unravel, extricate, disentangle ; free, clear.*

En'terprise. Undertaking ; venture, adventure ; activity.
    ANT. *Inactivity, inertness, apathy.*

Entertain'. Harbour, lodge, treat ; amuse, cheer.
    ANT. *Refuse shelter, exclude ; refuse welcome ; depress.*

Entertain'ment. Hospitality, feast ; amusement.
    ANT. *Inhospitality, mirthlessness.*

Enthu'siasm. Fanaticism; frenzy, ardour, interest.

    ANT. *Religious sanity ; coldness, indifference.*

Enthu'siast. Visionary, dreamer, zealot.
    ANT. *Practical person, Laodicean.*

Enthusias'tic. Ardent, zealous, fervent, visionary.
    ANT. *Cool, calculating, critical.*

Entice'. See ALLURE.

Entice'ment. Allurement, attraction, temptation, inducement.
    ANT. *Repulsion.*

Entire'. Whole, complete, perfect, undivided.
    ANT. *Partial, incomplete, imperfect, divided.*

Enti'tle. Name, designate ; style ; qualify, fit.
    ANT. *Disqualify.*

Ent'rance. Ingress, entry, passage, portal.
    ANT. *Exit, outlet, egress.*

Entrance' (*vb.*). See BEWITCH.

Entrap'. Ensnare, inveigle. See also ENTANGLE.
    ANT. *Set free, liberate.*

Entreat'. See BESEECH.

Entreat'y. Solicitation, suit, petition, prayer.
    ANT. *Command.*

En'try. See ENTRANCE.

Entwine'. Twist round, encircle surround.
    ANT. *Disentangle, loose.*

Enu'merate. Count, number, reckon ; detail.

Enun'ciate. Declare, propound, state, publish.
    ANT. *Conceal, suppress.*

Envel'op. Enwrap, inclose, surround.
    ANT. *Unwrap ; exclude.*

Enven'omed. Poisoned ; enraged, noxious.
    ANT. *Harmless ; kindly.*

En'vious. See JEALOUS.

En'voy. Messenger, legate, ambassador.

En'vy. Jealousy, ill-will, grudging, invidiousness.
    ANT. *Goodwill ; contentedness.*

Ephe'meral. Short-lived, transient, momentary, evanescent.

ANT. *Long-lived, everlasting.*

Ep'icure. Sensualist, voluptuary, Sybarite.

ANT. *Ascetic.*

Epidem'ic. Prevalent, general.

ANT. *Sporadic.*

Epigrammat'ic. Terse, short, concise, pointed.

ANT. *Diffuse, pointless.*

Epis'tle. Letter, missive, note.

ANT. *Oral message.*

Epit'ome. See ABRIDGMENT.

Epit'omize. See ABRIDGE.

Ep'och. Era, period, time, date.

E'quable. Regular, even, steady, calm.

ANT. *Irregular, variable, excitable.*

E'qual. Alike, uniform, equivalent ; proportionate ; impartial ; fit, able.

ANT. *Unequal, disproportionate ; partial ; unfit, incapable.*

Equanim'ity. Composure, calmness, coolness.

ANT. *Agitation, excitability.*

Equip'. Array, furnish, provide, arm, accoutre.

ANT. *Divest, withhold supplies.*

Equ'itable. Just, fair, impartial, proportionate.

ANT. *Unfair, unjust, partial, disproportionate.*

Equ'ity. Justice, impartiality, fairness.

ANT. *Injustice, partiality, unfairness.*

Equiv'alent. Commensurate, equal, tantamount, synonymous.

ANT. *Incommensurate, unequal, opposed.*

Equiv'ocal. Doubtful, ambiguous, uncertain, questionable.

ANT. *Unambiguous, certain, unquestionable.*

Equiv'ocate. Prevaricate, shuffle, quibble, evade.

ANT. *Admit, confess, speak straight out.*

E'ra. See EPOCH.

Erad'icate. Root out, extirpate. See also ANNIHILATE.

ANT. *Leave alone, spare.*

Erase'. See ANNUL.

Erect'. Build, raise, lift, found.

ANT. *Pull down, sink, lower.*

Err'. Deviate, wander ; go wrong, sin ; mistake.

ANT. *Keep straight, do right ; be correct.*

Er'ror. Blunder, mistake, sin, inaccuracy, fallacy.

ANT. *Correctness, accuracy, faultlessness, truth.*

Errat'ic. Wandering, nomadic ; eccentric.

ANT. *Straight-going, steady, natural.*

Erro'neous. Wrong, false, incorrect, inaccurate, mistaken.

ANT. *Right, true, correct, accurate.*

Er'ror. Mistake, trespass, fault, sin.

ANT. *Correctness, truth.*

Er'udite. Learned, scholarly, deeply read, lettered.

ANT. *Unlearned, unscholarly, ill-read, unlettered.*

Erudi'tion. See KNOWLEDGE.

Erup'tion. Outburst, outbreak, explosion, rush.

ANT. *Tranquillity.*

Escape'. See AVOID.

Escort'. Accompany, conduct, convey.

ANT. *Abandon.*

Es'culent. See EATABLE.

Espe'cial. Special, peculiar, particular, chief.

ANT. *General, least.*

Espouse'. Betroth ; marry, wed ; support.

ANT. *Refuse ; oppose.*

Espy'. Discover, descry, see ; perceive.

ANT. *Miss, fail to see.*

Essay' (*vb.*). See ATTEMPT.

Es'say. Attempt, endeavour. See also DISQUISITION.

Es'sence. Being, substance, essential part, scent, perfume.
ANT. *Accidents.*

Essen'tial. Inherent, vital, necessary, requisite.
ANT. *Non-essential, unnecessary.*

Estab'lish. Fix, settle, found. See also ERECT.
ANT. *Disestablish, unsettle, destroy.*

Estate'. Rank, state, position; property, possessions.

Esteem'. See ADMIRE and APPRECIATE.

Es'timable. Worthy, good, honourable.
ANT. *Dishonourable, worthless.*

Es'timate. See APPRAISE and APPRECIATE.

Estima'tion. Valuation, calculation; esteem, regard.
ANT. *Disregard, disapproval.*

Eter'nal. Endless, everlasting, perpetual, interminable.
ANT. *Transient, temporary, ephemeral.*

Ethe'real. Airy, celestial; rare, volatile.
ANT. *Earthly; dense.*

Eth'ics. Morals, morality, moral philosophy.

Eulogist'ic. Laudatory, encomiastic, panegyric.
ANT. *Condemnatory, disparaging.*

Eu'logy. Laudation, encomium, panegyric.
ANT. *Dispraise, condemnation.*

Evade'. See AVOID.

Evanes'cent. Vanishing, fleeting, transitive, fugitive.
ANT. *Permanent, constant.*

Evap'orate. Dissolve, disappear.
ANT. *Consolidate.*

Eva'sion. Equivocation, prevarication, shuffling, excuse.
ANT. *Straightforwardness, confession, admission.*

Eva'sive. Shuffling, equivocal, prevaricating.

ANT. *Straightforward, frank, honest.*

E'ven. Level, smooth, plain, flat; equable, calm; not odd.
ANT. *Unlevel, rough, raised, ruffled, excitable; odd.*

Event'. Occurrence, circumstance; issue, consequence. See also ENTERPRISE.
ANT. *Antecedent.*

Everlast'ing. See ENDLESS.

Ev'idence. Testimony, witness, proof, deposition.
ANT. *Disproof.*

Ev'ident. Clear, manifest, patent, plain.
ANT. *Obscure, unintelligible.*

E'vil. Bad, ill, wicked, vicious, corrupt. See also ABANDONED.
ANT. *Good, virtuous, genuine.*

Evince'. Manifest, show, demonstrate.
ANT. *Conceal, disprove.*

Evolve'. Develop, unfold, expound.

Exac'erbate. Exasperate, irritate, vex, embitter.
ANT. *Soothe, propitiate.*

Exact'. Accurate, correct, precise; strict, methodical.
ANT. *Inaccurate, careless, loose, unmethodical.*

Exact' (*vb.*). See EXTORT.

Exac'tion. Extortion, oppression, rapacity.
ANT. *Fairness, mildness.*

Exag'gerate. Amplify, magnify, overstate.
ANT. *Minimize; understate.*

Exalt'. Lift up, raise, elevate, dignify. See also ENNOBLE.
ANT. *Cast down, lower, humiliate.*

Examina'tion. Inspection, inquiry, investigation, scrutiny; trial.

Exam'ine. Inquire, inspect, scrutinize, question.
ANT. *Pass over, ignore.*

Exam′ple. Sample, model; instance, precedent.

Exas′perate. See ENRAGE.

Exceed′. Surpass, excel, go beyond, overstep.

ANT. *Fall short, be inferior.*

Excel′. Surpass, be superior, be eminent.

ANT. *Fail, be inferior.*

Ex′cellence. Superiority, eminence; worth, fine quality, perfection.

ANT. *Inferiority, poor quality, imperfectness.*

Except′. Exclude, omit, reject; raise objection.

ANT. *Include, admit; give in, accede.*

Excep′tionable. Objectionable, undesirable.

ANT. *Unobjectionable, desirable.*

Excep′tional. Unusual, abnormal, peculiar, rare.

ANT. *Usual, ordinary, commonplace.*

Ex′cerpt. Extract, selected passage, quotation.

Excess′. Superabundance, superfluity, overplus; intemperance.

ANT. *Lack, falling short, defeat; sobriety.*

Excess′ive. Superabundant, exuberant; extravagant, unreasonable, too great.

ANT. *Defective, lacking; sober.*

Exchange′. Change, commute, truck, barter, trade, interchange.

Exci′table. Irritable, passionate, hot-tempered, hyper-sensitive.

ANT. *Placid, calm, even-tempered.* See also EQUABLE.

Excite′. See AROUSE and FLUSTER.

Excite′ment. See AGITATION.

Exclaim′. Call out, vociferate, shout out, cry.

ANT. *Be silent.*

Exclude′. Shut out, eject. See also DEBAR and EXCEPT.

ANT. *Include, admit.*

Exclu′sive. Excluding, excepting; sole, special; stand off.

ANT. *Inclusive; sociable.*

Excommu′nicate. Expel, denounce, anathematize.

ANT. *Communicate, reconcile, absolve.*

Excres′cence. Swelling, growth, lump.

Excru′ciate. Torture, agonize, rack, torment.

ANT. *Comfort, alleviate.*

Ex′culpate. Exonerate, absolve, pardon, acquit.

ANT. *Blame, accuse.*

Excur′sion. Journey, jaunt, tour, trip, expedition; digression.

Excu′sable. Pardonable, allowable, venial.

ANT. *Inexcusable, unpardonable, sinful.*

Excuse′ (*vb.*). See EXCULPATE.

Excuse (*n.*). Apology, pretext, justification, defence, extenuation.

ANT. *Aggravation.*

Ex′ecrable. Abominable, detestable, hateful, accursed.

ANT. *Agreeable, delightful, blessed.*

Ex′ecute. Accomplish, effect, fulfil, finish; hang, behead.

ANT. *Attempt, begin, fail; acquit.*

Execu′tion. Accomplishment, performance; workmanship; capital punishment.

ANT. *Failure, attempt; pardon, acquittal.*

Exem′plary. Commendable, praiseworthy, laudable.

ANT. *Blameworthy, culpable.*

Exemp′lify. Illustrate, evidence, show.

ANT. *Contradict, conflict with.*

Exemp′tion. Immunity, privilege, freedom.

ANT. *Obligation.*

Ex′ercise (*n.*). Use, employment, application; practice, exertion.

ANT. *Disuse, slackness, neglect.*

Ex'ercise (*vb.*). Exert, apply, train, drill ; trouble.

ANT. *Disuse ; cheer.*

Exert'. Exercise, strive, employ.

Exer'tion. Effort, struggle, labour, strain.

ANT. *Apathy, inertness ; ease.*

Exhale'. Breathe out, evaporate.

ANT. *Inhale.*

Exhaust'. Drain, empty ; weaken, enfeeble, tire ; consume, spend.

ANT. *Fill up ; strengthen, refresh ; save up, economize.*

Exhib'it. See DISPLAY.

Exhibi'tion. Display, show, spectacle, representation.

Exhil'arate. See CHEER.

Exhort'. See ADVISE.

Ex'igency. Urgency, distress, requirement. See also CRISIS.

ANT. *Easiness.*

Ex'ile. Expulsion, banishment, expatriation.

ANT. *Home, repatriation.*

Exile' (*vb.*). See EXPATRIATE.

Exist'. Be, live; occur, endure, continue.

ANT. *Be dead, cease.*

Ex'it. Egress ; departure, withdrawal.

ANT. *Ingress, entrance.*

Exon'erate. See ACQUIT.

Exor'bitant. See EXCESSIVE.

Exot'ic. Foreign, not native.

ANT. *Native, not foreign.*

Expand'. Unfold, extend, widen, spread.

ANT. *Fold, narrow, contract.*

Expa'tiate. See DILATE.

Expa'triate. Exile, expel, banish.

ANT. *Repatriate, recall.*

Expect'. Await, hope for, look for.

ANT. *Despair.*

Expe'dient. Fitting, suitable, advantageous, useful.

ANT. *Inexpedient, unadvisable, unprofitable.*

Ex'pedite. Hasten, accelerate, forward, advance, facilitate.

Expedi'tious. Prompt, quick, active.

ANT. *Slow, tardy, slack.*

Expel'. See EJECT and EXCLUDE.

Expend'. Spend, disburse, use, empty.

ANT. *Husband, save.*

Expen'sive. Costly, dear, highpriced.

ANT. *Cheap, low-priced.*

Expe'rience. Trial, proof, practice, test.

ANT. *Inexperience.*

Expect'. See ADROIT and ADEPT.

Expi'ration. Exhalation ; death ; close, end, termination.

ANT. *Inspiration ; beginning.*

Expire'. Die, decease ; end, terminate. See also EXHALE.

ANT. *Live ; begin.*

Explain'. See ELUCIDATE.

Explana'tion. Exposition, interpretation, account ; meaning.

ANT. *Obscuration.*

Explic'it. Express, positive, definite, unequivocal, plain.

ANT. *Implicit, vague, indefinite.*

Ex'ploit. Feat, achievement, adventure.

ANT. *Failure.*

Explore'. See EXAMINE.

Expose'. Lay bare, disclose, exhibit ; subject, make liable.

ANT. *Conceal, cover.*

Expos'ition. See EXPLANATION.

Expound'. See ELUCIDATE.

Express'. See EXPLICIT.

Express'ive. Significant, telling, lively, striking.

ANT. *Inexpressive, dull, insignificant.*

Expunge'. See ANNUL and ANNIHILATE.

Ex'quisite. Choice, perfect, rare, delicate, refined.

ANT. *Common, unrefined.*

Extend'. See EXPAND.

Exten'sive. Large, broad, wide, comprehensive.
  ANT. *Narrow, confined.*

Extent'. Length, reach, width, bulk.

Exten'uate. Lessen, reduce, qualify, excuse.
  ANT. *Heighten, intensify.*

Exter'minate. See ANNIHILATE.

Exter'nal. Outward, outer, exterior.
  ANT. *Internal, inward.*

Extin'guish. Quench. See also ANNIHILATE.
  ANT. *Light, kindle.*

Ex'tirpate. See ANNIHILATE.

Extol'. See APPLAUD.

Extort'. Exact, squeeze out, get by force.

Extor'tion. See EXACTION.

Extract'. Pull out, draw out ; distil ; cite, quote.
  ANT. *Insert.*

Extra'neous. Extrinsic, foreign.
  ANT. *Native, intrinsic.*

Extraord'inary. Uncommon, unprecedented, marvellous, rare.
  ANT. *Common, usual, ordinary.*

Extrav'agant. Excessive, prodigal, lavish, wild ; absurd.
  ANT. *Restrained, limited, economical ; reasonable.*

Extreme'. Utmost, farthest, most distant, final.
  ANT. *Nearest, least distant.*

Extrem'ity. Verge, end ; great distress.
  ANT. *Middle ; ease.*

Ex'tricate. See DISENTANGLE and EMANCIPATE.

Extrude'. See EJECT.

Exu'berant. See ABUNDANT.

Exult'. Triumph, delight, rejoice.
  ANT. *Grieve, despair.*

F

Fa'ble. Story, legend, myth ; fiction, figment.
  ANT. *Fact, truth.*

Fab'ric. Structure, building ; material, texture.

Fab'ricate. Construct, forge, invent, coin, produce.

Fab'ulous. Fictitious, not real, false, mythical.
  ANT. *True, real, based on fact, actual.*

Face'. Front, countenance, visage, surface ; assurance.
  ANT. *Back.*

Face' (*vb.*). See COMBAT.

Face'tious. Merry, jesting, jocular, droll, funny, humorous.
  ANT. *Dull, serious.*

Fac'ile. Pliable, docile, tractable, easy.
  ANT. *Difficult, intractable.*

Facil'itate. See EXPEDITE.

Facil'ity. Dexterity, expertness, opportunity. See also ABILITY.

  ANT. *Clumsiness ; disability.*

Fact'. Deed, performance, act ; event, occurrence ; truth.
  ANT. *Fiction.*

Fac'tion. Clique, cabal, junto ; discord. See also CABAL.
  ANT. *Harmony, agreement.*

Facti'tious. Artificial, unreal.
  ANT. *Real, genuine.*

Fac'ulty. Talent, endowment, gift, knack. See also ABILITY.
  ANT. *Disability.*

Fade'. Wither, decay, droop, pale.
  ANT. *Flourish, revive.*

Fag. See JADE.

Fail'ing. Fault, defect, weakness.
  ANT. *Merit, virtue.*

Fail'ure. Miscarriage, default, shortening, neglect.
  ANT. *Success, performance.*

Faint'. Weak, languid ; dim ; slight, small.
  ANT. *Strong ; clear ; great.*

Fair'. Unblemished, untarnished; open, honest, equitable, impartial; moderately good; clear, not cloudy.

ANT. *Blemished; unfair, inequitable, biased; good; cloudy.*

Faith'. See BELIEF.

Faith'ful. Trusty, trustworthy, constant, true, loyal.

ANT. *Faithless, inconstant, disloyal.*

Fall'. Drop, sink, decline, descend; die; sin.

ANT. *Rise, ascend.*

Falla'cious. Deceptive, misleading, delusive, mocking, false.

ANT. *True, real, actual.*

Fall'acy. Deception, illusion; sophism. See also ERROR.

ANT. *Truth.*

Fall'ible. Erring, uncertain, liable to mistakes.

ANT. *Certain, infallible.*

False'. Untrue, lying, mendacious; dishonest, treacherous; spurious, supposititious.

ANT. *True, truthful, loyal.*

False'hood. Lie, untruth, fabrication, fiction.

ANT. *Truth, fact.*

Falt'er. Waver, totter, hesitate, stutter, vacillate.

ANT. *Be firm.*

Fame'. Rumour, hearsay; glory, reputation, honour, renown.

ANT. *Fact; shame, dishonour; ignominy.*

Famil'iar. Friendly, affable; accustomed, wonted; conversant with.

ANT. *Unfriendly, unsociable; unaccustomed, strange; ignorant of.*

Familiar'ity. Acquaintance, intimacy; freedom.

ANT. *Unfamiliarity; modesty.*

Fam'ily. Household; kindred, ancestry, clan; group, order.

ANT. *Individual.*

Fam'ine. Dearth, hunger, starvation.

ANT. *Plenty, satiety.*

Fa'mous. See CELEBRATED.

Fanat'ical. Visionary, bigoted, enthusiastic.

ANT. *Sedate, practical, broad-minded.*

Fanci'ful. Imaginative, fantastic, ideal, capricious, chimerical.

ANT. *Practical, steady.*

Fan'cy. Conceit, conception; liking, taste; whim, caprice.

ANT. *Reality; dislike.*

Fantas'tic. Fanciful, imaginative, visionary, queer.

ANT. *Real, practical.*

Far'cical. Ludicrous, droll, comic, laughable, extravagant.

ANT. *Tragic, serious.*

Fare'. Travel, journey; subsist, live.

Farewell'. Valediction, leave-taking, adieu, good-bye.

ANT. *Greeting, good morning, how do you do?*

Farm'er. Husbandman; agriculturist; collector.

Farra'go. See HODGE-PODGE.

Far'thest. See EXTREME.

Fas'cinate. See BEWITCH.

Fascina'tion. See ENCHANTMENT.

Fash'ion. See CUSTOM.

Fash'ion (*vb.*). Make, shape, form, create, mould.

Fash'ionable. Current, prevailing; stylish, modish.

ANT. *Unfashionable, dowdy.*

Fast'. Firm, constant, immovable; secure; quick, rapid; dissipated.

ANT. *Loose, unbound; unsafe; slow; sober.*

Fast'en. Fix, join, tie, bind.

ANT. *Unfix, disjoin, untie.*

Fastid'ious. Particular, over-nice, squeamish, dainty, finical, meticulous.

ANT. *Indifferent, careless, easy-going.*

39

Fat′. Corpulent, plump, fleshy, obese, gross; greasy, unctuous; stupid.

ANT. *Lean, thin; intelligent.*

Fate′. Destiny, lot, doom, chance, death.

Fa′tal. Destined, doomed; deadly, lethal, mortal.

ANT. *Unordained; harmless.*

Fath′omless. Bottomless, unfathomable, abysmal, profound.

ANT. *Shallow, fathomable.*

Fatigue′. Weariness, exhaustion, tiredness, lassitude.

ANT. *Rest.*

Fatigue′ (*vb.*). Weary, tire, exhaust, jade.

ANT. *Rest, refresh.*

Fat′uous. Silly, weak, idiotic, imbecile.

ANT. *Sensible, serious.*

Fault′. Defect, blemish, flaw; sin, error, blunder; default.

ANT. *Merit, flawlessness.*

Fault′less. See IMMACULATE.

Fault′y. Defective, imperfect, bad; wrong.

ANT. *Perfect, sound, good.*

Fa′vour. Grace, countenance, patronage, gift, boon.

ANT. *Disfavour, disapproval.*

Fe′alty. Loyalty, fidelity, allegiance.

ANT. *Disloyalty, treachery.*

Fear′. Dread, horror, fright, alarm, anxiety, awe.

ANT. *Courage; unconcern; irreverence.*

Fear′ (*vb.*). Dread, apprehend; reverence, venerate.

ANT. *Be bold, be unconcerned; contemn, mock.*

Fear′ful. Apprehensive, timid. See also AWFUL.

ANT. *Bold, courageous.*

Fear′less. See BOLD.

Feas′ible. Practicable, possible, doable.

ANT. *Impracticable, impossible.*

Feast′. Festival, holiday; banquet, entertainment, carousal; pleasure, delight. See also BANQUET.

ANT. *Fast, ferial, disappointment.*

Feat′. See EXPLOIT.

Feat′ure. Lineament, appearance, aspect; peculiarity, characteristic.

Fecund′ity. Productiveness, fertility, fruitfulness.

ANT. *Barrenness, infertility.*

Federa′tion. See ALLIANCE.

Fee′. Recompense, pay, reward, bribe.

Fee′ble. Weak, frail, debilitated, imbecile; dim, faint.

ANT. *Strong, vigorous, sane.*

Feel′. Touch, handle; experience, suffer; be moved by.

Feel′ing. Touch, sensation; emotion; impression, notion; tenderness, conviction.

ANT. *Hardness, mercilessness.*

Feign′. Pretend, dissemble, affect.

Felic′itate. See CONGRATULATE.

Felic′ity. Joy, happiness, good luck, bliss; appropriateness.

ANT. *Misfortune, sorrow, infelicity.*

Fell′. Barbarous, inhuman, savage, pitiless.

ANT. *Gentle, mild, kind.*

Fel′low. Companion, comrade, associate, mate, counterpart.

ANT. *Stranger.*

Fel′lowship. Brotherhood, intimacy, association, sociability.

ANT. *Isolation, aloofness.*

Fel′on. See CRIMINAL.

Fem′inine. Womanly, soft, modest; unmanly, womanish.

ANT. *Manly, strong, masculine, virile.*

Fen′. Moor, marsh, bog, slough.

ANT. *Dry land.*

Fence′. Palisade, barrier, guard.

Ferment'. Concoct, brew ; excite, agitate.
 ANT. *Calm, soothe.*

Fero'cious. Fierce, savage, wild, barbarous.
 ANT. *Mild, gentle.*

Fero'city. Cruelty, savagery, fierceness.
 ANT. *Kindness, gentleness.*

Fer'tile. See EXUBERANT and ABUNDANT.
 ANT. *Unfertile, unproductive.*

Fer'vent. Glowing, heated, vehement, impassioned.
 ANT. *Cool, unimpassioned.*

Fer'vid. See FERVENT.

Fer'vour. W a r m t h, g l o w, ardour, vehemence.
 ANT. *Coolness, imperturbability.*

Fest'al. Festive, joyous, merry, gay.
 ANT. *Everyday ; gloomy, sad.*

Fest'ival. See FEAST.

Festiv'ity. Merrymaking, gaiety, conviviality.
 ANT. *Mourning.*

Fe'tid. Stinking, foul, corrupt, noisome.
 ANT. *Sweet-scented, pure, wholesome.*

Fet'ter. Shackle, bind, enchain ; hinder, confine.
 ANT. *Loose, set free, advance.*

Feud'. Strife, contention, broil.
 ANT. *Peace, amity.*

Fe'ver. Heat, fervour, agitation.
 ANT. *Coolness, calmness.*

Fi'bre. Thread, filament; toughness, strength.
 ANT. *Weakness.*

Fick'le. See CHANGEABLE.

Fic'tion. Invention, fabrication, figment. See FABLE.
 ANT. *Truth, fact.*

Ficti'tious. False, untrue, supposititious, counterfeit.
 ANT. *True, genuine, actual.*

Fidel'ity. See FEALTY.

Fiend'ish. Devilish, diabolical, hellish, malignant.
 ANT. *Angelic, heavenly, benignant.*

Fierce'. Vehement, violent. See also FEROCIOUS.
 ANT. *Gentle, mild.*

Fi'ery. Igneous. See ARDENT.

Fight. See AFFRAY.

Fig'ment. See FICTION.

Fig'urative. Typical, emblematic, metaphysical.
 ANT. *Actual, straightforward.*

Fig'ure. Form, shape, fashion ; trope, metaphor, emblem, symbol.

Fil'ament. See FIBRE.

Filch'. Steal, purloin, pilfer.
 ANT. *Be honest.*

Fil'ibuster. Freebooter, pirate, buccaneer.

Fill'. Supply, replenish ; glut, satiate, satisfy.
 ANT. *Empty, leave unsatisfied.*

Filth'. Dirt, foulness, nastiness, impurity.
 ANT. *Cleanliness, purity.*

Fil'thy. Dirty, foul, nasty, impure.
 ANT. *Clean, pure.*

Fi'nal. Last, ending, ultimate ; conclusive, decisive.
 ANT. *First, beginning; inconclusive.*

Fine'. Thin ; light, airy, clear ; elegant, handsome, splendid ; subtle.
 ANT. *Coarse ; dull ; ugly ; stupid.*

Fin'ical. See FASTIDIOUS.

Fin'ish. End, conclude, close ; perform ; elaborate.
 ANT. *Begin ; leave unamended.*

Fi'nite. Bounded, limited, restricted, terminable.
 ANT. *Infinite, unlimited.*

Firm'. Strong, sturdy ; dense, solid ; steadfast, constant.
 ANT. *Weak, unsteady ; fluid, thin ; inconstant, fickle.*

First'. Primary, original ; highest, chief, foremost.

ANT. *Last, final ; lowest, hindmost.*

Fis′sure. See CREVICE.

Fit′. Fitting, proper, suitable. See also BECOMING and EXPEDIENT.

ANT. *Unfitting, improper, unsuitable.*

Fit′ful. See CHANGEABLE.

Fix′. Set, fasten, settle ; determine, appoint.

ANT. *Unfix, detach ; hesitate.*

Flac′cid. Soft, loose, weak, flabby.

ANT. *Firm, tight.*

Flag′. See DECLINE.

Flagi′tious. See ATROCIOUS.

Fla′grant. See ATROCIOUS.

Flame′. Blaze, brightness, fire ; ardour, passion, affection.

ANT. *Dullness, coldness.*

Flash′. Coruscation, gleam, sudden stroke.

ANT. *Steady light.*

Flash′y. Gaudy, showy, tawdry.

ANT. *Sober, refined.*

Flat′. Horizontal, level, even, smooth ; insipid, stale.

ANT. *Perpendicular ; unlevel, uneven, rough ; fresh.*

Flat′ter. See CAJOLE.

Flat′tery. Cajolery, adulation, fawning, sycophancy.

ANT. *Snubbing.*

Fla′vour. Taste, savour, relish, smack.

Flaw′. See BLEMISH.

Flay′. Skin, excoriate.

Fleck′. Spot, speck, streak.

Flee′. Fly, run away, escape ; avoid.

ANT. *Stand still, pursue.*

Fleece′. Shear, clip ; rob, despoil.

Fleet′. Quick, rapid, speedy.

ANT. *Slow, tardy.*

Fleet′ing. See EVANESCENT and EPHEMERAL.

Flesh′ly. Bodily, animal, carnal, sensual.

ANT. *Spiritual, pure.*

Flesh′y. See CORPULENT.

Flex′ible. Pliable, limber, lithe, yielding.

ANT. *Inflexible, stiff, unyielding.*

Flight′. Flying, fleeing, soaring, exodus.

Flight′y. Giddy, volatile, lightheaded. See also CHANGEABLE.

ANT. *Steady, sober.*

Flim′sy. Slight, thin ; trivial, superficial.

ANT. *Substantial ; serious, weighty.*

Flinch′. Shrink, swerve, wince.

ANT. *Stand firm.*

Fling′. Cast, hurl, throw.

ANT. *Catch.*

Flip′pant. Pert, saucy, forward, irreverent.

ANT. *Respectful, reverent, serious.*

Flirt′. Toss, jerk ; jeer ; coquette.

Flit′. Flutter, pass.

ANT. *Be steady, remain.*

Flock′. Drove, herd, multitude.

Flog′. See CASTIGATE.

Flood′. Deluge, inundation; superabundance, tidal flow.

ANT. *Drought ; ebb.*

Flood′ (*vb.*). See INUNDATE.

Flor′id. Flowery, ornate, bright-coloured.

ANT. *Plain ; dull.*

Flound′er. Roll about, wallow, stumble.

Flour′ish. Thrive, prosper, succeed.

ANT. *Fade, fail.*

Flout′. Ridicule, jeer at, taunt, insult.

ANT. *Treat with respect.*

Flow′. Stream, glide, emanate ; abound.

ANT. *Stand still.*

Flow′ery. See FLORID.

Fluct′uate. Waver, undulate ; vacillate.

ANT. *Be constant, be uniform.*

Flu′ent. Flowing, smooth, voluble, glib.

ANT. *Stuttering, hesitating.*

Flum'mery. Porridge ; trash, nonsense, flattery.
ANT. *Good sense.*

Flurr'y. Flutter, gust, tumult, confusion.
ANT. *Steadiness.*

Flust'er. Agitate, excite, perturb, confuse.
ANT. *Calm, allay.*

Flut'ter (*n.*) Quivering, agitation, tumult, confusion.
ANT. *Calm, coolness.*

Flut'ter (*vb.*). See HOVER.

Fly'. Soar, mount ; hasten ; escape, flee.
ANT. *Sink ; remain.*

Foam'. Froth, spume, spray.

Foe'. See ENEMY.

Foi'ble. Fault, weakness, defect, failing.
ANT. *Merit, good point.*

Foil'. See BAFFLE.

Fold'. Double over ; envelop, wrap.
ANT. *Unfold, unwrap.*

Fol'low. Pursue, come after, succeed ; result from, proceed ; imitate, copy.
ANT. *Precede, go before ; lead, initiate.*

Fol'lower. Adherent, dependent, associate, retainer ; imitator, successor.
ANT. *Leader, opponent ; predecessor.*

Fol'ly. Foolishness, absurdity, silliness, imprudence.
ANT. *Wisdom, sense.*

Foment'. Excite, stimulate, encourage.
ANT. *Allay.*

Fond'. Weak, foolish, doting, affectionate.
ANT. *Sensible ; severe.*

Fond'le. See CARESS.

Food'. Sustenance, aliment, support, meat, diet.
ANT. *Starvation, want.*

Fool'. Dolt, idiot, simpleton, imbecile.
ANT. *Wise man, sage.*

Fool'ery. Absurdity, nonsense, buffoonery.
ANT. *Good sense.*

Fool'hardy. Venturesome, rash, incautious, reckless.
ANT. *Cautious, prudent.*

Fool'ish. Absurd, senseless, irrational, ridiculous, nonsensical, indiscreet.
ANT. *Wise, sensible.*

Foot'. Paw ; bottom, base ; 12-in. measure.
ANT. *Head, top.*

Foot'step. Footprint, footmark, track.

Fop'. Dandy, coxcomb, puppy.

Fop'pish. Dandified, coxcombical, overdressed.
ANT. *Modest, sober.*

For'ay. Raid, incursion, invasion, inroad.

Forbear'. Abstain, cease, refrain, desist ; be lenient.
ANT. *Go on, continue ; treat harshly.*

Forbear'ance. Abstinence, refraining, indulgence, lenity.
ANT. *Harshness.*

Forbid'. Prohibit, inhibit, disallow, debar.
ANT. *Allow, command.*

Forbid'ding. Repulsive, disagreeable, offensive, odious.
ANT. *Attractive, pleasant, likable.*

Force'. See ENFORCE.

Force' (*n.*). Strength, vigour, violence, emphasis ; army, troops.
ANT. *Weakness, gentleness.*

Forc'ible. Strong, active, effective, energetic ; emphatic, cogent.
ANT. *Weak, ineffective, unemphatic.*

Forebode'. See BETOKEN.

Forecast'. Predict, anticipate, announce beforehand, reckon in advance.
ANT. *Be retrospective.*

Forego'. Precede, go before.
ANT. *Follow, succeed.*

Fore'going. See ANTERIOR.

For'eign. See EXOTIC.

Fore'most. First, leading, highest.
ANT. *Last, lowest, hindmost.*

43

Forerunn'er. Precursor, harbinger, herald.

ANT. *Follower.*

Foreshad'ow. See BETOKEN.

Fore'sight. Prescience ; foreknowledge ; caution, prudence.

ANT. *Imprudence, carelessness.*

Forestall'. See ANTICIPATE.

Foretell'. Predict, prophesy, augur.

ANT. *Record, give retrospect.*

For'feit. Fine, mulct, loss.

ANT. *Remission, gain.*

Forge'. See FABRICATE.

Forget'. Overlook, neglect, lose memory of.

ANT. *Remember, recall, regard.*

Forget'ful. Heedless, careless, neglectful, oblivious.

ANT. *Mindful, careful.*

Forgive'. Pardon, absolve, acquit, remit.

ANT. *Punish, condemn, excommunicate.*

Forgo'. Give up, relinquish, resign, abandon.

ANT. *Hold, keep, retain.*

Forlorn'. See DISCONSOLATE.

Form'. Fashion, mould, shape, configuration, figure ; rite ; manner, order.

Form' (*vb.*). Fashion, mould, create ; constitute.

ANT. *Unmake.*

Form'al. Ceremonious, stiff, exact, punctilious, affected.

ANT. *Informal, easy, unceremonious.*

Form'er. See ANTERIOR.

For'midable. See DREADFUL.

Forsake'. See ABANDON.

Forswear'. See ABANDON and DENY.

Forthwith'. At once, immediately, straightway, instantly.

ANT. *Later.*

For'tify. Secure, strengthen, entrench ; encourage, brace.

ANT. *Weaken ; discourage, unnerve.*

For'titude. See ENDURANCE.

Fortu'itous. See CASUAL.

For'tunate. Successful. See also AUSPICIOUS.

ANT. *Unsuccessful.*

For'tune. Chance, accident, luck ; estate, possessions, property.

ANT. *Misfortune.*

For'ward. Onward, advanced, progressive ; ready, prompt ; bold, confident.

ANT. *Backward ; dilatory ; timid.*

For'ward (*vb.*). See ACCELERATE.

Fost'er. See CHERISH.

Foul'. See FILTHY.

Found'. Set, build, base, institute, ground ; cast in a mould.

Founda'tion. See BASE.

Founder'. Creator, originator, author, beginner.

ANT. *Follower, imitator.*

Fount'. Spring, source.

Fount'ain. See FOUNT.

Frac'tious. See CROSS.

Frac'ture. See BREAK.

Frag'ile. Weak, slender. See also BRITTLE.

ANT. *Strong, steady.*

Frag'ment. Piece, bit, portion, morsel, scrap.

ANT. *Whole.*

Fra'grant. See BALMY.

Frail'. See FRAGILE.

Frail'ty. Weakness, frailness, fault ; sinful tendency.

ANT. *Strength, firmness, consistency.*

Frame'. See FABRICATE.

Frank'. See CANDID.

Fran'tic. Frenzied, mad, distracted, wild.

ANT. *Calm, sane.*

Frat'ernize. Consort, co-operate, associate.

ANT. *Quarrel, disagree, stand aloof.*

Fraud'. Deceit, guile, knavery, wile, trickery, cheating.

ANT. *Honesty.*

Fraud'ulent. Dishonest, cheating, knavish, deceptive.

ANT. *Honest.*

Fraught'. Filled, laden, charged, pregnant.

ANT. *Empty.*

Fray'. See AFFRAY and COMBAT.

Freak. See CAPRICE.

Freak'ish. See CHANGEABLE.

Free'. Unrestrained, at liberty, released, exempt ; frank, ingenuous ; generous, liberal ; casual.

ANT. *Bound, confined, imprisoned ; disingenuous ; close ; precise.*

Free' (*vb.*). Set free, liberate, release, rescue, deliver.

ANT. *Bind, confine, enslave.*

Free'dom. Liberty, release, independence ; frankness, openness ; scope, opportunity, familiarity, licence.

ANT. *Slavery, dependence ; disingenuousness ; formality.*

Freight'. Burden, cargo, load.

Fren'zy. Madness, fury, rage.

ANT. *Sanity, calm.*

Fresh'. New, novel ; raw ; healthy ; inexperienced.

ANT. *Old, stale ; uncooked ; unhealthy ; experienced.*

Fret'. Rub, chafe ; vex, gall ; worry.

ANT. *Smoothe, soothe ; be cheerful.*

Fret'ful. See CAPTIOUS and CROSS.

Fric'tion. Rubbing, grating, attrition.

Friend'. Intimate, associate, familiar ; benefactor.

ANT. *Enemy, opponent, adversary.*

Friend'ly. See AMICABLE.

Friend'ship. Affection, intimacy, familiarity, love.

ANT. *Hostility, opposition, hatred.*

Fright'. See FEAR.

Fright'en. See AFFRIGHT.

Fright'ful. See AWFUL.

Frig'id. Cold, chilling ; unfeeling, repellent.

ANT. *Warm ; sympathetic.*

Frisk'. Skip, dance, hop, caper, frolic.

ANT. *Stand still.*

Frit'ter. Shred ; waste, dissipate, idle.

ANT. *Use profitably.*

Frivol'ity. See LEVITY.

Friv'olous. Foolish, vain, trivial.

ANT. *Grave, serious.*

Frol'ic. See FRISK.

Front'. See FACE.

Froth'y. Foamy. See also FRIVOLOUS.

Fro'ward. Untoward, perverse, refractory, petulant. See also CROSS.

ANT. *Obedient, amenable.*

Fru'gal. Thrifty, economical.

ANT. *Extravagant, prodigal, wasteful.*

Fruit'ful. See ABUNDANT.

Fruit'less. Useless, vain, idle, futile, barren, bootless.

ANT. *Fruitful, advantageous, profitable.*

Frustrate'. See BAFFLE.

Fulfil'. See ACCOMPLISH.

Full'. Replete, satiated, stocked, complete.

ANT. *Empty, unsatisfied, incomplete.*

Full'ness. Repletion, satiety, plenitude ; copiousness.

ANT. *Emptiness, incompleteness.*

Full'y. Completely, entirely, sufficiently, wholly, quite.

ANT. *Imperfectly, incompletely.*

Ful'some. Offensive, rank, sickening, loathsome.

ANT. *Agreeable, pleasant.*

Func'tion. Performance, exercise ; office, duty, occupation ; ceremony.

ANT. *Neglect.*

Fundament'al. Primary, basic, important.

ANT. *Unimportant, superstructural.*

Fune'real. Dismal, gloomy, lugubrious, mournful.

ANT. *Cheerful, bright.*

Fur'bish. Polish, burnish, brighten.

Fu'rious. See FEROCIOUS.

Furn'ish. Provide, supply; fit up, equip.
 ANT. *Strip; withhold.*

Fur'niture. Movables, fittings, chattels.

Fur'ther. See AID.

Fur'tive. Stealthy, secret, sly.
 ANT. *Open, aboveboard.*

Fu'ry. See FRENZY and ANGER.

Fust'ian. Rant, bombast, rhodomontade, nonsense.
 ANT. *Good sense.*

Fu'tile. See FRUITLESS.

Futil'ity. Uselessness, vanity, worthlessness, unprofitableness.
 ANT. *Utility, advantage, profitableness.*

Fu'ture. Coming, forthcoming.
 ANT. *Past.*

G

Gab'ble. See BABBLE.

Gag'. Muzzle, silence, stifle.
 ANT. *Unmuzzle.*

Gai'ety. Joyousness, hilarity, festivity, jollity.
 ANT. *Sadness, mourning, dullness.*

Gain'. See ACQUIRE.

Gain' (*n.*). See ADVANTAGE.

Gain'say. Contradict, controvert, dispute, oppugn.
 ANT. *Agree, defend.*

Gal'axy. Group, cluster, constellation.

Gale'. Blast, storm, hurricane.
 ANT. *Calm.*

Gal'lant. See CHIVALROUS.

Gal'lantry. Courage, bravery, heroism, chivalry; politeness, courtesy.
 ANT. *Cowardice, poltroonery; discourtesy.*

Gamb'ol. See FRISK.

Game'. Play, amusement, pastime, sport, diversion.
 ANT. *Work.*

Gang'. Band, troop, crew, horde.

Gap'. See BREACH.

Garb'. See ATTIRE.

Gar'bage. Offal, refuse, filth.

Gar'ble. Pick over, sieve; misquote, distort, pervert.

Ga'rish. Gaudy, glittering, flaring, flashy.
 ANT. *Dull, sober, quiet.*

Gar'land. Wreath, chaplet.

Garn'er. Hoard, gather, accumulate.
 ANT. *Dissipate, scatter.*

Garn'ish. See EMBELLISH.

Gar'rulous. Talkative, loquacious, prattling, chattering.
 ANT. *Silent.*

Gath'er. Collect, pluck, glean; deduce, conclude. See also ASSEMBLE.
 ANT. *Scatter.*

Gaud'y. See GARISH.

Gaunt'. Lean, attenuated, emaciated, lank, thin.
 ANT. *Stout, healthy-looking.*

Gawk'y. Clumsy, awkward, ungainly.
 ANT. *Graceful, nimble.*

Gay. See BLITHE.

Gear'. Equipment, accoutrements, furniture, apparatus, tackle.

Gen'eral. Universal, catholic, usual, prevalent.
 ANT. *Particular, rare, uncommon.*

Gen'erate. Engender, beget, produce.
 ANT. *Be born.*

Genera'tion. Propagation, procreation, production; era, time, age.

Generos'ity. Kindness, beneficence, liberality, bountifulness.
 ANT. *Stinginess, illiberality, unkindness.*

Gen′erous. Noble, magnanimous ; munificent, open-handed, liberal, kind.

ANT. *Ignoble, poor-spirited, stingy, close-fisted.*

Ge′nial. See CORDIAL.

Ge′nius. Talent, cleverness, ability ; bent, aptness.

ANT. *Stupidity, incapacity.*

Genteel′. Polite, courteous, well-bred.

ANT. *Ill-bred, rude, impolite.*

Gent′le. Well-bred ; mild, placid, tender; docile, meek.

ANT. *Ill-bred ; hard, pitiless ; intractable.*

Gen′uine. Real, true, authentic, sincere, unadulterated.

ANT. *False, sham, fictitious.*

Ge′nus. Class, group, race, sort, kind.

ANT. *Species.*

Germ′. Seed, embryo, origin, first principle.

ANT. *Full growth, maturity.*

Germane′. Allied, kindred, related, relevant.

ANT. *Unrelated, irrelevant.*

Ges′ture. Gesticulation, posture, action.

Get′. See ACQUIRE.

Gew′gaw. See BAUBLE.

Ghast′ly. Spectral ; pallid, cadaverous, wan ; horrible.

ANT. *Corporeal, alive ; high coloured ; pleasing.*

Ghost′. Spectre, apparition, spirit, phantom.

ANT. *Living person, body, reality.*

Gib′berish. See BABBLE.

Gib′e. See DERIDE.

Gid′dy. Dizzy, flighty, inconstant.

ANT. *Steady, constant.*

Gift′. Boon, grant, bounty, largess, present ; talent, faculty.

Gift′ed. Able, talented, clever.

ANT. *Feeble, ignorant, incapable.*

Gigan′tic. See COLOSSAL.

Gild. See EMBELLISH.

Gim′crack. See BAUBLE.

Gird′. Belt, encircle, environ, inclose, surround.

Gist′. Meaning, point, substance, pith.

Give. See IMPART.

Glad′. Delighted, pleased, gratified, happy, joyous.

ANT. *Sorry, displeased, unhappy.*

Glad′den. See CHEER.

Glad′ness. See GAIETY.

Glam′our. See ENCHANTMENT.

Glance′. See GLIMPSE.

Glare′. Dazzle, gleam, flame, glower.

ANT. *Be dim.*

Gleam′. Glimmer, shine, flash.

ANT. *Be dull.*

Glee′. Part-song. See also GAIETY.

Glide′. Flow, slip, slide.

ANT. *Stand still, rest.*

Glim′mer. See GLEAM.

Glimpse′. Glance, gleam, rapid look.

ANT. *Steady look, full view.*

Glist′en. Beam, shine, twinkle.

ANT. *Be dark.*

Glit′ter. See GLISTEN and GLEAM.

Gloom′. Darkness, cloudiness, dimness ; melancholy, depression.

ANT. *Brightness, cloudlessness ; cheerfulness.*

Gloom′y. Dim, dark, cloudy, dismal, depressing.

ANT. *Bright, light, cloudless ; gay, cheery.*

Glo′rify. See EXALT.

Glo′rious. See CELEBRATED.

Glo′ry. Splendour, magnificence, fame, renown, celebrity, honour.

ANT. *Dimness, shabbiness, obscurity, dishonour.*

Glow′ing. See ARDENT.

Gloze′. Smooth over, extenuate. See also CAJOLE.

ANT. *Aggravate.*

Glut′. Cloy, gorge, cram, surfeit, satiate.

ANT. *Leave unsatisfied.*

Glu'tinous. Sticky, viscous, ropy.
ANT. *Liquid, smooth.*
Glut'ton. Gormandizer, gourmand, greedy fellow.
ANT. *Ascetic, temperate eater.*
Glut'tonous. Greedy, gorging, gormandizing.
ANT. *Temperate, ascetic.*
Go'. Proceed, advance, depart, move.
ANT. *Stay, remain, rest.*
Goad'. See AROUSE.
God'ly. Godlike, religious, pious, holy.
ANT. *Ungodly, irreligious, profane.*
Good'. Virtuous, excellent, religious, fitting, kind.
ANT. *Wicked, bad, unfitting, unkind.*
Good' (*n.*). Benefit, advantage, blessing.
ANT. *Harm, disadvantage.*
Good'ly. Comely, pleasant, agreeable ; comparatively large.
ANT. *Ugly, unpleasing ; trifling.*
Good'ness. Excellence, worth ; virtue ; kindness, benevolence.
ANT. *Badness, wickedness ; unkindness.*
Gorge'. See GLUT.
Gor'geous. Splendid, magnificent, sumptuous, superb.
ANT. *Shabby, mean, cheap.*
Gos'sip. Tattle, chatter.
Gov'ern. Rule, direct, command.
ANT. *Misrule, misdirect, misgovern.*
Gov'ernment. Rule, control, sway, administration.
ANT. *Disorder, anarchy.*
Grab'. See GRASP.
Grace'. Favour, permission, mercy ; beauty, elegance.
ANT. *Disfavour, refusal ; ungainliness.*
Grace'ful. Beautiful, elegant, natural, easy.
ANT. *Ungainly, inelegant.*

Grace'less. See CORRUPT and BASE.
Gra'cious. See AFFABLE.
Grad'ual. Slow, progressive, regular.
ANT. *Rapid, spasmodic, jerky.*
Grand'. Tall, great, majestic, pompous, stately, chief.
ANT. *Short, small, insignificant ; inferior.*
Grand'eur. Splendour, magnificence, majesty, greatness.
ANT. *Shabbiness, sordidness, lowliness.*
Grant'. Give, bestow ; concede, admit.
ANT. *Withhold, refuse.*
Graph'ic. Pictorial, vivid, lively, picturesque.
ANT. *Dull, tedious, unpicturesque.*
Grap'ple. Seize, gripe, wrestle ; cope with.
ANT. *Let go, release ; shrink from.*
Grasp'. Catch, clasp, seize, clutch, hold.
ANT. *Let go, release.*
Grasp'ing. Avaricious, greedy, covetous.
ANT. *Unenvious, generous.*
Grate'ful. Thankful, beholden ; acceptable, agreeable, welcome.
ANT. *Thankless, ungrateful ; unwelcome.*
Gratifica'tion. Enjoyment, delight, indulgence, satisfaction.
ANT. *Disappointment, dissatisfaction.*
Grat'ify. Indulge, please, delight.
ANT. *Refuse, displease.*
Gratu'itous. Voluntary, spontaneous ; unwarranted.
ANT. *Mercenary, paid for, compulsory.*
Grave'. Serious, staid, solemn ; weighty, important.
ANT. *Trivial, frivolous, undignified.*
Grav'ity. Centrifugal force,

48

weight, importance, seriousness, sedateness.
ANT. *Lightness, unimportance, triviality.*

Great'. Big, huge, vast ; noble,
sublime, high ; principal.
ANT. *Small, little, unimportant, minor.*

Great'ness. Magnitude ; eminence, fame ; nobility.
ANT. *Smallness, obscurity.*

Greed'iness. Avidity, voracity,
eagerness.
ANT. *Generosity, coolness.*

Greed'y. Voracious, ravenous,
avaricious, covetous. See
also GLUTTONOUS and GRASP-
ING.
ANT. *Self- restrained, unenvious.*

Green'. Verdant, emerald ;
fresh, blooming ; unripe, immature.
ANT. *Faded, ripe.*

Green'ness. Vividity, freshness,
immaturity.
ANT. *Withered state, decay.*

Greet'. Address, hail, welcome.
ANT. *Bid farewell, avoid.*

Grief'. See AFFLICTION.

Griev'ance. Hardship, trouble,
injustice, ground of com-
plaint.
ANT. *Justice.*

Griev'ous. Painful, hurtful,
harmful, sad, deplorable.
ANT. *Painless, easy, cheerful.*

Grim'. Sullen, surly. See also
FEROCIOUS.
ANT. *Mild, gentle.*

Grind'. Pulverize, pound, crush;
afflict, oppress.
ANT. *Comfort, relieve.*

Gripe'. See GRASP.

Gris'ly. Hideous, frightful. See
also GHASTLY.
ANT. *Agreeable, pleasant
looking.*

Groan'. Moan, lament.

Grope'. Fumble, feel one's way,
grabble.
ANT. *Go confidently.*

Gross'. Big, bulky ; thick,

dense ; coarse, sensual; impure, glaring ; entire.
ANT. *Small, light ; decent ;
net.*

Gross'ness. Coarseness, indelicacy.
ANT. *Decency, delicacy.*

Grotesque'. Whimsical, odd,
bizarre, unnatural.
ANT. *Regular, ordinary,
natural.*

Ground'. Soil, earth ; land ;
foundation, base ; motive,
reason, cause.

Ground' (*vb.*). Base, establish,
found ; instruct.

Group'. Cluster, assemblage,
association. See also GENUS.
ANT. *Individual.*

Grov'el. See COWER.

Grow'. Increase, develop, advance, wax.
ANT. *Decrease, decline.*

Growl'. Snarl ; grumble,
complain.
ANT. *Purr ; be cheerful.*

Growth'. Increase, augmentation, development, progress.
ANT. *Decrease, decline.*

Grudge'. Begrudge, envy.
ANT. *Be generous.*

Grudge' (*n.*). See ENVY.

Gruff'. Harsh, rugged, surly,
brusque.
ANT. *Smooth, soft.*

Grumb'le. Complain, growl,
murmur.
ANT. *Be uncomplaining.*

Guarantee'. Warrant, insure,
pledge.
ANT. *Refuse, deny.*

Guard'. Defence, protection ;
sentry, watchman ; vigilance,
keeping.
ANT. *Defencelessness, insecurity.*

Guard' (*vb.*). See DEFEND.

Guard'ed. See CIRCUMSPECT.

Guard'ian. Keeper, protector,
warden, custodian.
ANT. *Ward.*

Guerd'on. Reward, prize, recompense.
ANT. *Loss.*

Guess' (*n.*). See CONJECTURE.

Guess' (*vb.*). Surmise, divine, reckon, imagine, fancy.

　ANT. *Know certainly.*

Guide'. Lead, conduct, direct, regulate.

　ANT. *Follow.*

Guide' (*n.*). Leader, conductor, director, counsellor.

　ANT. *Follower, pupil.*

Guild'. Association, fraternity, company.

Guile'. See FRAUD.

Guilt'. See CRIME.

Guilt'y. Criminal, wicked, culpable.

　ANT. *Innocent, blameless.*

Guise'. See FASHION.

Gull'. See CHEAT.

Gullibil'ity. Simplicity, credulity.

　ANT. *Astuteness.*

Gump'tion. Acuteness, astuteness, shrewdness.

　ANT. *Simplicity.*

Gush'. Flow, stream, spout.

　ANT. *Stop, cease.*

Gust'. Breeze, blow, blast, squall.

　ANT. *Calm, lull.*

Gus'to. Relish, savour, zest.

　ANT. *Distaste, dislike.*

Guz'zle. Drink, swill, tope.

Gyve. Fetter, chain, manacle.

H

Habil'iments. See ATTIRE.

Hab'it. Custom, usage, practice, wont. See also ATTIRE.

　ANT. *Unwontedness.*

Habita'tion. See ABODE.

Habit'ual. Accustomed, ordinary, wonted, customary.

　ANT. *Unwonted, unusual, unaccustomed.*

Habit'uate. See INURE.

Hack'neyed. Trite, common, stale, threadbare.

　ANT. *Novel, fresh.*

Hag'gard. See GAUNT.

Hag'gle. Higgle, chaffer, bargain.

　ANT. *Buy outright.*

Hail'. See GREET.

Hale'. Healthy, sound, hearty, robust, vigorous.

　ANT. *Unhealthy-looking, weakly.*

Hal'low. See CONSECRATE.

Hallucina'tion. Delusion, illusion ; mistake.

　ANT. *Reality, truth.*

Halt'. Pause, rest, stop ; falter, hobble.

　ANT. *Go on, walk easily.*

Hamp'er. Shackle, fetter, clog, impede, encumber.

　ANT. *Release, disencumber, accelerate.*

Hand'. Paw ; agency ; workman, employee.

　ANT. *Employer.*

Hand'le. Wield, manage, manipulate ; treat ; discuss.

Hand'some. See BEAUTIFUL.

Hand'y. Convenient. See also ADROIT.

　ANT. *Inconvenient.* See also AWKWARD.

Hap'. Accident, fortune, fate.

Hap'less. Unfortunate, unlucky, unhappy. [*happy.*

　ANT. *Lucky, fortunate,*

Hap'pen. Occur, befall, chance, take place.

Hap'piness. Pleasure. See also GRATIFICATION.

　ANT. *Sadness, sorrow, misfortune.*

Harangue'. Speech, oration.

Har'ass. See ANNOY.

Har'binger. See HERALD.

Har'bour. Asylum, refuge, shelter, haven.

Har'bour (*vb.*). Shelter, lodge ; cherish, entertain.

　ANT. *Eject, banish.*

Hard'. Firm, solid ; difficult ; harsh, cruel, severe ; unyielding.

　ANT. *Soft, easy ; gentle, mild ; yielding.*

Hard'ened. See CALLOUS.

Hard'ihood. See EFFRONTERY.

Hard'ship. See ADVERSITY.

Hard'y. Brave, intrepid, courageous, robust, stout-hearted.

ANT. *Timid ; weakly ; faint-hearted.*

Harm'. Injury, hurt, loss, mischief, evil.

ANT. *Profit, good.*

Harm' (vb.). Injure, hurt, damage.

ANT. *Profit, benefit.*

Harm'ful. See BANEFUL.

Harm'less. Inoffensive, innocuous, innocent.

ANT. *Harmful, noxious, offensive.*

Harmo'nious. Concordant, consonant ; musical ; amiable, friendly.

ANT. *Discordant, unmusical ; unfriendly.*

Har'monize. Accord, agree, correspond ; arrange in parts.

ANT. *Disagree, be out of accord.*

Har'mony. Concord, agreement, peace, friendship.

ANT. *Discord, disagreement, quarrelling.*

Har'row. See ANNOY.

Harsh'. Rough, discordant ; bitter ; cruel, brutal.

ANT. *Smooth, harmonious, gentle.*

Harsh'ness. See ASPERITY.

Haste'. Quickness, speed, hurry, celerity, vehemence.

ANT. *Slowness, tardiness ; apathy.*

Hast'en. See ACCELERATE.

Hast'y. Precipitate, rash, irritable ; speedy ; passionate.

ANT. *Circumspect, deliberate, dispassionate.*

Hate'. See ABHOR.

Hate' (n.). See ENMITY.

Hate'ful. See EXECRABLE.

Ha'tred. See ENMITY and AVERSION.

Haught'iness. Arrogance, pride, hauteur, loftiness, insolence.

ANT. *Humility, condescension, geniality.*

Haught'y. See ARROGANT.

Haul'. See DRAW.

Haunt'. Frequent, resort to, visit often.

ANT. *Desert, keep away from.*

Hauteur'. See HAUGHTINESS.

Ha'ven. See HARBOUR.

Hav'oc. Devastation, ruin, destruction, desolation.

ANT. *Reconstruction, restoration.*

Haz'ard. See DANGER and ACCIDENT.

Haz'ard (vb.). Risk, endanger, adventure, imperil.

ANT. *Secure, make safe, preserve.*

Haz'ardous. Adventurous, bold; dangerous, perilous, precarious.

ANT. *Timid, safe, certain.*

Ha'zy. Foggy, misty, cloudy ; vague.

ANT. *Clear, unclouded.*

Head'. Top, summit ; chief, ruler ; intelligence, brain.

ANT. *Foot, bottom ; subordinate.*

Head'long. Precipitately, hastily, rashly, pell-mell.

ANT. *Slowly, deliberately.*

Head'strong. Obstinate, self-willed, stubborn ; venturesome.

ANT. *Complaisant, yielding ; cautious.*

Heal'. Restore, remedy, cure ; reconcile.

ANT. *Injure ; set at enmity.*

Health'. Salubrity, soundness, robustness, vigour.

ANT. *Insalubrity, unhealthiness, weakness.*

Health'y. See HALE.

Heap'. Accumulate, pile, mass.

ANT. *Throw down, lay level.*

Hear'. Listen, hearken, attend, heed.

ANT. *Be deaf, disobey.*

Heart'. Core, centre ; mind, will ; courage ; enthusiasm.

ANT. *Circumference, exterior ; apathy.*

Heart'ily. Cordially, sincerely, actively, ardently.

ANT. *Indifferently, coldly.*

Heart'y. Sincere, warm, cordial. See also HALE.

ANT. *Insincere, cold.*

Heat'. Warmth, caloric ; passion, rage, excitement.

ANT. *Cold, coolness, calmness.*

Heat'ed. Excited, angry, passionate.

ANT. *Calm, passionless, unimpassioned.*

Heave'. Raise, lift, throw.

ANT. *Drop, depress.*

Heav'en. Firmament, sky, welkin.

ANT. *Earth, ground, hell.*

Heav'enly. See CELESTIAL and DIVINE.

Heav'iness. Gravity ; depression, despondency. See also DESPAIR.

ANT. *Lightness ; gaiety, good spirits.*

Heav'y. Weighty, ponderous ; oppressive, grievous ; dull, stupid ; drowsy.

ANT. *Light ; comforting ; easy ; intelligent ; wideawake.*

Hec'tor. Threaten, menace, bully. See also BLUFF.

ANT. *Speak gently, encourage.*

Hedge'. Fence, hem in ; bet both ways, play double part.

ANT. *Leave open, admit.*

Heed'. Mind, pay attention, note, consider.

ANT. *Disregard, be careless, neglect.*

Heed'ful. See CAREFUL.

Height'. Top, summit, acme. See also ALTITUDE.

ANT. *Depth, bottom.*

Height'en. See ENHANCE and AGGRAVATE

ANT. *Detract from, lower.*

Hein'ous. See ATROCIOUS.

Hell'ish. See FIENDISH.

Help'. See AID.

Help'less. Weak, feeble, defenceless, irremediable.

ANT. *Strong, resourceful ; remediable.*

Hem'. Border, edge, fringe.

ANT. *Surface.*

Her'ald. Proclaimer, precursor, forerunner, harbinger.

Her'ald (*vb.*). See ADVERTISE.

Hercu'lean. Laborious, toilsome, colossal.

ANT. *Slight, easy.*

Heret'ical. Unorthodox, heterodox, impious.

ANT. *Orthodox, sound.*

Her'itage. Inheritance, patrimony, estate.

Her'mit. Eremite, recluse ; solitary, anchoret.

Hero'ic. See BOLD.

Her'oism. See COURAGE.

Hes'itate. See FALTER.

Hesita'tion. See DOUBT.

He'terodox. See HERETICAL.

Heteroge'neous. Unlike, dissimilar, miscellaneous.

ANT. *Alike, homogeneous.*

Hew'. Cut, chop ; shape.

Hia'tus. See BREACH.

Hidd'en. Covert, concealed ; mysterious, occult, abstruse.

ANT. *Open, revealed, plain.*

Hide'. Cover, conceal, secrete, bury, veil.

ANT. *Uncover, reveal, disclose.*

Hid'eous. See GHASTLY and GRISLY.

Hig'gle. See HAGGLE.

High'. Tall, lofty, elevated ; eminent, exalted, superior ; loud ; acute.

ANT. *Low, short, humble ; low-pitched.*

High'ly. Much, greatly, exceedingly.

ANT. *Slightly, by no means.*

Hila'rious. See CONVIVIAL.

Hilar'ity. See GAIETY.

Hind'. Peasant, farm-servant, herdsman.

Hind′er. Impede, stop, prevent, arrest, delay.

ANT. *Urge on, facilitate.*

Hind′rance. Impediment, prevention, obstruction, restraint.

ANT. *Facility, liberty.*

Hint′. Suggest, intimate, imply. See also ALLUDE.

ANT. *Speak out.*

Hint′ (*n.*). Suggestion, intimation, allusion.

Hire′. Pay, wages, allowance.

Hir′sute. Hairy, shaggy, bearded.

ANT. *Smooth, hairless, beardless.*

Histrion′ic. Theatrical, dramatic.

Hit′. See BEAT.

Hoard′. See GARNER.

Hoarse′. Husky, raucous, rough, grating.

ANT. *Smooth, soft.*

Hoar′y. Gray, silvery, frosty.

Hoax′. Befool, dupe, trick, cheat.

Hob′ble. See LIMP.

Hodge′-podge. Hotch-potch, medley, miscellany, farrago.

Hoist. See HEAVE.

Hold′. Grasp, seize ; contain ; possess, keep ; detain ; last, endure ; avail.

ANT. *Let go, loose : fail.*

Hole′. Aperture, opening, excavation, rent.

ANT. *Stopper, unbroken surface.*

Hol′low. Concave, sunken ; empty, void ; insincere, false.

ANT. *Solid ; full ; sincere, genuine.*

Ho′ly. Pure, sacred, religious.

ANT. *Unholy, impure, irreligious, profane.*

Hom′age. Fealty, obeisance, deference, duty ; worship.

Home′. See ABODE.

Home′ly. Homelike, simple, plain ; commonplace.

ANT. *Splendid, costly, extravagant, elaborate.*

Home′spun. Home-made ; plain, coarse.

ANT. *Shop-made, fine.*

Hom′ily. Sermon, discourse, lecture.

Homoge′neous. Uniform, similar, akin.

ANT. *Heterogeneous.*

Hon′est. Upright, truthful, faithful, sincere, trustworthy,

ANT. *Untruthful, untrustworthy, false.*

Hon′esty. Integrity, trustworthiness, sincerity, rectitude, uprightness.

ANT. *Dishonesty, insincerity, turpitude.*

Hon′our. Glory, credit, renown ; dignity ; truthfulness, word, principle.

ANT. *Dishonour, disgrace ; dishonesty.*

Hon′our (*vb.*). Respect, esteem, venerate ; dignify, elevate.

ANT. *Dishonour, disparage, depreciate, lower.*

Hon′ourable. Trustworthy, upright, honest, just ; illustrious.

ANT. *Dishonourable.*

Hood′wink. See HOAX and CHEAT.

Hooked′. Curved, bent, aquiline.

ANT. *Straight.*

Hop′. Jump, skip, caper, dance.

ANT. *Stand still, be steady.*

Hope′. Expectation, look for, confidence, reliance.

ANT. *Despair, distrust.*

Hope′ (*vb.*). Expect, look for, be confident.

ANT. *Despair of, distrust.*

Hope′ful. Expectant, confident, cheerful ; promising.

ANT. *Despairing, cheerless, unpromising.*

Hope′less. Desperate, despairing ; impossible, impracticable.

ANT. *Expectant, confident ; possible, practicable.*

Hori′zon. Limit, bound, verge.

Hor′rible. See GRISLY.

Hor′rid. Bristly, prickly. See also GRISLY.

ANT. *Smooth.*

Hor'rify. See AFFRIGHT.

Hor'ror. See FEAR.

Hos'pitable. Kind, liberal, welcoming.
  ANT. *Inhospitable, unfriendly.*

Hospital'ity. Welcome, kindly reception, shelter.
  ANT. *Inhospitality, dismissal.*

Host'. Landlord, inn-keeper, entertainer.
  ANT. *Guest, inmate, lodger.*

Host'. Army, crowd, multitude.

Host'ile. See ADVERSE.

Hostil'ity. See ENMITY.

Hot'. Heated, warm. See also ARDENT.
  ANT. *Cold, cool.*

Hound'. Chase, pursue, urge on.
  ANT. *Flee.*

House' (*n.*). Family, line, lineage. See also DOMICILE and ABODE.

House' (*vb.*). Shelter, harbour ; contain.
  ANT. *Shut out, exclude.*

Hov'el. Hut, cabin, poor dwelling.
  ANT. *Palace, mansion.*

Hov'er. Flutter, waver over, fly about.
  ANT. *Pause, rest.*

Hub'bub. Din, tumult, uproar. disturbance.
  ANT. *Peace, quiet, calm.*

Hue'. See COLOUR.

Hug'. See CLASP.

Huge'. See COLOSSAL.

Humane'. Gentle, kind, benevolent, tender, compassionate.
  ANT. *Cruel, ungentle, hard.*

Human'ity. Mankind ; kindness, charity, benevolence, compassion.
  ANT. *Divinity , cruelty, unkindness.*

Hu'manize. Civilize, refine, soften.
  ANT. *Corrupt, harden.*

Hum'ble. Low, lowly, poor, mean ; meek, modest.
  ANT. *High, lofty, grand, proud.*

Hum'ble (*vb.*). See ABASE.

Hum'bug (*vb.*). See HOAX.

Hu'mid. Damp, dank, watery, wet.
  ANT. *Dry, arid.*

Humil'iate. See ABASE.

Humil'ity. Humbleness, modesty, meekness.
  ANT. *Pride, arrogance.*

Hu'morous. Whimsical, jocose, comical.
  ANT. *Dull, stolid.*

Hu'mour. Bent, mood ; drollery, comicality.
  ANT. *Gravity.*

Hu'mour (*vb.*). Gratify, yield to, comply with.
  ANT. *Disappoint, refuse, oppose.*

Hunt'. Chase, pursue, hound.
  ANT. *Flee, run.*

Hurl'. See FLING.

Hurri'cane. Tempest, tornado.

Hur'ry. See HASTE.

Hurt'. See DAMAGE.

Hurt'ful. See BANEFUL.

Hus'band. Consort, spouse.
  ANT. *Wife.*

Hus'bandry. Agriculture, farming, tillage ; economy.

Hus'ky. See HOARSE.

Hussy'. See JADE.

Hust'le. Push, shove, jostle.
  ANT. *Give way.*

Hypercrit'ical. See CAPTIOUS.

Hypoc'risy. Deceit, imposture, pretence, cant.
  ANT. *Honesty, sincerity.*

Hypocrit'ical. Deceitful, false, canting.
  ANT. *Honest, sincere.*

I

I'cy. Cold, frozen, chilling; frigid.
ANT. *Warm, genial.*

Ide'a. Conception, notion, fancy, impression; plan; archetype.
ANT. *Fact; individual thing.*

Ide'al. Imaginary; visionary, unreal; standard.
ANT. *Actual; ordinary.*

Ident'ity. Sameness, oneness, individuality.
ANT. *Difference.*

I'dle. Indolent, lazy; unoccupied; vain, unprofitable; foolish.
ANT. *Active, industrious; busy; useful, profitable; sensible.*

I'dolize. Worship, adore, deify.
ANT. *Execrate, blaspheme.*

Igno'ble. See BASE.

Ignomin'ious. Disgraceful, dishonourable, shameful, humiliating.
ANT. *Honourable, creditable.*

Ig'nominy. Disgrace, opprobrium, contempt, shame.
ANT. *Honour, credit, praise.*

Ig'norant. Unlearned, illiterate, unenlightened, ill-informed.
ANT. *Learned, lettered, literate, well-informed.*

Ignore'. Disregard, neglect, reject.
ANT. *Regard, consider, heed.*

Ill'. Wicked, evil, bad; sick.
ANT. *Good; well, cured.*

Ille'gal. Unlawful, illicit, prohibited.
ANT. *Legal, lawful.*

Illeg'ible. Unreadable, undecipherable.
ANT. *Readable, legible, plain.*

Illegit'imate. Unlawful, bastard.
ANT. *Legitimate, lawful.*

Illi'cit. See ILLEGAL.

Illim'itable. Boundless, unbounded, immense, infinite.
ANT. *Limited, finite, small.*

Illit'erate. See IGNORANT.

Ill'ness. Ailment, malady. See also DISEASE.
ANT. *Health.*

Illog'ical. Inconsequent, unsound, fallacious.
ANT. *Logical, sound, consequent.*

Illu'minate. See ENLIGHTEN.

Illu'sion. See HALLUCINATION.

Ill'ustrate. See ELUCIDATE.

Illust'rious. See CELEBRATED.

Im'age. Figure, likeness, effigy, statue, picture.

Imag'inary. See IDEAL and CHIMERICAL.

Imag'inative. Poetical, creative; fanciful, visionary.
ANT. *Unpoetical; prosaic.*

Im'becile. Weak, feeble, silly, idiotic.
ANT. *Strong, sane.*

Imbibe'. See ABSORB.

Im'itate. Copy, follow; counterfeit, ape, mimic.
ANT. *Lead, initiate.*

Immac'ulate. Spotless, stainless, unblemished, faultless.
ANT. *Spotted, stained, blemished, faulty.*

Immate'rial. Incorporeal; unimportant, insignificant, trifling.
ANT. *Substantial, material; important, significant.*

Immature'. See CRUDE.

Immeas'urable. See ILLIMITABLE.

Imme'diate. Close, proximate; direct; instantaneous.
ANT. *Remote; mediate.*

Imme'diately. Forthwith, directly, straightway.
ANT. *Later.*

Immense'. See ILLIMITABLE.

Immerse'. Dip, plunge, douse ; overwhelm, drown.

ANT. *Draw out.*

Im'minent. Threatening, impending, near.

ANT. *Remote.*

Immod'erate. See EXCESSIVE.

Immod'est. Indelicate, shameless, indecent, indecorous, unchaste.

ANT. *Modest, decent, chaste.*

Immor'al. See ABANDONED.

Immoral'ity. Wickedness, sin, vice, depravity.

ANT. *Virtue, morality.*

Immort'al. Undying, imperishable, endless, everlasting.

ANT. *Mortal, perishable, human.*

Immu'nity. Exemption, release, freedom, privilege.

ANT. *Subjection, obligation, liability.*

Immu'table. Unchanging, changeless, unalterable, fixed.

ANT. *Mutable, changing.*

Impair'. See DIMINISH.

Impart'. Give, bestow, afford. See also DISCLOSE.

ANT. *Withhold, refuse.*

Impar'tial. See EQUITABLE and FAIR.

Impas'sioned. See FERVENT.

Impa'tient. Restless, hasty, intolerant, unsubmissive.

ANT. *Patient, tolerant, submissive, resigned.*

Impeach'. Accuse, denounce, arraign, censure ; question.

ANT. *Defend, justify ; believe.*

Impeach'ment. See IMPUTATION.

Impede'. See HINDER.

Imped'iment. See HINDRANCE.

Impel'. See DRIVE and ACTUATE.

Impend'ing. See IMMINENT.

Impen'etrable. Impervious, impassable, dense.

ANT. *Pervious, penetrable.*

Imper'ative. Commanding, authoritative ; obligatory, binding.

ANT. *Submissive ; unimportant.*

Impercep'tible. Invisible, impalpable, inaudible ; exceedingly small.

ANT. *Perceptible, visible, audible.*

Imper'fect. Defective, unfinished, incomplete. See also FAULTY.

ANT. *Complete, perfect, finished.*

Imper'il. See ENDANGER.

Impe'rious. Domineering, commanding, arrogant, authoritative, dictatorial, arbitrary.

ANT. *Considerate, condescending.*

Imper'meable. See IMPENETRABLE.

Impert'inent. Irrelevant ; rude, impudent, saucy, pert.

ANT. *Pertinent, relevant, polite, courteous.*

Imper'vious. See IMPENETRABLE.

Impet'uous. Precipitate, vehement. See also BOISTEROUS.

ANT. *Calm, quiet, apathetic.*

Im'pious. Irreligious, ungodly, profane, blasphemous.

ANT. *Religious, pious, godly.*

Implac'able. Unappeasable, irreconcilable, unrelenting, remorseless, inexorable.

ANT. *Placable, reconcilable, remorseful.*

Im'plicate. Entangle, involve, compromise.

ANT. *Exclude.*

Implic'it. Implied, inferred ; unreserved, full.

ANT. *Expressed ; reserved.*

Imply'. Involve ; mean, import. See also DENOTE.

ANT. *Exclude.*

Impolite'. Rude, discourteous, uncivil.

ANT. *Polite, courteous, civil.*

Import'. Introduce, bring in ; denote, imply, mean ; interest.

ANT. *Export.*

Im'port (*n.*). Importation ; purport, drift, gist.
ANT. *Export.*

Import'ance. Weight, consequence, moment, value.
ANT. *Unimportance, insignificance.*

Import'ant. Weighty, momentous, significant, serious.
ANT. *Unimportant, insignificant, trivial.*

Importune'. See BESEECH.

Impose'. Lay, fix, appoint ; trick, deceive.

Impo'sing. See GRAND.

Imposi'tion. See FRAUD.

Im'post. Tax, levy, tribute, duty.
ANT. *Exemption.*

Impos'tor. Cheat, charlatan, rogue, knave.
ANT. *Honest man.*

Im'potent. See FEEBLE.

Impract'icable. Impossible, not feasible.
ANT. *Possible, feasible, practicable.*

Impreca'tion. See CURSE.

Impreg'nate. Fecundate, imbue, fill, infuse.

Im'press (*n.*). Stamp, mark, device.

Impress'. Engrave, stamp ; inculcate ; cause admiration.

Impres'sion. Printing, edition, stamp, mark ; notion, feeling.

Impress'ive. Affecting, striking, exciting.
ANT. *Unimpressive, commonplace, ordinary.*

Impris'on. Incarcerate, confine, immure.
ANT. *Liberate, enlarge, let out.*

Improp'er. Unsuitable, unfit ; unseemly, indecorous, wrong.
ANT. *Proper, fit, suitable ; decorous ; right.*

Improve'. See AMEND.

Improv'ident. Prodigal ; imprudent, short-sighted, careless.
ANT. *Saving, economical, prudent.*

Impru'dence. Thoughtlessness,

short-sightedness, heedlessness, rashness.
ANT. *Prudence, carefulness, caution.*

Im'pudence. See EFFRONTERY.

Im'pudent. See AUDACIOUS.

Impugn'. See GAINSAY.

Im'pulse. Push, thrust ; incentive, motive ; sudden resolve.
ANT. *Pull ; premeditated act.*

Impul'sive. See IMPETUOUS.

Impure'. Mixed ; foul, unclean ; corrupt ; unchaste.
ANT. *Pure, unmixed, clean, chaste.*

Imputa'tion. Accusation, charge ; attribution ; slur.

Inacces'sible. Unapproachable, out of reach.
ANT. *Approachable, accessible.*

Inac'curate. Inexact, faulty, careless, erroneous.
ANT. *Accurate, exact, correct, careful.*

Inact'ive. Sluggish, inert, idle, slothful.
ANT. *Active, vigorous, busy.*

Inadvert'ent. Inattentive, unobservant, careless, negligent.
ANT. *Attentive, observant, heedful.*

Inan'imate. Lifeless, dead ; apathetic, inert.
ANT. *Lively, living.*

Inane'. Empty, silly, frivolous, idiotic.
ANT. *Full ; sane, sensible.*

Inappro'priate. See IMPROPER.

Inattent'ive. See INADVERTENT.

Inaug'urate. Install, begin, commence.

Inauspi'cious. See AUSPICIOUS.

Inca'pable. Unqualified, incompetent, unable, disabled.
ANT. *Capable, competent, qualified.*

Incapa'city. Inability, disqualification, unfitness, incompetency.
ANT. *Capacity, ability, fitness, competency.*

Incar'cerate. See IMPRISON.

Incense' (*vb.*). See ENRAGE.

Incent'ive. Motive, stimulus, spur, impulse.

ANT. *Discouragement, hindrance.*

Incess'ant. Ceaseless, unceasing, continual, constant.

ANT. *Temporary, short-lived.*

In'cident. See CIRCUMSTANCE.

Incident'al. Contingent, casual, occasional.

ANT. *Essential.*

Inci'sive. Sharp, biting, trenchant.

ANT. *Mild, gentle.*

Incite'. See AROUSE.

Incite'ment. See INCENTIVE.

Inclem'ent. Unmerciful, harsh; rough, stormy.

ANT. *Clement, merciful, pitiful ; mild, calm.*

Inclina'tion. Bias, bent, disposition ; liking, affection.

Incline'. Bend, slope, slant ; tend.

Include'. See COMPREHEND and COMPRISE.

Incohe'rent. Loose, unconnected ; wandering, unintelligible.

ANT. *Coherent, connected, intelligible.*

Incommode'. Inconvenience, disturb, embarrass.

ANT. *Convenience, relieve.*

Incommo'dious. See COMMODIOUS.

Incom'parable. Unrivalled, inimitable, matchless, peerless, unequalled.

Incom'petent. See INCAPABLE.

Incon'gruous. Inconsistent, unsuited, discrepant.

ANT. *Congruous, fitting, consistent.*

Inconsid'erate. See CONSIDERATE.

Inconsistent. See CONSISTENT and COMPATIBLE.

Incon'stancy. See INSTABILITY.

Incon'stant. See CHANGEABLE.

Incontrovert'ible. See IRREFRAGABLE.

Inconve'nient. See FIT and COMMODIOUS.

Incor'porate. See EMBODY.

Incorrect'. See CORRECT.

Increase' (*vb.*). See AUGMENT.

In'crease (*n.*). Addition, growth, extension, augmentation.

ANT. *Diminution, decay, loss.*

In'culcate. Instil, enforce, impress.

In'culpate. See BLAME.

Incum'bent. Binding, compulsory, obligatory.

ANT. *Unnecessary, non-compulsory.*

Incur'sion. See FORAY.

Indeci'sion. Irresoluteness, hesitation, wavering.

ANT. *Decision, firmness.*

Indefat'igable. Unwearied, untiring, assiduous.

ANT. *Tired, weary, lax.*

Indefens'ible. Untenable, unwarranted, inexcusable.

ANT. *Justifiable, tenable, warranted.*

Indef'inite. See DEFINITE.

Indem'nify. Compensate, satisfy, reimburse, requite.

ANT. *Inflict loss, injure.*

Independ'ent. Unconnected, unrelated, free.

ANT. *Dependent, related, servile.*

In'dicate. Show, denote, signify.

Indica'tion. Mark, sign, token, symptom.

Indict'. See IMPEACH.

Indict'ment. See CHARGE.

Indiff'erence. Carelessness, apathy, unconcern, disregard, callousness, unimportance.

ANT. *Concern, regard ; importance.*

Indiff'erent. Impartial, neutral ; unconcerned ; tolerable, middling.

ANT. *Partial, biased ; concerned, sympathetic ; excellent.*

In'digent. Needy, poor, necessitous.

ANT. *Well off, well-to-do, rich.*

Indigna′tion. See ANGER.

Indig′nant. Angry, wrathful, exasperated, incensed.

ANT. *Peaceful, gentle.*

Indig′nity. See AFFRONT.

Indirect′. See DIRECT.

Indiscre′tion. Imprudence, rashness, recklessness ; error, mistake.

ANT. *Prudence, caution, discretion.*

Indiscrim′inate. Mixed up, confused, undistinguished, promiscuous.

ANT. *Distinguished, classified.*

Indisposi′tion. Aversion, dislike, disinclination ; sickness, ailment.

ANT. *Liking, willingness ; health.*

Indis′putable. Unarguable, incontestable, unquestionable, irrefutable.

ANT. *Doubtful, questionable, disputable.*

Indistinct′. Dim, vague, confused, imperfect, ambiguous.

ANT. *Distinct, clear, certain.*

Indite′. Dictate, write, compose, pen, frame.

Individ′ual. Single, separate, personal, distinctive.

ANT. *General, common ; impersonal.*

Indoc′trinate. See INITIATE.

In′dolence. Apathy, inactivity, laziness, sloth.

ANT. *Activity, keenness.*

In′dolent. Inactive, idle, lazy, slothful, inert.

ANT. *Active, strenuous, zealous.*

Indorse′. See ENDORSE.

Indu′bitable. See INDISPUTABLE.

Induce′. Lead, persuade, influence, actuate.

ANT. *Dissuade, discourage, put off.*

Induce′ment. See INCENTIVE.

Indulge′. Gratify, cherish, foster, humour, pamper.

ANT. *Deny, repel, treat harshly.*

Indul′gent. Compliant, pampering, lenient, tender, kind.

ANT. *Unyielding, hard, unkind.*

Indus′trious. Busy, active, laborious, assiduous, sedulous.

ANT. *Idle, slothful, lazy.*

Ineffi′cient. See INCAPABLE.

Inert′. Inactive, apathetic, torpid, listless, sluggish, idle.

ANT. *Active, vigorous, alert.*

Ines′timable. Priceless, invaluable.

ANT. *Worthless, valueless.*

Inev′itable. Unavoidable, necessary, certain.

ANT. *Avoidable, unnecessary, uncertain.*

Inex′orable. See IMPLACABLE.

Inexpe′dient. See EXPEDIENT.

Infall′ible. Unerring, certain, sure, unfailing.

ANT. *Fallible, erring, uncertain.*

In′famous. See DISREPUTABLE.

Infect′. Poison, corrupt, vitiate, contaminate.

ANT. *Purify, cleanse.*

Infec′tious. Catching, contaminating, corrupting.

ANT. *Harmless.*

Infer′. Gather, conclude, deduce.

In′ference. Conclusion, deduction, corollary, consequence.

Infe′rior. Lower, subordinate, secondary ; mean.

ANT. *Higher, superior, chief ; excellent.*

Infer′nal. Hellish, diabolical, fiendish, Stygian.

ANT. *Supernal, celestial.*

Infest′. See ANNOY.

In′finite. See ILLIMITABLE

Infirm′. Debilitated, sickly, feeble, weak ; decrepit.

ANT. *Strong, healthy.*

Infirm′ity. See DISEASE.

In′fluence (*vb.*). Move, impel, bias, persuade, sway.

ANT. *Dissuade ; prevent.*

In′fluence(*n.*). Authority, sway, power, weight, interest.

ANT. *Weakness ; obscurity.*

Influen'tial. Powerful, forcible, leading.

ANT. *Weak, uninfluential.*

Inform'. Inspire. See also APPRIZE.

Informa'tion. Intelligence, news, advice; accusation, charge.

Infrac'tion. Breach, violation, infringement, transgression.

ANT. *Compliance.*

Infringe'. Break, violate, transgress; encroach.

ANT. *Submit, obey; observe bounds.*

Infu'riate. See ENRAGE.

Inge'nious. Inventive, contriving, clever, able.

ANT. *Uninventive, unskilful, unhandy.*

Ingenu'ity. Inventiveness, ingeniousness, skill, ability.

ANT. *Clumsiness, unhandiness.*

Ingen'uous. Noble, generous; open, sincere. See also ARTLESS.

ANT. *Low-born; artificial, insincere.*

Ingre'dient. Constituent, component, element.

ANT. *Mixture, whole.*

Inhab'it. Dwell, live in, occupy, reside in.

ANT. *Desert, avoid.*

Inhe'rent. Innate, inborn, native.

Inhib'it. See FORBID.

Inim'ical. See ADVERSE.

Inim'itable. See INCOMPARABLE.

Iniq'uitous. Sinful, wicked, unjust, unrighteous.

ANT. *Equitable, fair, righteous.*

Ini'tiate. Begin, start, inaugurate, indoctrinate.

ANT. *End, finish.*

Injudi'cious. See JUDICIOUS.

Injunc'tion. Command, order, precept.

In'jure. See HARM.

Inju'rious. See BANEFUL.

In'jury. Wrong, harm, hurt, damage.

ANT. *Right, benefit.*

Injust'ice. Wrong, unfairness, iniquity. See also GRIEVANCE.

ANT. *Right, fairness, equity.*

In'let. Entrance, passage, entry; bight, cove.

ANT. *Outlet.*

Innate'. See INHERENT.

In'nocence. Harmlessness; blamelessness, simplicity, ignorance.

ANT. *Guilt, cunning, artfulness, knowledge.*

In'nocent. Harmless, blameless, guiltless; simple, ignorant.

ANT. *Harmful, guilty; artful, knowing.*

Innoc'uous. See HARMLESS.

Innu'merable. Countless, numberless, unnumbered.

ANT. *Few.*

Inoffens'ive. See HARMLESS.

Inord'inate. See REGULAR; also EXCESSIVE.

ANT. *Regular.*

Inqui'ry. Question, query, interrogation; investigation, scrutiny.

Inquis'itive. See CURIOUS.

In'road. Irruption. See also FORAY.

Insane'. Mad, crazy, demented, raving, deranged, lunatic.

ANT. *Sane, sensible.*

Insan'ity. Lunacy, madness, mania, frenzy, dementia.

ANT. *Sanity.*

Inscribe'. Write, engrave, imprint.

Insens'ate. Stupid, unreasoning, unfeeling.

ANT. *Sensible, considerate.*

Insid'ious. Crafty, sly, treacherous, deceitful.

ANT. *Honest, simple, loyal.*

In'sight. Perception, observation, penetration, discernment.

Insin'uate. Ingratiate (oneself), hint, intimate, suggest.

ANT. *Speak plainly, say outright.*

Insip'id. Tasteless, vapid, flavourless, dull, lifeless.

ANT. *Tasty, well-flavoured ; animated.*

Insnare'. See ENSNARE and ALLURE.

In'solence. See EFFRONTERY.

In'solent. See ARROGANT.

Inspect'. Look into, examine, investigate, oversee, superintend.

Inspire'. Inhale, breathe ; instil ; animate, influence.

ANT. *Exhale ; discourage.*

Inspir'it. See ENCOURAGE.

Instabil'ity. Changeableness, fickleness, inconstancy.

ANT. *Stability, firmness, constancy.*

In'stance. Prompting, instigation, incitement ; example, case ; occasion.

In'stant. Urgent, solicitous ; immediate ; present.

ANT. *Half-hearted ; future.*

Instanta'neous. Immediate, quick, momentary.

ANT. *Future, remote, tardy.*

In'stantly. Directly, immediately, quickly, at once.

ANT. *Later, slowly.*

In'stigate. See AROUSE and INSPIRE.

Instil'. Infuse, impress, inculcate.

Instinct'ive. Natural, spontaneous, intuitional.

ANT. *Acquired, reasoned.*

In'stitute. See APPOINT and FOUND.

Instruct'. Teach, inform, educate ; command.

Instruct'ion. Teaching, information, education ; advice, command.

In'strument. Tool, implement ; means, medium ; deed, charter.

In'sult. See AFFRONT.

Insult'ing. See ARROGANT.

Insurrec'tion. Revolt, rising, rebellion, sedition.

Intact'. Untouched, unbroken, whole, scatheless ; virgin.

ANT. *Broken, injured, soiled.*

Intan'gible. Impalpable, unreal, vague, unsubstantial.

ANT. *Tangible, solid, real.*

Integ'rity. Entirety, completeness. See also HONESTY.

Integ'ument. Cover, skin, envelope.

In'tellect. Mind, reason, understanding, brains.

Intellect'ual. Intelligent; rational, mental.

ANT. *Unintelligent ; physical.*

Intel'ligence. Mental ability, understanding, instruction ; advice, information.

ANT. *Ignorance, stupidity.*

Intel'ligible. Comprehensible, plain, perspicuous,

ANT. *Unintelligible, incomprehensible, obscure.*

Intem'perate. Uncontrolled, unrestrained, excessive, passionate.

ANT. *Temperate, self-controlled, moderate.*

Intend'. See CONTEMPLATE.

Intent'. See ARDENT and EARNEST.

Intent' (*n.*). Intention, aim, purpose, resolve.

Inten'tion. See INTENT (*n.*).

Inten'tional. Intended, designed, purposed.

ANT. *Undesigned, unintentional.*

Interces'sion. Mediation ; prayer, advocacy.

In'tercourse. Communication, association, intimacy. See also COMMERCE.

ANT. *Separation, seclusion.*

In'terest. Affect, concern, touch.

In'terest (*n.*). Concern, regard ; advantage ; influence.

ANT. *Indifference, unconcern ; impotence.*

Interfere'. Intervene, meddle, prevent.

ANT. *Leave alone.*

Interm'inable. Limitless, boundless ; never ending.

ANT. *Limited, terminable ; brief.*

Intermis'sion. Suspension, stoppage, pause, cessation.
ANT. *Continuance.*

Intermit'. Stop, leave off, discontinue.
ANT. *Continue, go on.*

Interne'cine. Deadly, to the death, mortal.

Interpose'. Insert, intrude, interfere ; mediate, intercede.

Inter'pret. Translate, render. See also ELUCIDATE.

Interpreta'tion. Exposition, explanation, version ; meaning, sense.

Inter'rogate. Question, inquire of, ask.
ANT. *Answer, reply.*

Interrupt'. Break, divide ; stop, put a stop to, hinder.
ANT. *Join ; accelerate.*

Intervene'. See INTERPOSE.

Interven'tion. Interposition, mediation, agency.
ANT. *Neglect, hindrance.*

Intes'tine. Inner, inward, domestic, not alien.
ANT. *External, alien, foreign.*

In'timate (*vb.*). Hint, impart, announce, tell.
ANT. *Say nothing, be silent.*

In'timate. Familiar, close, inward, friendly.
ANT. *Unfamiliar, distant, unfriendly.*

Intim'idate. See AFFRIGHT.

Intol'erable. Unbearable, unendurable, insufferable.
ANT. *Tolerable, bearable, agreeable.*

Intol'erant. See ARBITRARY and ARROGANT.

Intract'able. Obstinate, perverse, unmanageable, unruly.
ANT. *Yielding, docile, manageable, tractable.*

Intrep'id. See BOLD.

In'tricate. Involved, complicated, obscure.
ANT. *Straightforward, simple, clear.*

Intrigue' (*vb.*). Plot, scheme, cabal, conspire.

Intrigue' (*n.*). Cabal, plot, scheme, conspiracy.

Intrin'sic. Inherent, internal, material, native.
ANT. *Extrinsic, unessential.*

Introduce'. Bring in, present, begin, usher in, recommend.
ANT. *Remove, withdraw, disparage.*

Introduc'tion. Presentation, recommendation ; beginning, prelude, preface.
ANT. *Withdrawal, disparagement ; finale.*

Intrude'. Invade, interfere. See also ENCROACH.

Intui'tion. Insight, instinct, direct perception.
ANT. *Calculation, inference.*

In'undate. Flood, deluge, submerge.
ANT. *Subside.*

Inure'. Habituate, accustom, train.

Invade'. See ASSAIL.

Inval'idate. See ANNUL.

Inva'sion. See INROAD and FORAY.

Invect'ive. Abuse, vituperation, railing.
ANT. *Compliment, praise.*

Inveigh'. See DENOUNCE.

Invei'gle. See ALLURE.

Invent'. Find out, discover, contrive, design, originate.

Invent'ive. See INGENIOUS.

Invert'. Upset, turn upside down, overturn.
ANT. *Set upright.*

Invest'. Dress, array, endow ; blockade, besiege.
ANT. *Divest ; raise siege.*

Invest'igate. See INSPECT.

Investiga'tion. Inspection, examination, research, inquiry.

Invet'erate. Habitual, confirmed, ingrained, rooted.
ANT. *Unwonted, newly acquired.*

Invid'ious. Envious, offensive, hateful.
ANT. *Unenvious, charitable.*

Invig′orate. Brace, strengthen, nerve, stimulate.

ANT. *Weaken, unnerve.*

Invinc′ible. Unconquerable, insuperable, impregnable.

ANT. *Superable, surmountable.*

Invi′olable. Sacred, holy, sacrosanct.

ANT. *Violable, profane.*

Invi′olate. See INTACT.

Invis′ible. Unseen, imperceptible.

ANT. *Visible, perceptible.*

Invita′tion. Asking, bidding, solicitation, summons.

ANT. *Repulse, dismissal.*

Invite′. Ask, call, summon, solicit ; allure.

ANT. *Dismiss ; repel.*

Invoke′. See APPEAL.

Invol′untary. Compulsory, not willed ; automatic.

ANT. *Voluntary, spontaneous ; conscious.*

Involve′. See IMPLICATE and IMPLY.

Irasc′ible. See CHOLERIC.

Ire. See ANGER.

Irk′some. Tiresome, tedious, disagreeable, annoying.

ANT. *Pleasant, easy, agreeable.*

Irra′tional. See ABSURD.

Irra′diate. See ENLIGHTEN.

Irreconcil′able. See IMPLACABLE.

Irre′fragable. Indubitable, indisputable, incontestable, irrefutable.

ANT. *Questionable, doubtful, disputable.*

Irreg′ular. Anomalous, abnormal, unmethodical, unpunctual.

ANT. *Regular, normal, systematic, punctual.*

Irregular′ity. Abnormality, anomaly ; vice ; unpunctuality.

ANT. *Regularity, propriety ; punctuality.*

Irrel′evant. Inappropriate, unrelated, inapplicable.

ANT. *Relevant, apt, related.*

Irrelig′ious. Impious, profane, wicked.

ANT. *Pious, religious.*

Irreme′diable. Incurable, irreparable, irretrievable.

ANT. *Remediable, curable.*

Irreproach′able. See INNOCENT.

Irres′olute. Undecided, vacillating, wavering.

ANT. *Resolute, firm, decided.*

Ir′ritable. See CHOLERIC.

Ir′ritate. See ANNOY.

Isola′tion. Segregation, separation, solitude.

ANT. *Company.*

Is′sue (*vb.*). Emanate, arise, proceed ; end ; send out.

Is′sue (*n.*). Exit ; result, event, end ; offspring, progeny.

Itin′erant. Wandering, roving, nomadic.

ANT. *Stationary, stay-at-home, settled.*

J

Jab′ber. See BABBLE.

Jade′ (*n.*). Hussy, slut.

Jade′ (*vb.*). Weary, tire, exhaust, fag.

ANT. *Refresh, ease.*

Jag′ged. Uneven, broken ; notched, indented.

ANT. *Even, smooth.*

Jar′. Clash, conflict ; wrangle ; jolt.

Jaun′diced. Biased, prepossessed, prejudiced.

ANT. *Unprejudiced, unbiased.*

Jaunt′. Trip, ramble, excursion.

Jaunt′y. Affected, gay, airy, finical.

ANT. *Unaffected, serious.*

Jeal′ous. Envious, emulous, suspicious.

ANT. *Unenvious, unsuspicious.*

Jeal'ousy. See ENVY.

Jeer'. Flout, sneer, deride, mock, gibe.

ANT. *Compliment, praise.*

Jeop'ardize. See HAZARD.

Jeop'ardy. See DANGER.

Jest'. Joke, witticism ; play, fun.

ANT. *Earnest, solemnity.*

Jew'el. Gem, precious stone.

Jilt'. Discard lover, flirt.

Jing'le. Rattle, tinkle, clink.

Jocose'. See FACETIOUS.

Joc'und. Gay, blithe, festive, merry, joyous.

ANT. *Sad, low-spirited.*

Jog'gle. See JOSTLE.

Join'. Fasten, attach, connect ; confederate, associate ; add.

ANT. *Loose, unfasten ; stand aloof.*

Joint'. Concerted, united, combined.

ANT. *Unconcerted, separate.*

Joke'. See JEST.

Joll'y. Jovial, festive, plump. See also JOCUND.

ANT. *Miserable, dull; gaunt.*

Jos'tle. Hustle, joggle, thrust, push.

Jot'. Whit, tittle, scrap, atom, particle.

Journ'ey. Travel, trip, excursion, pilgrimage.

ANT. *Stay at home.*

Joy'. Delight, pleasure, bliss, transport, felicity.

ANT. *Sadness, gloom, depression.*

Joy'ful. Joyous, delighted, delightful.

ANT. *Sad, gloomy, out of spirits ; depressed.*

Ju'bilant. Exulting, exultant, triumphant, rejoicing.

ANT. *Despondent, despairing.*

Judge'. Magistrate, justice ; umpire, referee ; connoisseur, expert.

ANT. *Prisoner, plaintiff.*

Judg'ment. Verdict, doom decree ; discrimination, discernment, sagacity.

ANT. *Stupidity.*

Judge (*vb.*). Decide, sit in judgment, try ; be of opinion, reckon.

Judi'cious. Discriminating, discreet, prudent, well-advised, sagacious. See also CIRCUMSPECT.

ANT. *Indiscreet, imprudent, undiscriminating.*

Jum'ble. Confuse, mix together, disorder.

ANT. *Order, arrange.*

Jump'. Leap, skip, caper, vault, spring.

ANT. *Stand still.*

Junc'tion. Union, juncture, connection, alliance.

ANT. *Separation, fraction.*

Junc'ture. Joining, junction ; emergency, crisis.

Ju'rist. Lawyer, civilian.

ANT. *Layman.*

Just'. Lawful, fair, equitable, exact.

ANT. *Unjust, unlawful ; incorrect.*

Just'ice. Equity, right, impartiality, fairness.

ANT. *Wrong, partiality.*

Just'ifiable. Defensible, excusable, warrantable.

ANT. *Indefensible, inexcusable, unwarrantable.*

Justifica'tion. Vindication, defence, excuse.

ANT. *Condemnation.*

Just'ify. Defend, excuse, vindicate, exculpate.

ANT. *Condemn, blame.*

Ju'venile. Youthful, childish, young.

ANT. *Senile, old.*

Juxtaposi'tion. Contact, contiguity, proximity.

ANT. *Separation, remoteness.*

K

Keen'. Sharp-edged, acute, penetrating, eager, zealous ; poignant ; discerning, shrewd.
ANT. *Blunt, apathetic ; dull.*

Keep'. Hold, retain, detain ; observe, celebrate ; feed, support ; remain fresh.
ANT. *Release, give away ; neglect, profane ; starve ; grow stale.*

Keep'ing. Care, charge, custody ; harmony, congruity.

Key'. Clue, guide, solution ; tonality.

Kick'shaw. Toy, trifle.

Kid'nap. Abduct, carry off, steal (child).
ANT. *Restore.*

Kill'. Murder, destroy, assassinate, slay, slaughter.
ANT. *Save, spare, save life.*

Kin'. Kindred, affinity, consanguinity, kinsfolk.
ANT. *Alien, unrelated, strangers.*

Kind'. See BENEVOLENT and GENEROUS.

Kind' (*n.*). Class, genus, sort, family.

Kind'le. Ignite, light, set fire to ; stimulate, fire, excite.
ANT. *Extinguish ; calm, soothe.*

Kind'liness. See GENEROSITY.

Kind'ly. See BENEVOLENT.

Kind'ness. See GENEROSITY and BENEFICENCE.

Kind'red. See KIN.

King'dom. Realm, monarchy, sovereignty.
ANT. *Republic.*

King'ly. King-like, royal, regal, majestic.
ANT. *Undignified, base-born.*

Knack'. Trick, art, feat, dexterity.
ANT. *Clumsiness, unhandiness.*

Knave'. Rascal, scoundrel, scamp, rogue, base fellow.
ANT. *Honest man.*

Kna'very. See FRAUD.

Knav'ish. See FRAUDULENT.

Knit'. Tie, fasten, loop, bind closely, contract.
ANT. *Relax.*

Knock'. Strike, smite, rap, clap.

Knot'. Tie ; joint, node ; group, cluster.

Knott'y. Gnarled ; hard, intricate.
ANT. *Smooth, easy, simple.*

Know'ing. Learned, clever ; cunning.
ANT. *Simple-minded, unintelligent.*

Know'ledge. Apprehension, comprehension, understanding ; learning, erudition ; cognizance.
ANT. *Ignorance.*

L

Labo'rious. Toilsome, wearisome, arduous, fatiguing, tiring ; industrious, assiduous.
ANT. *Easy, light ; idle.*

La'bour. Toil, work, effort, drudgery, pains ; task ; childbirth.
ANT. *Rest, repose, relaxation.*

La'bour (*vb.*). Toil, work, take pains ; suffer ; travail.
ANT. *Idle, rest.*

Labyrin'thine. Mazy, confused, intricate.
ANT. *Straightforward, plain, simple.*

Lac'erate. Afflict, wound, mangle, rend.
ANT. *Heal.*

Lack'. Want, scarcity, need.
ANT. *Plenty, supply.*

Lack' (*vb.*). Want, be without,
need ; fail.
ANT. *Abound in, have,
possess ; abound.*

Lack'ey. } Footman, servant,
Lac'quey. } hanger-on.
ANT. *Master, mistress.*

Lacon'ic. Short, terse, brief,
curt.
ANT. *Long-winded, ver-
bose.*

Lade'. Load, freight, pile on.
ANT. *Unlade.*

Lag'. Loiter, hang back, linger.
ANT. *Hurry, hasten.*

Lag'gard. Loitering, sluggish,
tardy.
ANT. *Quick, prompt, has-
tening.*

Lame'. Limp, crippled, hob-
bling, halt ; feeble.
ANT. *Able-bodied.*

Lament'. Wail, bewail, mourn,
grieve, complain, deplore.
ANT. *Rejoice ; approve.*

Lamenta'tion. Wailing, mourning, grief, sorrow.
ANT. *Rejoicing, joy.*

Lampoon'. Defame, l i b e l,
satirize.
ANT. *Eulogize, panegyrize.*

Land'. Country, fatherland.
See also GROUND.

Land'lord. Owner, proprietor,
host, innkeeper.
ANT. *Tenant ; guest.*

Lang'uage. Speech, tongue,
idiom, diction, phraseology.
ANT. *Dumbness.*

Lan'guid. Faint, weak, feeble ;
listless, torpid.
ANT. *Vigorous, cheerful.*

Lan'guish. Faint, pine, droop,
sink.
ANT. *Flourish, revive.*

Lan'guor. Faintness, weakness,
lassitude, apathy.
ANT. *Vigour, alacrity,
enthusiasm.*

Lank'. See GAUNT.

Lapse'. Flow, glide, slip.
ANT. *Stand still.*

Large'. See BIG and GREAT.

Larg'ess. See GIFT.

Lasciv'ious. Wanton, lustful,
lewd, libidinous.
ANT. *Chaste, pure.*

Lash'. Flog, whip, scourge ;
satirize ; bind together.

Lass'. Girl, maiden, damsel.
ANT. *Boy, youth, lad.*

Las'situde. See FATIGUE.

Last'. Hindmost, latest ; ultimate, final.
ANT. *First ; initial.*

Last' (*vb.*). Continue, endure,
abide.
ANT. *Cease, expire.*

Last'ing. See ABIDING.

Late'. Tardy, slow, after time ;
dead, deceased ; recent.
ANT. *Quick, prompt, up to
time ; living ; old.*

La'tent. Hidden, concealed.
ANT. *Patent, open.*

Lat'itude. Distance (from the
equator) ; width, breadth ;
scope, freedom.
ANT. *Longitude ; narrow-
ness ; limit.*

Laud'. See APPLAUD.

Laud'able. Praiseworthy, meritorious, commendable.
ANT. *Blameworthy, detestable.*

Laugh'able. See COMIC and
DROLL.

Lav'ish. See EXCESSIVE and
EXTRAVAGANT.

Law'ful. Legitimate, legal, constitutional, authorized ; right-
ful.
ANT. *Unlawful, lawless,
unauthorized, improper.*

Lax'ity. Looseness, slackness ;
dissoluteness.
ANT. *Tightness, firmness ;
temperance.*

Lay'er. Stratum, row.

La'zy. See IDLE and INDOLENT.

Lead'. See GUIDE.

Lead'er. See GUIDE.

Lead'ing. Principal, chief,
ruling, foremost.
ANT. *Subordinate, inferior.*

League'. See ALLIANCE.

Leal'. Faithful, true, loyal.

ANT. *Disloyal, unfaithful.*

Lean. See GAUNT.

Lean' (*vb.*). See INCLINE.

Leap'. See JUMP.

Learn'ed. See ERUDITE.

Learn'ing. Knowledge, erudition, scholarship, lore.

ANT. *Ignorance.*

Least'. Smallest, lowest.

ANT. *Greatest, largest, highest.*

Leave' (*vb.*). See ABANDON.

Leave' (*n.*). Allowance, permission, liberty ; departure.

ANT. *Prohibition ; arrival.*

Leav'en. Raise, lighten ; infect ; influence.

Lech'erous. See LASCIVIOUS.

Lec'ture. Reading, reproof, address, lesson.

ANT. *Commendation, approval.*

Lees'. Dregs, sediment, leavings.

Le'gal. See LAWFUL.

Le'galize. Make lawful, legitimatize, authorize.

ANT. *Prohibit.*

Leg'ate. Envoy, ambassador, nuncio.

Leg'end. Myth, fable, tradition ; inscription, motto.

ANT. *True story, fact.*

Leg'endary. Traditional, mythical, fabulous.

ANT. *Actual, true.*

Leg'ible. Readable, decipherable, distinct.

ANT. *Illegible, unreadable, indistinct.*

Legit'imate. See LAWFUL.

Leis'ure. Rest, vacation, ease, spare time.

ANT. *Work, employment.*

Length'en. Extend, stretch, pull out, prolong.

ANT. *Shorten, contract.*

Le'niency. See CLEMENCY.

Le'nient. Gentle, forbearing, mild, clement.

ANT. *Harsh, unforbearing, inclement.*

Le'nity. See CLEMENCY.

Les'sen. See ABATE.

Les'son. Instruction, lection, task ; reproof, warning.

Let'. Allow, permit, suffer ; lease ; hinder.

ANT. *Forbid, prohibit.*

Let'. Hindrance, prohibition, impediment.

ANT. *Permission, freedom.*

Le'thal. Deadly, mortal, fatal.

ANT. *Harmless.*

Leth'argy. Torpor, stupor ; apathy.

ANT. *Activity, vigorousness.*

Letter'. Alphabetical character. See also EPISTLE.

Let'ters. Literature, erudition, learning.

ANT. *Ignorance.*

Let'tered. See ERUDITE.

Lev'el. Flat, plain, even, smooth, horizontal.

ANT. *Hilly, mountainous ; uneven, rough ; perpendicular.*

Lev'el (*vb.*). Make even, make horizontal, pull down, raze ; aim, point.

ANT. *Make uneven ; lift up, restore.*

Lev'ity. Light weight, lightness ; fickleness, inconstancy, flightiness ; frivolity.

ANT. *Gravity, constancy, seriousness, steadiness.*

Lev'y. Raise, collect, exact.

Lewd'. See LASCIVIOUS.

Liabil'ity. Responsibility, accountableness ; being exposed to.

ANT. *Immunity.*

Li'able. Accountable, responsible, exposed to.

ANT. *Irresponsible, immune.*

Li'bel. See LAMPOON.

Lib'eral. Open-minded, tolerant. See also GENEROUS.

ANT. *Intolerant, bigoted.*

Liberal'ity. Tolerance, open-mindedness. See also HUMANITY.

ANT. *Bigotry, intolerance.*

Lib'erate. See FREE (*vb.*).

Lib′ertine. Rake, debauchee, profligate.

ANT. *Ascetic.*

Lib′erty. Freedom, independence ; licence, permission, leave.

ANT. *Serfdom, slavery ; prohibition.*

Libid′inous. See LASCIVIOUS.

Li′cence. Laxity ; authority, permission, liberty.

ANT. *Propriety, moderation ; prohibition.*

Li′cense. Authorize, sanction, warrant.

ANT. *Prohibit, forbid.*

Licen′tious. See LASCIVIOUS.

Lie′. See FALSEHOOD.

Lie′ (*vb.*). Tell lies, deceive.

ANT. *Be truthful, speak truth.*

Lie′ (*vb.*). Recline, be placed, rest, remain.

ANT. *Stand, sit up.*

Life′less. See DEAD.

Lift′. Hoist, heave, raise, elevate.

ANT. *Lower, depress.*

Light′. Radiance, luminosity, gleam, dawn.

ANT. *Darkness ; sunset.*

Light′. Imponderous ; easy ; inconsiderable, flimsy ; trivial, frivolous. See also LUMINOUS.

ANT. *Heavy, ponderous, onerous ; difficult ; serious, grave ; dark.*

Light′en. Light, kindle ; shine, grow light ; flash ; alleviate.

ANT. *Darken ; aggravate.*

Like′. Similar, resembling, related, parallel.

ANT. *Dissimilar, unlike, unrelated.*

Like′ly. Probable ; well-favoured.

ANT. *Improbable, unlikely ; unattractive.*

Like′ness. Resemblance, similarity ; counterpart ; semblance, appearance ; portrait, picture.

ANT. *Dissimilarity.*

Lim′ber. Pliant, flexible, supple.

ANT. *Stiff, unbending.*

Lim′it. Bound, boundary, border ; end, stop, restriction.

Lim′it (*vb.*). See CIRCUMSCRIBE.

Limp′. Hobble, go lamely, halt.

ANT. *Walk firmly.*

Lin′eage. Descent, ancestry, family, house, line.

Lin′ger. Dally, delay, loiter, wait, tarry.

ANT. *Hurry, hasten.*

Link′. Tie, bond, connection.

Link′ (*vb.*). Tie, bind, connect, unite, join.

ANT. *Untie, disconnect.*

Liq′uid. Fluid ; mellifluous, dulcet.

ANT. *Solid ; raucous.*

Liq′uidate. Pay up, clear off, discharge, settle.

ANT. *Owe.*

List′. Catalogue, register, inventory, schedule, roll.

List′en. Hear, hearken, attend, obey.

ANT. *Shut ears, disobey.*

List′less. See APATHETIC and INERT.

Lit′erary. See ERUDITE.

Lit′erate. See ERUDITE.

Lithe′. See LIMBER.

Litig′ious. Quarrelsome, contentious.

Lit′tle. Small, minute, diminutive, slight, scanty, inconsiderable, mean.

ANT. *Great, big, important.*

Live′. Exist, be, dwell, abide ; be fed.

ANT. *Die, starve.*

Live′liness. Sprightliness, gaiety, vivacity, animation.

ANT. *Dullness, depression, dispiritedness.*

Live′ly. Active, quick, smart, animated, vivacious.

ANT. *Slow, tardy ; depressed.*

Liv′ing (*n.*). Livelihood, support, sustenance.

Load′. Freight, cargo, burden, weight.

Loath′. See LOTH.

Loathe′. Detest, abhor, abominate.

ANT. *Like, delight in, prefer.*

Loathing′ (*n.*). Detestation, abhorrence, abomination, disgust.

ANT. *Liking, preference.*

Loath′some. Detestable, disgusting, nauseating, revolting.

ANT. *Desirable, pleasing.*

Lod′ging. Shelter, habitation, dwelling, protection.

Loft′y. High, tall, towering; stately, proud.

ANT. *Low, depressed; humble.*

Loi′ter. Dawdle, linger, delay, tarry, saunter.

ANT. *Hurry, hasten, hustle.*

Lone′liness. Solitude, solitariness, desolation.

ANT. *Company, crowd.*

Long′. Produced, extended, prolonged; slow, tardy.

ANT. *Short, contracted; quick.*

Look′ (*n.*). View, sight; aspect, appearance, air; complexion.

Look′ (*vb.*). Behold, observe, regard; take care; seem.

ANT. *Disregard, overlook.*

Loose′ (*a.*). Untied, unbound, free; rambling, diffuse; immoral, dissolute.

ANT. *Bound, tied, captive; coherent, concise; moral.*

Loose′ (*vb.*). Unbind, untie, detach, set free, liberate.

ANT. *Bind, tie, attach; imprison.*

Loqua′cious. Talkative, garrulous, glib, voluble.

ANT. *Silent, reserved, morose.*

Loquac′ity. Talkativeness, garrulity, glibness, volubility.

ANT. *Silence, reserve, moroseness.*

Lord′. See MASTER.

Lord′ship. Dominion, domination, rule, command.

ANT. *Subjection, slavery.*

Lore′. Learning, erudition, letters, knowledge.

ANT. *Ignorance.*

Lose′. Forfeit, miss, mislay, let slip.

ANT. *Gain, acquire.*

Loss′. Deprivation, damage, forfeiture, failure.

ANT. *Gain, advantage, profit, success.*

Lot′. Chance, fortune, destiny, fate; portion, share; number.

Loth′. Unwilling, reluctant, indisposed, disinclined.

ANT. *Willing, ready, inclined.*

Loud′. Sonorous, resonant, noisy, stentorian; blustering, vehement; glaring, vulgar.

ANT. *Soft, quiet; sober, in good taste.*

Love′. Affection, fondness, tenderness. See also BENEVOLENCE.

ANT. *Hate, dislike.*

Love′ly. Charming, delightful, beautiful, adorable.

ANT. *Unlovely, ugly, displeasing, unpleasant.*

Lov′ing. Affectionate, devoted, attached, tender.

ANT. *Unloving, unamiable, unkind.*

Low′. Depressed, deep; short, stunted; deep-toned; mean, base; vulgar, coarse.

ANT. *High, tall; high-pitched; exalted; refined.*

Low′er (*vb.*). Take down, debase, degrade, humble, humiliate; diminish.

ANT. *Raise, exalt; increase.*

Low′ering. Threatening, darkening, gloomy, sullen.

ANT. *Bright, clear, cheerful.*

Low′ly. Humble, meek, simple, unassuming, unpretentious.

ANT. *High, proud, exalted, pretentious.*

Loy′al. Faithful, devoted, constant, true.

ANT. *Disloyal, unfaithful, treacherous.*

Loy'alty. See FEALTY.

Lu'cid. See CLEAR.

Luck. Chance, fortune, hazard, fate, hap.

Luck'less. Ill-starred, unfortunate, unsuccessful, ill-fated.

Luck'y. Favoured, fortunate, successful, prosperous ; auspicious.
ANT. *Unlucky, unfortunate.* See LUCKLESS.

Lu'crative. Profitable, remunerative, paying.
ANT. *Unprofitable, unremunerative ; losing.*

Lu'cre. Gain, profit, pay, money.
ANT. *Loss.*

Lu'dicrous. Laughable, ridiculous, absurd, comic.
ANT. *Serious, grave, tragic.*

Lugu'brious. Mournful, sad, doleful, melancholy.
ANT. *Cheerful, blithe, gay.*

Lull'. Tranquillize, calm, still ; abate, pause.
ANT. *Agitate, disturb ; increase.*

Lum'ber. Trash, trumpery, rubbish.

Lu'minous. Light, bright ; pale ; clear.
ANT. *Dark ; obscure.*

Lu'nacy. Insanity, madness, derangement.
ANT. *Sanity, mental soundness.*

Lure'. Attract, entice, allure, tempt.
ANT. *Repel, shock.*

Lu'rid. Dismal, murky, gloomy. See also LOWERING.
ANT. *Cheerful, bright.*

Lurk'. Hide, skulk, lie hidden.
ANT. *Appear, be seen.*

Lus'cious. Sweet, honeyed, rich, delicious.
ANT. *Unappetizing, sour.*

Lust'. Craving, desire, cupidity ; concupiscence.
ANT. *Self-control.*

Lust'ful. Sensual, lascivious, lewd, passionate.
ANT. *Self-controlled, ascetic.*

Lust're. Brilliance, sheen, splendour, brightness, glory.
ANT. *Dimness ; plainness.*

Lust'y. Strong, robust, stout, vigorous, hearty.
ANT. *Weak, flabby, anaemic.*

Luxu'riant. Abundant, superabundant, flourishing, profuse.
ANT. *Scanty, barren.*

Luxu'riate. Flourish, abound ; indulge in, enjoy.
ANT. *Decay, wither.*

Luxu'rious. Voluptuous, sensual, pleasure-loving ; comfortable, dainty.
ANT. *Ascetic ; uncomfortable, plain.*

Lux'ury. Voluptuousness, sensuality ; daintiness ; pleasure, gratification.
ANT. *Asceticism ; inelegance, discomfort.*

M

Machina'tion. Intrigue, plot ; stratagem ; contrivance.

Mad'. Insane, lunatic, frenzied, furious, frantic, rabid.
ANT. *Sane, calm.*

Mad'den. See ENRAGE.

Mad'ness. See LUNACY.

Mag'ic. Sorcery, witchcraft, enchantment, the black art.

Magiste'rial. Authoritative, pompous, commanding.
ANT. *Unassuming, simple.*

Magnan'imous. Generous, noble, disinterested, unselfish.
ANT. *Ungenerous, mean, selfish.*

Magnif'icence. Splendour, pomp, grandeur, gorgeousness.
ANT. *Shabbiness, meanness.*

Mag'nify. Increase, amplify ; praise, extol.
> ANT. *Diminish, lessen ; depreciate, disparage.*

Magnil'oquent. Bombastic, turgid, inflated.
> ANT. *Plain-spoken, direct.*

Mag'nitude. Size, bulk, largeness, grandeur.
> ANT. *Smallness.*

Maim'. Cripple, lame, dismember, mutilate.

Maintain'. Support, uphold ; carry on ; affirm, assert ; contend.
> ANT. *Undermine, bring down ; deny.*

Main'tenance. See LIVING.

Majest'ic. August, kingly, grand, stately.
> ANT. *Undignified, humble, lowly.*

Maj'esty. Grandeur, splendour, stateliness.
> ANT. *Lowliness, poverty.*

Make'. See CREATE.

Ma'ker. Creator, framer, fashioner, manufacturer ; poet, artist.
> ANT. *Destroyer.*

Mal'ady. Illness, ailment, disorder, distemper.
> ANT. *Remedy, cure.*

Maledict'ion. See CURSE.

Mal'efactor. See CRIMINAL.

Malev'olence. See BENEVOLENCE.

Malev'olent. Malignant, spiteful, rancorous, malicious.
> ANT. *Benevolent, kindly, generous.*

Mal'ice. Spite, hate, ill-will, malevolence.
> ANT. *Charity, love, goodwill.*

Malic'ious. Envious, mischievous. See also MALEVOLENT.
> ANT. *Unenvious, harmless.*

Malign'. Traduce, vilify, calumniate, defame.
> ANT. *Defend, excuse, praise.*

Malig'nant. See MALEVOLENT.

Malig'nity. See MALICE.

Man'age. Govern, regulate, construct, administer ; contrive.
> ANT. *Mismanage, neglect.*

Man'agement. Direction, control, regulation, administration ; contrivance.
> ANT. *Mismanagement, misdirection.*

Man'date. Order, command, edict, commission.

Mang'le. Crush, tear. See also MAIM.

Man'hood. Full age, maturity ; courage, bravery. See also MANLINESS.
> ANT. *Infancy, childhood ; cowardice.*

Ma'nia. See LUNACY.

Man'ifest. Exhibit, show, display, evince, express.
> ANT. *Conceal, suppress.*

Man'ifest (*a.*). Evident, clear, apparent, patent, obvious.
> ANT. *Obscure, dark, puzzling.*

Mankind'. Man, human beings, humanity, society.

Man'liness. Boldness, firmness, independence.
> ANT. *Cowardice, servility.*

Man'ly. See BOLD.

Man'ner. Style, fashion, mode, way ; custom ; sort ; demeanour.

Manufac'ture (*vb.*). Make, produce, fabricate, construct.

Manufact'urer. See MAKER.

Man'y. Multiplied, divers, manifold.
> ANT. *None, few.*

Mar'. Disfigure, harm, damage, spoil, impair.
> ANT. *Improve, repair.*

Maraud'er. Robber, plunderer, raider, pillager.

Mar'gin. Brink, edge, border, brim, verge, limit.
> ANT. *Surface, space.*

Marine'. Pelagic, maritime, naval, nautical.
> ANT. *Terrestrial, land.*

Mar'iner. Seaman, sailor, salt.
> ANT. *Landsman.*

71

Mar'ital. Conjugal, connubial, matrimonial.

Mar'itime. See MARINE.

Mark'. Brand, stamp, impression ; sign, proof, symptom.

Mark' (*vb.*). Brand, stamp ; note, notice, observe ; evince, prove ; characterize.

Mar'riage. Wedlock, matrimony ; wedding, nuptials.

ANT. *Celibacy.*

Marsh'. Fen, bog, morass, swamp.

ANT. *Land.*

Mar'shal. Array, order, dispose, range, muster.

ANT. *Disarray, disarrange, disorder.*

Mar'tial. Warlike, military, brave.

ANT. *Civil ; timid, cowardly.*

Mar'vel. Wonder, prodigy, miracle ; surprise ; astonishment.

ANT. *Ordinary occurrence ; indifference, calmness.*

Mar'vellous. Amazing, astonishing, surprising, prodigious, incredible.

ANT. *Ordinary, commonplace.*

Mas'culine. Male, manly, virile, bold.

ANT. *Feminine, female ; timid.*

Mask'. Visor ; disguise, screen, pretext.

Mass'. Heap, lump, bunch ; bulk, size ; aggregate.

ANT. *Individuals.*

Mass'acre. Carnage, slaughter, butchery.

Mass'ive. Solid, compacted ; heavy, bulky, ponderous.

ANT. *Thin, light, small.*

Mas'ter. Lord, ruler ; teacher, instructor ; adept.

ANT. *Servant, subject, subordinate ; pupil, apprentice ; novice.*

Mas'ter (*vb.*). Learn thoroughly, become adept in. See also SUBDUE.

Mas'terly. Consummate, expert, adept, adroit.

ANT. *Inexpert, 'prentice, feeble.*

Mas'tery. Proficiency, expertness. See also LORDSHIP.

Match'. Equal, compare, rival.

Match'less. Unrivalled, unequalled, incomparable, unparalleled, peerless.

ANT. *Ordinary, commonplace.*

Mate'. Companion, co-worker, associate, comrade, assistant.

ANT. *Master.*

Mate'rial (*a.*). Corporeal, substantial ; weighty, important, essential.

ANT. *Spiritual ; slight, immaterial.*

Mate'rial (*n.*). See MATTER.

Mat'rimony. See MARRIAGE.

Matt'er. Substance, body, material ; topic ; affair, concern ; consequence, importance.

ANT. *Spirit, essence.*

Mature'. Ripe, mellow, perfect, fit, developed.

ANT. *Unripe, crude, imperfect, undeveloped, immature.*

Mature' (*vb.*). Ripen, develop, perfect.

Matu'rity. Ripeness, full age, perfection, completion.

ANT. *Unripeness, immaturity, incompleteness, youth.*

Mawk'ish. Stale, flat, insipid, vapid.

ANT. *Well flavoured.*

Max'im. Precept, proverb, apophthegm, adage.

Maze'. Labyrinth ; intricacy, puzzle, perplexity.

Ma'zy. Labyrinthine ; intricate, puzzling, confused.

ANT. *Straight, direct, intelligible.*

Mea'gre. Gaunt, emaciated, lank ; scanty, poor ; uninteresting.

ANT. *Plump, stout ; plentiful ; interesting.*

Mean'. Abject, low, base ; servile, grovelling ; stingy, niggardly ; paltry, insignificant.
   ANT. *Proud, exalted ; lordly ; generous, liberal.*

Mean' (*vb.*). Import, imply, signify ; purpose, intend.

Mean'ing (*n.*). Purport, import, sense, implication ; intention, purpose, design.

Meas'ure (*vb.*). Mete, gauge, appraise ; distribute.

Meat'. Victuals, food, fare, nourishment ; flesh-food.
   ANT. *Want, hunger.*

Mechan'ic. Artisan, artificer, skilled worker, craftsman.
   ANT. *Unskilled workman.*

Med'dlesome. Officious, interfering, intrusive, mischievous.
   ANT. *Harmless, non-interfering.*

Me'diate. Intercede, arbitrate.

Med'icine. Remedy, drug, physic ; healing.

Me'diocre. Indifferent, commonplace, ordinary, inferior.
   ANT. *Superior, great, valuable.*

Med'itate. Contemplate, ponder, muse, consider ; intend.

Medita'tion. Contemplation, reflection, musing, rumination.

Me'dium. Means, instrument, channel.

Med'ley. Jumble, miscellany, farrago.

Meed'. Reward, due, prize, recompense.
   ANT. *Loss, penalty.*

Meek'. See GENTLE.

Meek'ness. See HUMILITY.

Meet' (*a.*). Fit, suitable, apt, proper, appropriate.
   ANT. *Unmeet, unfit, inappropriate.*

Meet' (*vb.*). Encounter, come upon ; join ; suit ; assemble, come together.
   ANT. *Miss ; stay apart ; disperse.*

Mel'ancholy. (*n.*). Depression, dejection, gloominess, dolefulness.
   ANT. *Gaiety, cheerfulness, high spirits.*

Mel'ancholy (*a.*). Sad, gloomy, dejected, depressed, doleful, woebegone.
   ANT. *Gay, joyous, jolly.*

Mell'ow. Mellifluous ; tipsy. See also MATURE.
   ANT. *Raucous ; sober.*

Melo'dious. Tuneful, musical, sweet.
   ANT. *Unmelodious, tuneless, harsh.*

Mel'ody. Song, air, tune, music.

Melt'. Dissolve, liquefy, thaw ; grow softer.
   ANT. *Solidify, freeze ; harden.*

Memen'to. Remembrance, memorial, souvenir.
   ANT. *Oblivion.*

Mem'oir. Life, biography, record.

Mem'orable. Remarkable, distinguished, notable, signal, famous.
   ANT. *Insignificant, undistinguished, infamous.*

Memo'rial. Monument ; petition. See also MEMENTO.

Mem'ory. Remembrance, recollection ; fame.
   ANT. *Forgetfulness ; oblivion.*

Men'ace. Threaten, denounce, intimidate.

Mend'. Repair, patch ; improve, amend, restore.
   ANT. *Unmend, break.*

Menda'cious. Lying, untruthful, false.
   ANT. *Truthful, true.*

Mendac'ity. Lying, untruthfulness, deceit, lie.
   ANT. *Truthfulness, truth.*

Me'nial (*n.*). Servant, domestic, attendant, flunkey.
   ANT. *Master, mistress.*

Ment'al. Rational, intellectual.
   ANT. *Bodily, physical.*

Men'tion. Name, report, cite ; reveal, impart.
   ANT. *Conceal, withhold.*

Mer′cenary. Hired, venal ; mean, sordid, avaricious.

ANT. *Voluntary ; honourable, generous.*

Mer′chant. Trader, dealer, trafficker.

Mer′ciful. Tender, compassionate, forgiving, lenient, pitiful.

ANT. *Merciless, pitiless, hard, unforgiving.*

Mer′cy. See CLEMENCY.

Mere′. Pure, simple, entire, bare.

Mere′ly. Only, simply, purely, barely.

Meretri′cious. Unchaste; gaudy, showy, flashy, false.

ANT. *Chaste ; simple, plain, good.*

Mer′it. Desert, worth, worthiness, virtue.

ANT. *Demerit, worthlessness.*

Mer′riment. Joy, jollity, gaiety, mirth, hilarity.

ANT. *Sadness, grief, gravity.*

Merry′. See BLITHE.

Mes′sage. Missive, notice, communication.

Mes′senger. Courier, emissary, express ; herald, forerunner.

Mete′. Measure, allot, apportion.

Meth′od. System ; way, mode, manner, process.

ANT. *Disorderliness, irregularity.*

Method′ical. Systematic, orderly, precise.

ANT. *Unsystematic, disorderly, casual.*

Mett′le. Spirit, ardour, courage, fire.

ANT. *Timidity, weakness, apathy.*

Met′tlesome. Spirited, ardent, fiery, courageous.

ANT. *Timid, apathetic, cold.*

Midd′ling. See MEDIOCRE.

Mien′. See ASPECT.

Might′y. Strong, powerful, exalted ; huge ; momentous.

ANT. *Weak ; lowly ; small, unimportant.*

Mi′gratory. Wandering, roving, unsettled, nomadic.

ANT. *Settled, stationary.*

Mild′. Equable, soft, kind, clement, calm.

ANT. *Fierce, harsh, blustering.*

Mil′itary. See MARTIAL.

Mim′ic. See IMITATE.

Mind′ (*vb.*). Attend, look, note, mark, heed ; care.

ANT. *Overlook, be inattentive, neglect.*

Mind′ (*n.*). Soul, intellect, understanding ; opinion ; intention, purpose.

ANT. *Body.*

Ming′le. Mix, blend, compound, confuse.

ANT. *Dissolve, disentangle.*

Min′ion. Pet, favourite, parasite, sycophant.

Min′ister. Servant, assistant ; administrator, ambassador , priest.

ANT. *Master, superior.*

Min′ister (*vb.*). Supply, give, afford ; serve.

ANT. *Neglect, refuse.*

Minst′rel. Harper, bard, player, singer.

Minute′. Tiny, slight, fine ; particular, circumstantial.

ANT. *Large, coarse ; vague.*

Mir′acle. Wonder, marvel, prodigy, portent.

ANT. *Ordinary occurrence.*

Mirac′ulous. Marvellous, preternatural, wonderful, abnormal.

ANT. *Normal, natural.*

Mirth. See MERRIMENT.

Misadvent′ure. Accident, mishap, disaster, mischance.

Miscar′riage. Failure. See also MISADVENTURE.

ANT. *Success, accomplishment.*

Miscella′neous. Mixed, various, promiscuous, mingled.

ANT. *Individual, separate.*

Miscell′any. See MEDLEY.

Mischance′. See MISADVENTURE.

Mis′chief. Harm, injury, damage, detriment.
ANT. *Benefit, advantage.*

Mis′chievous. Harmful, troublous, damaging, detrimental, impish.
ANT. *Harmless, innocuous ; sober, steady.*

Mis′creant. Knave, caitiff, villain, rascal.

Misdeed′. Transgression, crime, offence, trespass.

Misdemean′our. See MISDEED.

Mi′ser. See NIGGARD.

Mis′erable. See ABJECT.

Mi′serly. Sordid, niggardly, avaricious, penurious, parsimonious.
ANT. *Generous, lavish, liberal, open-handed.*

Mis′ery. Sorrow, distress, destitution, wretchedness, pain, affliction.
ANT. *Joy, comfort, relief.*

Misfort′une. See ADVERSITY.

Mishap′. See MISADVENTURE.

Mislead′. Deceive, misguide, delude.
ANT. *Help, lead, guide.*

Misguide′. See MISLEAD.

Miss′. Lose, forgo, omit ; lack ; fail.
ANT. *Gain, obtain ; regain ; succeed.*

Miss′ion. Charge, errand, commission, duty ; embassy, legation.

Mistake′. See ERROR.

Mistake′ (*vb.*). Misunderstand, blunder, err.
ANT. *Understand, be right ; keep straight.*

Mistrust′. Doubt, suspicion, distrust, fear.
ANT. *Confidence, trust, reliance.*

Mist′y. See OBSCURE.

Misunderstand′. See MISTAKE.

Mit′igate. See ALLAY.

Mitiga′tion. Relief, alleviation, abatement.
ANT. *Aggravation, increase.*

Mix′. See MINGLE.

Mix′ture. Admixture, compound. See also MEDLEY.
ANT. *Solution.*

Moan′. Lament, mourn, groan.

Mob′. Crowd, mass, multitude, populace, rabble, throng.
ANT. *Individuals.*

Mock′. Jeer, deride, ridicule.
ANT. *Applaud, cheer, encourage.*

Mock′ery. Derision, ridicule, jeering ; counterfeit.
ANT. *Applause, favour, approval ; real thing, reality.*

Mode′. Fashion, manner, method, way.

Mod′el. Pattern, standard, example, specimen.
ANT. *Copy, reproduction.*

Mod′erate (*a.*). Restrained, limited ; abstinent, temperate ; ordinary, mediocre.
ANT. *Immoderate, excessive ; intemperate ; great.*

Mod′erate (*vb.*). Control, regulate, lessen, allay.
ANT. *Aggravate, increase.*

Mod′est. Restrained, bashful, unassuming, chaste. See also MODERATE (*a.*).
ANT. *Immodest, unreserved, bold, impudent, unchaste.*

Mod′ify. Change, vary. See also MODERATE (*vb.*).

Mo′dish. Fashionable, stylish.
ANT. *Unfashionable, dowdy.*

Molest′. See ANNOY.

Moll′ify. Soften, assuage, appease, pacify.
ANT. *Harden ; anger, provoke.*

Mo′ment. Instant, second, trice ; force ; importance.
ANT. *Eternity ; unimportance.*

Moment′ous. Important, significant, weighty, grave.
ANT. *Unimportant, trifling.*

Mon′itor. Adviser, counsellor, mentor.
ANT. *Pupil, disciple.*

Monot′onous. Uninflected, uniform, boring, dull.

ANT. *Melodious, varied, cheerful.*

Monot'ony. Dullness, boredom, sameness.

ANT. *Variety, cheerfulness.*

Mon'ster. Prodigy ; fright, atrocity ; savage, ruffian, brute.

Mon'strous. Prodigious, abnormal, horrible, fearful, shocking.

ANT. *Ordinary, normal, agreeable.*

Mood'. Vein, humour, temper.

Mood'y. Sullen, morose, sulky, gloomy.

ANT. *Cheerful, affable.*

Mor'al. Ethical ; virtuous, upright, strict.

ANT. *Immoral, loose.*

Morass'. See MARSH.

Mor'bid. Sick, unhealthy, unsound, depressed.

ANT. *Healthy, natural.*

Morose'. Sullen, moody, surly, gloomy, ill-tempered.

ANT. *Gay, pleasant, civil.*

Mor'sel. See FRAGMENT.

Mor'tal. Perishable ; human ; fatal, deadly.

ANT. *Immortal, imperishable ; divine ; harmless.*

Mort'ify. Gangrene ; humiliate ; vex, disappoint.

ANT. *Heal ; exalt, honour ; gratify.*

Mote'. See SPECK.

Mo'tion. Movement, action ; proposal.

ANT. *Station ; rest.*

Mo'tive. Stimulus, incitement, cause, influence, inducement.

Mot'ley. Speckled, mottled, mixed, heterogeneous.

ANT. *Homogeneous, unmixed.*

Mott'led. Speckled, specked, dappled.

ANT. *Plain, unmarked.*

Mould' (*vb.*). Form, shape, cast, fashion.

Mould' (*n.*). Cast, form, shape ; loam.

Mould'er. Crumble, perish, waste away.

ANT. *Last, flourish.*

Mount'. Climb, ascend, scale ; get on horse.

ANT. *Descend ; dismount.*

Mourn'. Lament, deplore, bewail.

ANT. *Rejoice.*

Mourn'ful. Sorrowful, sad, lugubrious ; deplorable.

ANT. *Cheerful, bright ; pleasing, joyous.*

Move'. Drive, impel, push, actuate, influence ; proceed, go on.

ANT. *Stop, arrest ; stand still.*

Much'. Plenteous, plentiful, abundant, ample.

ANT. *Scanty, little.*

Mud'dy. Miry, soiled, turbid ; muddled, confused.

ANT. *Clear, fresh ; lucid.*

Multi'tude. See MOB.

Munif'icent. See BENEFICENT.

Munif'icence. See BENEFICENCE.

Mur'der. See KILL.

Mur'derer. Slayer, assassin.

Mus'cular. Brawny, robust, sinewy, athletic.

ANT. *Flabby, weak.*

Muse'. See MEDITATE.

Mu'sical. See MELODIOUS.

Mu'sing. See MEDITATION.

Mus'ter. See MARSHAL.

Mu'table. Changeable, variable, alterable, unsettled.

ANT. *Settled, steady, unchanging.*

Mute'. Speechless, silent, dumb.

ANT. *Vocal, loud.*

Mu'tilate. See MAIM.

Mu'tinous. Seditious, insurgent, riotous, rebellious.

ANT. *Disciplined, obedient, quiet.*

Mu'tiny. Insubordination, rebellion, revolt, riot.

ANT. *Loyalty, subordination.*

Mu'tual. Reciprocal, interchangeable, correlative.
  ANT. *Separate, individual.*

Myste'rious. Obscure, occult, dark, mystical.
  ANT. *Open, clear, intelligible.*

Myst'ical. See MYSTERIOUS.

Myst'ify. Puzzle, perplex, bewilder, confuse.
  ANT. *Illuminate, enlighten.*

Myth'. Fable, legend, story ; figment.
  ANT. *History, fact.*

Myth'ical. Legendary, fabulous ; fictitious.
  ANT. *Historic, actual.*

N

Nag'. Scold, provoke, find fault.
  ANT. *Soothe, appease.*

Na'ked. Bare, nude, unclothed, undraped ; plain, manifest.
  ANT. *Clothed, draped.*

Name'. Appellation, designation ; fame, distinction.

Name'. (*vb.*). Call, style, denominate ; mention, specify.
  ANT. *Pass over.*

Narrate'. Recount, relate, tell, enumerate.
  ANT. *Omit, pass over, conceal.*

Nar'row. Strait, limited, circumscribed ; straitened ; miserly.
  ANT. *Broad, wide ; ample, comfortable ; liberal.*

Nast'y. See FILTHY.

Na'tion. Country, people, race, state.
  ANT. *Citizen, individual.*

Na'tive. Natural, inbred ; indigenous, original ; vernacular.
  ANT. *Exotic, imported, foreign.*

Nat'ural. Native ; characteristic ; ordinary, normal.
  ANT. *Unnatural ; unlike ; extraordinary, abnormal.*

Naught'y. Bad, wicked, perverse, froward, mischievous.
  ANT. *Good, well-behaved, obedient, harmless.*

Nau'sea. Sickness, qualm. See also AVERSION.

Nau'tical. See MARINE.

Na'val. See MARINE.

Near'. Close to, nigh, adjacent, neighbouring ; impending, forthcoming ; close-fisted.
  ANT. *Far, remote ; generous.*

Neat'. Tidy, cleanly, trim ; unmixed.
  ANT. *Slovenly, untidy ; mixed.*

Neb'ulous. Cloudy, misty, hazy, confused.
  ANT. *Clear, unclouded.*

Nec'essary. Needed, requisite, obligatory, unavoidable.
  ANT. *Needless, avoidable, unnecessary.*

Necess'itate. Compel, oblige, force, demand.

Necess'ity. Need, want ; force, compulsion ; indigence.
  ANT. *Supply ; persuasion ; affluence.*

Nec'romancy. See MAGIC.

Need' (*vb.*). Require, want, lack.
  ANT. *Possess, be content.*

Need'. Want, necessity, requirement ; poverty, straits, indigence.
  ANT. *Supply, abundance ; wealth, comfort.*

Need'ful. See NECESSARY.

Nefa'rious. See ATROCIOUS.

Neglect'. Overlook, disregard, omit ; slight.
  ANT. *Regard, perform ; respect, honour.*

Neglect' (*n.*). Carelessness, oversight, negligence, default, failure ; slight.
  ANT. *Care, carefulness, attention ; respect.*

Neglect'ful. See NEGLIGENT.

Neg'ligence. See NEGLECT.

Neg'ligent. Careless, heedless, indifferent, neglectful.
ANT. *Careful, attentive, punctilious.*

Neigh'bourhood. Vicinity, proximity, nearness.
ANT. *Distance, remoteness.*

Ne'ophyte. Tiro, novice, proselyte, beginner.
ANT. *Master, expert.*

Nerve'. Sinew ; courage, spirit, force, firmness.
ANT. *Cowardice, timidity.*

Nerv'ous. Sinewy ; vigorous, robust ; spirited ; timid, hysterical.
ANT. *Weak, powerless, nerveless.*

Nettle'. See ENRAGE.

Neut'ral. For neither, intermediate, indifferent, indistinct.
ANT. *Partial, partisan.*

Neut'ralize. Undo, counteract, countervail.
ANT. *Accomplish.*

New'. Novel, fresh, recent, modern.
ANT. *Old, faded, ancient, antiquated.*

News'. Tidings, message, intelligence, advice.

Nice'. Precise, exact ; fastidious, **exacting**; pleasant, agreeable.
ANT. *Inexact, inaccurate ; indifferent ; nasty.*

Ni'cety. Accuracy, precision ; fastidiousness.
ANT. *Carelessness ; indifference.*

Nig'gard. Miser, skinflint, screw, curmudgeon.
ANT. *Spendthrift.*

Nig'gardly. See MISERLY.

Nigh'. See NEAR.

Nim'ble. See ALERT.

Nobil'ity. Nobleness, grandeur, dignity ; high rank, aristocracy, peerage.
ANT. *Littleness, humility, lowliness ; the Commons.*

No'ble. Exalted, grand, lofty, stately ; patrician.
ANT. *Low, base, ignoble.*

Noi'some. Harmful, noxious, hurtful, offensive.
ANT. *Harmless, innocuous, agreeable.*

Noi'sy. See LOUD.

Nom'inate. Designate, present, name.

Non'plus. Embarrass, puzzle, confound.
ANT. *Help, enlighten, encourage.*

Nonsen'sical. See ABSURD.

Norm'al. Regular, standard, usual, ordinary.
ANT. *Abnormal, irregular, unusual, extraordinary.*

No'table. See MEMORABLE.

Note'. Mark, sign, token ; annotation, comment ; letter ; heed, notice ; distinction.
ANT. *Inattention ; obscurity.*

Note' (*vb.*). Notice, remark, observe ; record.
ANT. *Overlook, miss ; forget.*

No'ted. See CELEBRATED.

No'tice (*vb.*). See NOTE.

No'tice (*n.*). Observation, heed, attention ; advice, warning.
ANT. *Inattention.*

No'tify. See ADVERTISE.

No'tion. Idea, conception, belief ; knowledge, understanding.
ANT. *Fact, ignorance.*

Notori'ety. Publicity, bad name, repute.
ANT. *Obscurity, good name.*

Noto'rious. Well known, famous ; infamous, disreputable.
ANT. *Unknown, obscure, reputable, creditable.*

Nour'ish. See CHERISH.

Nour'ishment. See FOOD.

Nov'el. See NEW.

Nov'ice. See NEOPHYTE.

Nox'ious. See NOISOME.

Nude'. See NAKED.

Nu'gatory. Trifling, insignificant, futile, useless.
ANT. *Important, effective.*

Nui'sance. Annoyance, plague, trouble, pest, bother.
   ANT. *Pleasure, delight.*

Null'ify. See NEUTRALIZE.

Numb'. Benumbed, paralysed, torpid.
   ANT. *Active, warm, vigorous.*

Num'ber. Numeral, figure ; aggregate, multitude, throng.

Num'ber (*vb.*). Count, enumerate, reckon, total.

Nu'merous. Abundant, manifold, comprising many.

   ANT. *Small, scanty, containing few.*

Nup'tials. Wedding, marriage.

Nurse'. See CHERISH.

Nur'ture. Bringing-up, training, education, discipline.

Nu'triment. See FOOD.

Nutri'tion. Nourishment. See also FOOD.

Nutri'tious. See NUTRITIVE.

Nu'tritive. Nourishing, sustaining, nutritious, strengthening.
   ANT. *Innutritious, unsustaining.*

O

Ob'duracy. Obstinacy, stubbornness, perverseness.
   ANT. *Complaisance, docility.*

Ob'durate. Obstinate, stubborn, unyielding, hardened, perverse.
   ANT. *Complaisant, yielding.*

Obe'dience. Compliance, acquiescence, duty, respect.
   ANT. *Disobedience, refusal, rebellion, disrespect.*

Obe'dient. Compliant, dutiful, respectful, submissive.
   ANT. *Disobedient, undutiful, self-willed.*

Obey'. Comply, yield, acquiesce, submit.
   ANT. *Resist, disobey.*

Ob'ject. See PURPOSE.

Object' (*vb.*). Oppose, demur, refuse.
   ANT. *Agree, consent, acquiesce.*

Objec'tion. Opposition, exception, cavil, demurrer.
   ANT. *Agreement, consent, acquiescence.*

Obliga'tion. Bond, engagement ; responsibility ; favour, debt.
   ANT. *Freedom, liberty ; irresponsibility.*

Oblige'. Compel, force, bind ; do favour.
   ANT. *Release ; displease.*

Obli'ging. Helpful, willing, kindly.
   ANT. *Disobliging, unwilling, unkindly.*

Oblit'erate. Delete, blot out, expunge, efface.

Obliv'ion. Forgetfulness ; obscurity.
   ANT. *Memory, remembrance ; fame.*

Ob'loquy. Reproach, censure, calumny, disgrace, detraction.
   ANT. *Praise, encomium.*

Obnox'ious. Exposed, subject. See also HARMFUL.
   ANT. *Free.*

Obscene'. Filthy, foul, indecent, lewd, disgusting.
   ANT. *Pure, chaste, clean.*

Obscure'. Dark, murky, indistinct ; lowly, humble ; abstruse.
   ANT. *Bright, clear, light ; exalted ; lucid.*

Obscure' (*vb.*). Darken, dim, cloud, conceal.
   ANT. *Brighten, lighten, reveal.*

Obscur'ity. Darkness, dimness ; seclusion, oblivion.
   ANT. *Brightness, light; publicity, fame.*

Obse'quious. Deferential, servile, cringing.

ANT. *Independent, haughty.*

Observ'ance. Attention; celebration; fulfilment; ceremony.

ANT. *Inattention; neglect.*

Observ'ant. See ATTENTIVE.

Observa'tion. Remark, comment. See also OBSERVANCE.

Observe'. Mark, notice; obey; celebrate, perform; remark.

ANT. *Overlook, disregard; disobey; neglect.*

Ob'solete. Ancient, antiquated, out-of-date, disused.

ANT. *Modern, up-to-date.*

Ob'stacle. See HINDRANCE.

Ob'stinacy. See OBDURACY.

Ob'stinate. See OBDURATE.

Obstrep'erous. See LOUD.

Obstruct'. See HINDER.

Ob'struction. Bar, barrier, hindrance, opposition.

ANT. *Help, free passage.*

Obtain'. See ACQUIRE.

Obtrude'. Intrude, encroach, infringe, trespass.

ANT. *Retire.*

Obtuse'. Stupid, dull, unintelligent.

ANT. *Intelligent, bright, quick-witted.*

Ob'viate. Prevent, counteract, preclude.

ANT. *Help, advance.*

Ob'vious. See MANIFEST.

Occa'sion. Occurrence, happening; opening, opportunity; necessity; reason, ground.

Occa'sion (*vb.*). See CAUSE.

Occult'. See MYSTERIOUS.

Occupa'tion. Tenure, occupancy; business, employment, vocation.

Occ'upy. Hold, possess, take possession; employ.

Occur'. Appear, happen, arise; arise in mind.

Occur'rence. Event, incident, affair, happening.

Odd'. Uneven; additional, supernumerary, eccentric, queer, peculiar.

ANT. *Even; normal, ordinary.*

O'dious. See EXECRABLE.

O'dium. Hate, abhorrence; disgrace, obloquy.

ANT. *Love, liking; praise, credit.*

O'dorous. Fragrant, scented, sweet.

ANT. *Mal-odorous, smelling, disagreeable.*

Off'al. Refuse, dregs, garbage.

Offence'. Assault; umbrage; insult, affront; sin, transgression.

ANT. *Defence.*

Offend'. Affront, annoy, vex; transgress, sin.

ANT. *Defend; please; obey.*

Offens'ive. Assailing, attacking; disgusting, obnoxious; insulting.

ANT. *Defensive; pleasing; polite.*

Off'er. Present, show; propose, bid, proffer, sacrifice.

ANT. *Withdraw, refuse.*

Off'er (*n.*). Proposal, overture, proffer, bid.

ANT. *Withdrawal, refusal.*

Of'fice. Business, function; post, situation; bureau.

Off'icer. Official, functionary.

ANT. *Private person.*

Offic'ious. See MEDDLESOME.

Oft'en. Repeatedly, frequently.

ANT. *Seldom, rarely.*

Old'. Aged, ancient, antiquated, obsolete.

ANT. *Young, modern.*

O'men. Presage, sign, warning, prognostic, augury, foreboding.

O'minous. Foreboding, premonitory, inauspicious.

ANT. *Auspicious, promising.*

Omiss'ion. Failure, neglect, oversight.

ANT. *Fulfilment, performance.*

Omit'. Neglect, miss, leave out, overlook.

ANT. *Perform, fulfil, include.*

On'erous. Burdensome, oppressive, laborious.

ANT. *Light, easy, trifling.*

On'ly. Solely, singly, barely, merely.

ANT. *Generally ; quite.*

On'set. Attack, charge, assault.

ANT. *Retreat.*

On'ward. Forward, advancing, ahead.

ANT. *Backward, to rear.*

Ooze'. Drip, exude, percolate.

ANT. *Flow, gush.*

O'pen (*a.*). Unfolded, unclosed; public; frank, candid, unreserved ; exposed ; evident.

ANT. *Folded, closed ; private ; reserved, secretive ; obscure.*

O'pen (*vb.*). Unclose, unlock, unfold, expand, disclose; begin.

ANT. *Shut, close, conceal ; end, conclude.*

O'pening. Orifice, aperture, cleft, rent ; beginning ; opportunity, chance.

ANT. *Ending, conclusion.*

Opera'tion. Working, action, effect, manipulation, instrumentality.

ANT. *Inaction, suspension.*

Op'erative. See EFFECTIVE.

Opine'. Think, be of opinion, judge, believe.

ANT. *Know, be sure.*

Opin'ion. Feeling, conviction, impression, view.

ANT. *Certainty, knowledge.*

Opin'ionated. Dogmatic, self-assertive, obstinate.

ANT. *Undogmatic, modest.*

Opin'ionative. See OPINIONATED.

Oppo'nent. See ADVERSARY.

Opportune'. Timely, seasonable, convenient, felicitous.

ANT. *Inopportune, untimely, unseasonable, inconvenient.*

Opportu'nity. See OCCASION.

Oppose'. Resist, attack, bar, prevent.

ANT. *Defend, support, help.*

Opposi'tion. Resistance ; prevention, hindrance ; hostility.

ANT. *Support, help ; goodwill.*

Oppress'. Crush, harass, persecute.

ANT. *Relieve, help.*

Oppress'ion. Cruelty, persecution, hardship, misery, tyranny.

ANT. *Kindness ; freedom.*

Oppress'ive. Heavy, burdensome, overwhelming, cruel, tyrannical, unjust.

ANT. *Light, easy, just.*

Oppro'brious. Offensive, abusive, scurrilous.

ANT. *Courteous, polite.*

Oppro'brium. See OBLOQUY and ODIUM.

Op'tion. Preference, choice.

ANT. *Compulsion.*

Op'ulent. Rich, wealthy, affluent.

ANT. *Poor, penniless, needy.*

Orac'ular. Prophetic ; dogmatic ; ambiguous.

ANT. *Undogmatic ; clear, perspicuous.*

O'ral. Spoken, by word of mouth, verbal, not written.

ANT. *Written, unspoken.*

Ora'tion. Speech, address, harangue.

ANT. *Silence.*

Orb'. Sphere, globe, ball.

Ordain'. Appoint ; institute ; decree, command, order.

Ord'er. Arrangement, method, system ; rule, command ; class, rank, grade.

ANT. *Disorder, confusion, medley.*

Ord'er (*vb.*). Arrange, methodize ; command, prescribe.

ANT. *Disarrange, disorder.*

Ord'erly. See METHODICAL.

Ord'inance. Decree, appointment, edict, statute.

Ord'inary. Settled, ordered ; usual, wonted ; commonplace.

ANT. *Irregular, unusual,*

unwonted, extraordinary, uncommon.

Org'anize. Arrange, adjust, settle, establish, order.
ANT. *Disorganize, disorder, upset.*

Organiza'tion. Method, system, construction, structure, form.
ANT. *Disorganization, disorder, confusion.*

Or'ifice. See OPENING.

Or'igin. Beginning, rise, source, cause.
ANT. *End.*

Orig'inal. Primitive, first, primordial; eccentric, odd; inventive.
ANT. *Modern; ordinary; uninventive, unimaginative.*

Orig'inate. Make, cause, create; rise, spring.
ANT. *End.*

Orn'ament (*vb.*). See EMBELLISH.

Orn'ament (*n.*). Adornment, embellishment, decoration.
ANT. *Blemish, disfigurement.*

Ornate'. Decorated, embellished; florid.
ANT. *Plain, simple, unadorned.*

Ostenta'tion. Display, pomp, parade; boasting.
ANT. *Reticence, restraint; modesty.*

Ostenta'tious. Boastful, pretentious, pompous, extravagant.
ANT. *Reticent, restrained, modest, homely.*

Oust'. Eject, expel, displace, evict.
ANT. *Admit, replace, restore.*

Out'break. See AFFRAY.

Out'cry. See CLAMOUR.

Outdo'. Surpass, exceed, eclipse, excel.
ANT. *Fall short of.*

Outland'ish. Foreign, alien, strange, barbarous, rude.
ANT. *Native; civilized, cultivated.*

Out'let. Vent, egress, exit.
ANT. *Inlet.*

Out'line. Figure, contour; sketch, draft.
ANT. *Body, whole.*

Out'look. Prospect, watch; future.

Out'rage. See AFFRONT.

Outrage'ous. See MONSTROUS and ATROCIOUS.

Out'set. See BEGINNING.

Out'skirt. Environ, purlieu, suburb, border.

Out'ward. External, outer, exterior.
ANT. *Inward, internal, interior.*

O'ver. Above, upon; athwart, beyond, across; in excess of, more than.
ANT. *Under, beneath, within; less than.*

Overawe'. Terrify, intimidate, cow.
ANT. *Encourage, treat gently.*

O'vercast. Cloudy, beclouded, dark.
ANT. *Unclouded, clear, bright.*

Overcome'. See SUBDUE.

O'verflow. Deluge, inundation, flood.

Overflow'ing. See ABUNDANT.

Overlook'. Superintend, supervise; pardon, forgive. See also NEGLECT and OMIT.

Overpow'er. See SUBDUE.

Overreach'. See CHEAT.

Overrule'. Influence, control; supersede, annul.
ANT. *Leave alone, allow.*

O'versight. Charge, superintendence; direction; inadvertence, error, neglect. See also NEGLECT (*n.*).

O'vert. Open, patent, apparent.
ANT. *Covert, hidden, concealed.*

Overthrow' (*vb.*). Throw down, destroy, demolish; defeat, conquer.
ANT. *Restore, set up; spare.*

O'verthrow. Destruction, ruin; defeat, conquest.
ANT. *Restoration.*

O'verture. Offer, invitation,

proposal; prelude, musical introduction.

ANT. *Withdrawal ; finale.*

Overturn'. See OVERTHROW.

Overwhelm'. See SUBDUE and OVERTHROW.

Own'. Possess, hold ; acknowledge, admit.

ANT. *Lack possession ; repudiate ; deny.*

Own'er. Possessor, holder, proprietor.

P

Pace'. Step, stride, rate of movement.

ANT. *Rest, pause.*

Pacif'ic. Peaceful, gentle, friendly, conciliatory.

ANT. *Violent, hostile.*

Pac'ify. See APPEASE.

Pack'. Bundle, packet, load ; gang, set.

Pact'. Compact, league, bond, covenant.

Pa'gan. Heathen, non-Christian.

ANT. *Christian.*

Pain'. See PANG and AFFLICTION.

Pain' (*vb.*). See HARM.

Pain'ful. Distressing, hurting, grievous ; arduous, toilsome.

ANT. *Pleasant, harmless, painless ; easy.*

Paint'. Smear ; depict, picture, portray.

Pal'atable. Tasty, appetizing, delicious.

ANT. *Unpalatable, nauseous, unappetizing.*

Pale'. Pallid, light-coloured, wan, sallow ; dim.

ANT. *Florid, dark, healthy ; bright.*

Pall'iate. Cloak, cover ; excuse, extenuate.

ANT. *Reveal ; condemn.*

Pall'id. See PALE.

Palm'y. Flourishing, prosperous.

ANT. *Depressed, unfortunate.*

Palp'able. Tangible. See also MANIFEST.

ANT. *Impalpable, intangible.*

Palp'itate. Flutter, beat, throb, pulsate.

ANT. *Be steady.*

Pal'sy (*vb.*). Benumb, paralyse.

ANT. *Stimulate.*

Pal'ter. Quibble, equivocate, trifle, shuffle.

ANT. *Be straight.*

Pal'try. Contemptible, mean, despicable, beggarly ; little.

ANT. *Fine, honourable ; great.*

Pamp'er. Coddle, cocker, indulge.

ANT. *Neglect, discourage, refuse.*

Panegy'ric. See ENCOMIUM.

Pang'. Pain, twinge, agony, anguish.

ANT. *Relief, ease.*

Pant'. Gasp, blow, puff ; yearn for.

ANT. *Breathe steadily.*

Parade'. See OSTENTATION.

Par'allel. Equidistant ; similar, analogous.

ANT. *Unlike, dissimilar.*

Par'alyse. See PALSY.

Par'amount. Supreme, predominant, pre-eminent.

ANT. *Subordinate, inferior.*

Par'asite. Hanger-on, sycophant, flatterer.

Par'don. See FORGIVE.

Pa'rent. Begetter, producer, author, cause.

ANT. *Child, work.*

Par'oxysm. Fit, attack, convulsion.

Parsimo'nious. See MISERLY.

Par'son. Parish priest, rector, vicar, incumbent.

ANT. *Parishioner, people.*

Part'. Share, piece, portion ; ingredient, constituent ; office, function, duty.

ANT. *Whole.*

Part′ (*vb.*). Sever, divide, break ; allot, share ; depart, go away.
ANT. *Join, unite, reunite ; remain, stay.*

Partake′. Share, participate.
ANT. *Allot.*

Par′tial. Biased, unfair, one-sided, prejudiced.
ANT. *Impartial, unbiased, fair, indifferent.*

Partic′ipate. See PARTAKE.

Par′ticle. Atom, grain, minute part, mite.
ANT. *Whole.*

Partic′ular. Individual, distinctive, especial ; careful, precise.
ANT. *General ; careless, inexact.*

Partic′ularly. Especially, distinctly, chiefly.

Part′isan. Adherent, follower, backer, supporter.

Parti′tion. Division, distribution, allotment ; barrier, wall.

Part′ner. Colleague, associate, sharer, participator, companion ; wife or husband, spouse.

Part′nership. Association, corporation, union.

Par′ty. See ASSOCIATION.

Pass′. Go by, elapse ; disappear ; proceed ; exceed, surpass.
ANT. *Stand still, abide, remain ; fall short.*

Pass′able. Traversable ; tolerable, moderately good, fair.
ANT. *Impassable ; excellent.*

Pass′age. Course, road, journey ; entrance, channel ; clause, extract.
ANT. *Block, barrier.*

Pass′ion. Ardour, zeal, excitement ; emotion, love, devotion ; rage, anger.
ANT. *Indifference, coolness, phlegm.*

Pass′ionate. Fierce, ardent, angry, irascible ; tender.
ANT. *Cold, cool, indifferent ; good-tempered.*

Pass′ive. Suffering, enduring, unresisting, submissive, patient, inactive.
ANT. *Impassive, impatient, active, energetic.*

Pas′time. See GAME.

Pa′tent. Open, evident, obvious, manifest.
ANT. *Obscure, secret.*

Pater′nal. Fatherly, tender.
ANT. *Unfatherly.*

Path′. Road, route, track, course.

Pathet′ic. Touching, sad, moving, affecting, plaintive.
ANT. *Joyous, cheery.*

Pa′tient. See PASSIVE.

Pat′ronize. Favour, protect, befriend, countenance.
ANT. *Repel, neglect, oppose.*

Patt′ern. See MODEL.

Pau′city. Fewness, lack, deficiency.
ANT. *Multitude, abundance.*

Paup′erism. Indigence, penury, poverty, beggary, destitution.
ANT. *Wealth, affluence.*

Pause′. Stop, stay, interval, interruption, hesitation.
ANT. *Movement, action.*

Pay′. Liquidate, settle, discharge ; requite, reward.
ANT. *Owe.*

Peace′. Calm, quiet, silence, repose ; amity, concord.
ANT. *Noise, clamour ; strife, war.*

Peace′able. See PACIFIC.

Peace′ful. See PACIFIC.

Peas′ant. Countryman, rustic, swain, hind.
ANT. *Townsman, citizen.*

Pec′cant. Erring, sinful, guilty.
ANT. *Innocent.*

Pecu′liar. Exceptional, especial. See also PARTICULAR.
ANT. *Ordinary.*

Ped′igree. Lineage, descent, genealogy.

Peer′. Equal ; nobleman.

Peer′less. See MATCHLESS.

Peev′ish. See MOROSE and SURLY.

Pellu'cid. Transparent, clear, limpid.

ANT. *Turbid, muddy, dark.*

Pen'alty. Fine, punishment, forfeiture.

ANT. *Acquittal, release.*

Pen'etrate. Bore, pierce, enter, fathom.

Penetra'tion. Seeing, acumen.

Pen'itence. Repentance, compunction, contrition.

ANT. *Obstinacy, stubbornness, hardness of heart.*

Pen'itent. Repentant, contrite, remorseful.

ANT. *Unrepentant, remorseless.*

Pens'ive. Thoughtful, contemplative, dreamy ; sorrowful.

ANT. *Active ; gay.*

Penu'rious. See MISERLY.

Pen'ury. See PAUPERISM.

Peo'ple. Folk, nation, race ; public, populace, community ; mob.

Perceive'. See, feel, know, comprehend, discern.

ANT. *Miss, misunderstood.*

Percept'ible. Apparent, discernible, perceivable.

ANT. *Imperceptible, insensible.*

Percep'tion. Seeing, feeling, discernment, understanding, notion.

ANT. *Misunderstanding, blindness.*

Per'colate. See OOZE.

Perdi'tion. Ruin, destruction, damnation.

ANT. *Salvation.*

Per'emptory. See ARBITRARY.

Peren'nial. Everlasting, enduring, perpetual.

ANT. *Temporary, unenduring.*

Per'fect. Complete, finished, ripe ; entire, whole ; faultless, immaculate.

ANT. *Imperfect, incomplete ; faulty, defective.*

Perfec'tion. Completeness, perfectness, maturity, excellence.

ANT. *Imperfection, incompleteness, immaturity.*

Perfid'ious. See FALSE.

Per'fidy. Treachery, faithlessness, disloyalty.

ANT. *Loyalty.*

Per'forate. See PENETRATE.

Perform'. See ACCOMPLISH.

Perform'ance. See EXHIBITION.

Per'fume. Scent, odour, fragrance, smell, aroma.

Perhaps'. Possibly, peradventure, perchance, maybe.

ANT. *Certainly, doubtless.*

Per'il. See DANGER.

Per'ilous. See HAZARDOUS.

Pe'riod. Age, era, time, epoch ; end, conclusion ; full stop.

Per'ish. See DECAY.

Per'manent. Lasting, abiding, enduring, constant.

ANT. *Impermanent, passing, fleeting, inconstant.*

Permis'sible. Allowable, admissible, legitimate, lawful.

ANT. *Unallowable, inadmissible, unlawful.*

Permis'sion. Allowance, leave, licence, consent.

ANT. *Prohibition, refusal.*

Permit'. Allow, licence, consent, suffer, authorize.

ANT. *Prohibit, refuse.*

Pernic'ious. See NOISOME.

Perpet'ual. See PERMANENT and PERENNIAL.

Perplex'. See BEWILDER.

Perplex'ing. Puzzling, embarrassing, bewildering, confusing.

ANT. *Simple, intelligible, easy.*

Per'secute. See OPPRESS.

Persecu'tion. See OPPRESSION.

Perseve'rance. Persistence, steadiness, constancy.

ANT. *Slackness, inconstancy.*

Persevere'. Persist, continue, keep on.

ANT. *Give in, slacken.*

Persist'. Remain, last ; persevere.

ANT. *Pass, vanish ; give up.*

Per'sonal. Individual, private.
　ANT. *General, impersonal.*
Persuade'. Induce, lead, convince, prevail on, urge.
　ANT. *Dissuade.*
Persua'sion. Inducement, conviction, belief.
　ANT. *Dissuasion.*
Persua'sive. Convincing, cogent ; seductive.
　ANT. *Dissuasive, unconvincing, weak.*
Pert'. See AUDACIOUS.
Pertina'cious. Determined, persistent, obstinate.
　ANT. *Slack, inert.*
Per'tinent. See APPROPRIATE.
Perturb'. See ANNOY.
Perturba'tion. Disquietude, agitation, vexation.
　ANT. *Composure.*
Pervade'. Overspread, penetrate, fill.
Perverse'. See OBDURATE.
Pervert'. Twist, distort, corrupt, falsify.
　ANT. *Correct.*
Per'vious. Penetrable, passable, permeable.
　ANT. *Impervious, impenetrable.*
Pest'. Plague, pestilence ; annoyance, bother.
Pestilen'tial. Poisonous, contaminating, noxious, deadly.
　ANT. *Harmless, innocuous.*
Peti'tion. Request, appeal, entreaty, supplication, prayer.
　ANT. *Command.*
Pett'y. Trivial, small, insignificant, unimportant.
　ANT. *Great, important, significant.*
Pet'ulant. See CAPTIOUS.
Phant'om. Ghost, wraith, spectre.
　ANT. *Living being.*
Pharisa'ical. Hypocritical, sanctimonious, formal.
　ANT. *Sincere, humble.*
Phlegm'. Indifference, coldness, sluggishness.
　ANT. *Ardour, zeal, warmth.*

Phlegmat'ic. Cold, heavy, stolid, sluggish.
　ANT. *Warm, lively.*
Phys'ical. Natural, material, bodily.
　ANT. *Spiritual, mental.*
Pick'. Pluck, gather, choose, cull.
Pic'ture. Painting, drawing, sketch, portrait.
Picturesque'. Graphic, vivid, picture-like.
　ANT. *Dull, ugly.*
Piece'. Fragment, portion, part, bit, shred.
　ANT. *Whole.*
Pierce'. See PERFORATE.
Pier'cing. Sharp, acute, keen, penetrating, shrill.
　ANT. *Soft, low.*
Pi'ety. Filial love, religion, devotion, holiness.
　ANT. *Impiety, profanity, irreverence.*
Pile'. See HEAP.
Pil'fer. Filch, steal, thieve.
Pil'grim. Wanderer, traveller.
Pil'lage. Depredation, booty, plunder, looting, rapine.
Pil'lage (*vb.*). See PLUNDER.
Pinch'. Squeeze, press, gripe, nip.
Pine'. Wilt, droop, wither, flag.
　ANT. *Revive, flourish.*
Pi'ous. Dutiful, religious, devout, reverent, holy.
　ANT. *Impious, irreligious, irreverent, wicked.*
Pi'quant. Pungent, cutting, sharp ; racy.
　ANT. *Gentle, mild ; dull.*
Pique'. Umbrage, displeasure, irritation, offence.
　ANT. *Satisfaction, pleasure.*
Pitch'. See FLING.
Pit'eous. Sorrowful, distressing, mournful, sad, pitiable.
　ANT. *Cheerful, joyful.*
Pith'. Marrow, core, heart ; substance, meaning ; force, energy.
　ANT. *Stem ; weakness.*

Pith'y. Forcible, strong ; terse, concise.

ANT. *Weak, pointless ; wordy.*

Pit'iable. See PITEOUS.

Pit'iful. See MERCIFUL.

Pity.' See CLEMENCY.

Place'. Position, situation ; room, space.

Place' *(vb.).* Set, put, settle, arrange.

ANT. *Move, remove, displace.*

Plac'id. See CALM.

Plague'. See PEST.

Plague' *(vb.).* See ANNOY.

Plain'. Level, flat, even ; simple, homely. See also MANIFEST.

ANT. *Uneven, hilly, mountainous ; grand, rich.*

Plaint'ive. Sad, doleful, wailing.

ANT. *Cheerful, gay.*

Plan'. Draft, sketch, chart, design ; plot, project ; method.

Plant'. See PLACE *(vb.).*

Plas'tic. Formative ; flexile, easy to mould.

ANT. *Stiff, solid.*

Plau'sible. Specious, colourable.

ANT. *Unreasonable, unjustifiable.*

Play'. See ENTERTAINMENT and GAME.

Play' *(vb.).* Frolic, frisk ; act, perform.

ANT. *Work.*

Play'ful. Merry, joyous, mischievous, frolicsome.

ANT. *Serious, grave.*

Plea'. Legal action ; excuse, argument ; entreaty.

Pleas'ant. See DELECTABLE.

Please'. Delight, gratify, gladden, content.

ANT. *Displease, annoy, dissatisfy.*

Pleas'ure. Enjoyment, delight, gratification, satisfaction ; will, wish.

ANT. *Pain, dissatisfaction, discontent.*

Pledge'. Guarantee, earnest, pawn, security.

Plen'tiful. Abundant, copious, plenteous, ample.

ANT. *Scanty, scarce, few.*

Plent'y. Fullness, copiousness, abundance ; affluence.

ANT. *Lack, dearth, scarcity.*

Pli'able. Flexible, supple, yielding, docile, tractable.

ANT. *Stiff, unbending, intractable.*

Plight'. State, condition, situation ; predicament.

Plot'. See INTRIGUE *(n.).*

Plot' *(vb.).* Plan, scheme, cabal, intrigue.

ANT. *Counterplot.*

Pluck'. Courage, spirit, hardihood, mettle.

ANT. *Cowardice, faintheartedness.*

Plump'. Stout, buxom, round, fat.

ANT. *Thin, lean.*

Plund'er. Pillage, despoil, sack, rob, rifle.

Plunge'. See IMMERSE.

Poign'ant. Sharp, keen, intense, biting.

ANT. *Gentle, mild.*

Point'ed. Sharpened, sharp ; distinct ; full of meaning.

ANT. *Blunt ; vague ; meaningless.*

Poi'son. Virus, venom ; corruption.

ANT. *Antidote.*

Pol'ish. Burnish, brighten, rub up, furbish ; refine.

ANT. *Stain, sully.*

Polite'. Urbane, civil, courteous, affable ; refined, elegant.

ANT. *Impolite, uncivil, discourteous, rude.*

Polite'ness. Courtesy, urbanity, affability, civility.

ANT. *Impoliteness, discourtesy, incivility, rudeness.*

Pol'itic. Wise, judicious, diplomatic, wary.

ANT. *Impolitic, injudicious, unwise.*

Pollute'. Taint, corrupt, contaminate, defile.

ANT. *Purify, cleanse.*

Pollu'tion. Contamination, defilement, corruption, taint.

ANT. *Purification, cleansing.*

Poltroon'. Dastard, craven, coward.

ANT. *Hero, brave man.*

Pomp'. See OSTENTATION.

Pomp'ous. Stately, majestic, august; inflated ostentatious.

ANT. *Undignified; simple.*

Pond'er. See MEDITATE.

Pond'erous. Weighty, heavy, bulky.

ANT. *Light, small.*

Poor'. Needy, indigent, penniless; mean, paltry.

ANT. *Rich, wealthy, affluent; good, fine.*

Pop'ulace. See MOB.

Pop'ular. General, common; favoured; simple, plain.

ANT. *Unpopular; technical, difficult.*

Pop'ulous. Numerous, crowded, thickly inhabited.

Port'. Harbour, haven, roadstead; bearing, mien.

Por'tend. See BETOKEN.

Por'tent. See PRODIGY.

Por'tion. See PART.

Port'ly. Grand, stout, corpulent.

ANT. *Insignificant, thin, slight.*

Portray'. Delineate, draw, sketch, represent.

Pose'. Perplex, bewilder, puzzle; pretend.

ANT. *Explain; be natural.*

Posi'tion. Station, place, attitude, point of view; situation.

ANT. *Motion.*

Pos'itive. Real, actual; definite, precise, explicit; assertive, dogmatic.

ANT. *Unreal; vague; undogmatic.*

Possess'. See HOLD.

Possess'ion. Having, holding, ownership, tenure, occupation; treasure.

ANT. *Dispossession.*

Poss'ible. Potential, feasible, practicable.

ANT. *Impossible, impracticable.*

Poss'ibly. Peradventure, perhaps, perchance, maybe.

ANT. *Certainly, assuredly.*

Post'. Pillar, stake. See also POSITION.

Poste'rior. Later; hinder, rear.

ANT. *Anterior, earlier; fore, forward.*

Poster'ity. Successors, descendants, offspring; future.

ANT. *Ancestors; past.*

Post'ure. Attitude, position.

Po'tent. Powerful, mighty, influential, strong; cogent.

ANT. *Impotent, powerless, uninfluential, weak; unconvincing.*

Pov'erty. Need, want, indigence, penury; meagreness.

ANT. *Wealth, affluence, abundance.*

Pow'er. Strength, might, influence, rule, dominion.

ANT. *Weakness, impotence; subjection.*

Pow'erful. See POTENT.

Pract'icable. See POSSIBLE.

Pract'ical. Serviceable, useful; expert, skilful.

ANT. *Unserviceable, useless; clumsy, inexpert.*

Pract'ice (*n.*). See CUSTOM.

Pract'ise (*vb.*). Perform, pursue, apply, exercise.

ANT. *Neglect, omit.*

Praise'. Laud, approval, applause, encomium, eulogy; renown.

ANT. *Dispraise, blame; disgrace.*

Praise' (*vb.*). Applaud, extol, command, approve, eulogize, laud, worship.

ANT. *Condemn, disapprove, blame.*

Praise'worthy. Laudable, commendable, creditable.

ANT. *Blameworthy, discreditable.*

Pray'. See BESEECH.

Pray'er. Petition, entreaty, request, suit.

ANT. *Command, behest.*

Preamb'le. Introduction, preface, exordium.

ANT. *Conclusion, ending, peroration.*

Preca'rious. Risky, uncertain, doubtful, unsafe, dangerous.

ANT. *Safe, secure, certain.*

Precau'tion. Forethought, care.

ANT. *Carelessness.*

Precede'. Go before, lead.

ANT. *Follow, succeed.*

Prece'dence. Priority, pre-eminence, preference.

ANT. *Inferiority.*

Prece'dent (*adj.*). Preceding, anterior, pre-eminent.

ANT. *Following, posterior.*

Pre'cedent (*n.*). Previous decision, procedure, example, standard.

Pre'cept. Law, instruction, maxim, principle.

Precep'tor. Teacher, instructor, master, tutor.

ANT. *Pupil, scholar.*

Pre'cinct. Enclosure, limit, bounds, confines.

Prec'ious. Rare, costly, valuable, choice ; dear.

ANT. *Valueless, worthless, cheap ; hated.*

Precip'itate (*vb.*). Hasten, hurry, expedite, press.

ANT. *Delay, retard, check.*

Precip'itate (*adj.*). Hasty, rash, impetuous, premature.

ANT. *Cautious, considered, mature.*

Precip'itous. Steep, abrupt, headlong.

ANT. *Gentle, sloping.*

Precise'. See EXACT and PRIM.

Precis'ion. Exactness, accuracy, definiteness.

ANT. *Inexactness, inaccuracy, indefiniteness.*

Preclude'. Prevent, stop, hinder, prohibit, inhibit.

ANT. *Help, expedite, allow.*

Pred'atory. Rapacious, plundering.

Predic'ament. Plight, fix, state, dilemma.

Pre'dicate. Assert, affirm, state.

ANT. *Deny, doubt.*

Predict'. Foretell, prophesy, prognosticate, forecast.

Predilec'tion. Preference, choice, fondness, bias.

Predom'inant. Ascendant, overpowering, prevailing, paramount.

ANT. *Inferior, subordinate.*

Pre-em'inent. Supreme, chief, conspicuous.

ANT. *Inferior, subordinate, undistinguished.*

Pref'ace. See PREAMBLE.

Pref'atory. Introductory, opening, preliminary, prelusive.

ANT. *Concluding, final.*

Prefer'. Offer ; choose, select.

ANT. *Withdraw ; dislike.*

Pref'erence. See PREDILECTION.

Preg'nant. Full, teeming, big, fraught.

ANT. *Empty, meaningless.*

Pre'judice. Forejudgment, bias, prepossession ; damage, injury.

ANT. *Judgment, indifference, impartiality ; safety.*

Prejudic'ial. See HARMFUL.

Prelim'inary. See PREFATORY.

Prel'ude. See PREAMBLE.

Pre'mature. Untimely, unripe. See also PRECIPITATE (*adj.*).

ANT. *Mature, timely, ripe.*

Pre'mium. Recompense, reward, bonus, bribe.

ANT. *Discount, loss.*

Prepare'. Fit, get ready, equip, make.

ANT. *Dally.*

Prepond'erate. Outweigh, overbalance, prevail.

ANT. *Be outweighed.*

Prepossess'ing. Attractive, charming, engaging, fascinating.

ANT. *Unprepossessing, unattractive, ugly.*

Pres´age. Foreknowledge, betokening, prognostic, omen.

Pres´age (*vb.*). See BETOKEN.

Prescribe´. Order, appoint, enjoin, command, dictate.
ANT. *Obey, submit.*

Pres´ence. Being at a place ; attendance ; bearing, mien.
ANT. *Absence.*

Pres´ent (*adj.*). Existing, immediate, at hand, attending.
ANT. *Past ; absent.*

Pres´ent (*n.*). Gift, donation, presentation.

Present´ (*vb.*). Introduce ; show ; give, bestow, confer.
ANT. *Refuse.*

Presenta´tion. Introduction ; showing ; giving.

Present´iment. See PRESAGE.

Preserva´tion. Maintenance, security, safety, upholding.
ANT. *Destruction, ruin, peril.*

Preserve´. Save, guard, protect, secure, maintain, uphold.
ANT. *Destroy, abandon, violate.*

Press´. Compress, squeeze, crush ; urge, push, enforce.
ANT. *Loosen ; delay, hinder.*

Pres´sure. Force, compression ; urgency.
ANT. *Unimportance.*

Presume´. Surmise, conjecture, infer, suppose ; dare, take liberties.
ANT. *Know, be sure ; be respectful.*

Presump´tion. Surmise, conjecture, inference, supposition ; audacity, assurance.
ANT. *Knowledge, certainty ; deference.*

Presump´tuous. Audacious, forward, presuming, arrogant.
ANT. *Modest ; backward.*

Pretence´. Affectation, show, simulation ; excuse, pretext.
ANT. *Sincerity, reality, genuineness.*

Pretend´. Counterfeit, feign, simulate ; lay claim to.
ANT. *Be real ; renounce.*

Preternat´ural. See ABNORMAL.

Pre´text. See PRETENCE.

Pret´ty. See BEAUTIFUL.

Prevail´. Persuade, induce. See also SUBDUE and PREPONDERATE.
ANT. *Fail.*

Prevail´ing. Prevalent, predominant ; usual, established ; effective.
ANT. *Few, inferior ; unusual ; ineffective.*

Prev´alent. See PREVAILING.

Prevar´icate. Equivocate, quibble, cavil, shuffle.
ANT. *Speak truth.*

Prevent´. Stop, hinder, frustrate, thwart, anticipate.
ANT. *Help, forward, allow.*

Pre´vious. See ANTERIOR.

Prey´. Victim, capture. See also BOOTY.
ANT. *Captor, hunter.*

Price´. Cost, charge, worth, value, figure.
ANT. *Worthlessness.*

Prick´. Incite, spur. See also PERFORATE.
ANT. *Retard.*

Pride´. See HAUGHTINESS.

Prim´. Precise, formal, starched, demure.
ANT. *Casual, jolly, informal.*

Pri´mary. Original, radical ; best, chief.
ANT. *Latest, lowest.*

Prime´. See PRIMARY.

Prim´itive. See ANCIENT.

Prince´. Sovereign, ruler, monarch ; king's descendant.

Prince´ly. See AUGUST.

Prin´cipal. See CHIEF and CARDINAL.

Prin´ciple. See PRECEPT.

Pri´or. See ANTERIOR.

Prior´ity. See PRECEDENCE.

Pris´tine. See ANCIENT.

Pri´vacy. Retirement, solitude, retreat, secrecy.
ANT. *Publicity.*

Pri'vate. Retired, secluded, separate ; secret ; personal, individual.

ANT. *Public, open, common, general.*

Priva'tion. Loss, deprivation, need, destitution.

ANT. *Gain, possession ; comfort.*

Priv'ilege. Prerogative, advantage, permission, immunity.

ANT. *Disqualification, disadvantage.*

Prize'. R e w a r d. See also BOOTY.

Prize' (*vb.*). See APPRAISE and APPRECIATE.

Prob'able. Likely, reasonable. See also CREDIBLE.

ANT. *Unlikely, improbable, incredible.*

Probabil'ity. Likelihood, credibility, presumption.

ANT. *Improbability, unlikelihood.*

Probe'. Sound, search, examine.

Prob'ity. See HONESTY.

Problemat'ic. Doubtful, dubious, questionable, undecided.

ANT. *Certain, undoubted, unquestionable.*

Proce'dure. Process, practice, action.

Proceed'. Advance, go on, pass, arise.

ANT. *Recede, go back, stand.*

Proceed'ing. Transaction, measure, act, step.

Proces'sion. Advance, march, cavalcade, file.

ANT. *Station.*

Proclaim'. See ADVERTISE.

Proclama'tion. Announcement, edict, decree, ordinance.

ANT. *Silence.*

Procliv'ity. Tendency, disposition, propensity, bias, leaning, aptitude.

ANT. *Aversion from, opposition.*

Procras'tinate. Dally, defer, postpone, delay.

ANT. *Hasten, be prompt.*

Procrastina'tion. Delay, dallying, postponement, deferment.

ANT. *Speed, haste, promptness.*

Pro'create. Beget, engender, generate.

Procure'. See ACQUIRE.

Prod'igal. See EXTRAVAGANT and PROFUSE.

Prodig'ious. See COLOSSAL and MONSTROUS.

Prod'igy. Marvel, portent, miracle, wonder.

Produce'. Bring forth, show ; cause, occasion ; lengthen, prolong.

ANT. *Conceal, withhold ; result ; shorten, reduce.*

Prod'uce (*n.*). Fruit, product, profit, yield ; consequence.

ANT. *Seed, cause.*

Prod'uct. See PRODUCE (*n.*).

Product'ive. Fruitful, fertile, prolific ; causative.

ANT. *Unproductive, barren ; resultant.*

Profane'. Unconsecrated, secular ; godless, blasphemous, impious.

ANT. *Sacred, hallowed, consecrated ; religious, pious, reverent.*

Profan'ity. See BLASPHEMY.

Profess'. Acknowledge, avow, own ; pretend, affect.

ANT. *Disavow, deny.*

Profes'sion. Acknowledgment, avowal, vocation, business.

ANT. *Disavowal, denial.*

Prof'fer. Offer, propose, propound.

ANT. *Withdraw, withhold, refuse.*

Profic'iency. Improvement ; skill, mastery, dexterity.

ANT. *Deterioration ; awkwardness, clumsiness.*

Profic'ient. Skilful, skilled, dexterous, expert, accomplished.

ANT. *Unskilled, inexpert, amateurish.*

Prof'it. See ADVANTAGE.

Prof'itable. Advantageous, gainful, lucrative, beneficial.

91

ANT. *Unprofitable, disad-vantageous, non-paying.*

Prof'ligate. See ABANDONED.

Profound'. Deep, fathomless. See also ABSTRUSE.

ANT. *Shallow.* See also ABSTRUSE.

Profuse'. Lavish, prodigal, extravagant ; exuberant, excessive.

ANT. *Sparing, economical ; meagre, scanty.*

Prog'eny. Descendants, off-spring, children, issue.

ANT. *Ancestors, fathers.*

Prognost'icate. See BETOKEN.

Pro'gress. Advance, march, advancement, growth.

ANT. *Retrogression, decline.*

Prohib'it. Forbid. See also PRECLUDE.

ANT. *Command.* See also PRECLUDE.

Project' (*vb.*). Plan, scheme, purpose ; protrude, bulge.

ANT. *Turn inward.*

Proj'ect (*n.*). Plan, scheme, purpose, design.

Prolif'ic. See PRODUCTIVE.

Pro'lix. Verbose, long, diffuse, tedious, tiresome, boring.

ANT. *Terse, concise, laconic.*

Pro'logue. See PREAMBLE.

Prolong'. Lengthen, extend, continue, protract.

ANT. *Shorten, discontinue.*

Prom'inent. Protuberant, projecting ; eminent, conspicuous, foremost.

ANT. *Retiring, obscure.*

Promisc'uous. Mingled, confused, indiscriminate, mixed.

ANT. *Distinct, discriminate.*

Prom'ise. Pledge, word, assurance, undertaking.

ANT. *Refusal.*

Prom'ise (*vb.*). Pledge, undertake, engage, covenant.

ANT. *Refuse.*

Promote'. See ADVANCE and AID.

Prompt'. Expeditious. See also ACTIVE.

ANT. *Tardy.*

Prompt' (*vb.*). Incite, move, persuade, urge ; remind.

ANT. *Hinder, discourage, dissuade.*

Prompt'itude. Expedition. See also ALACRITY.

Prom'ulgate. See ADVERTISE.

Prone'. Prostrate ; inclined, apt, disposed.

ANT. *Upright ; not disposed, averse.*

Pronounce'. Articulate, speak, enunciate, express, utter.

ANT. *Mumble, be silent.*

Proof'. Assay, test ; demonstration, testimony, evidence.

ANT. *Disproof.*

Prop'. Support, stay, staff.

Prop' (*vb.*). Support, stay, buttress, sustain, shore up.

ANT. *Let down, undermine.*

Prop'agate. Breed, produce ; disseminate, circulate, spread.

ANT. *Be barren ; conceal, suppress.*

Propens'ity. See BENT.

Prop'er. Own, particular, peculiar ; fit, seemly, suitable, right.

ANT. *General, common ; improper, unseemly, unfit, wrong.*

Prop'erty. Quality, attribute ; wealth, possessions, estate.

Proph'ecy. Prediction, foretelling, vaticination.

ANT. *Retrospection.*

Proph'esy (*vb.*). See PREDICT.

Propin'quity. Neighbourhood, nearness, vicinity ; affinity.

ANT. *Remoteness, distance.*

Propi'tiate. See APPEASE.

Propi'tious. See AUSPICIOUS.

Propor'tionate. Commensurate, equal, adequate.

ANT. *Disproportionate, incommensurate, inadequate.*

Propo'sal. Offer, proposition, tender, suggestion.

ANT. *Withdrawal, rejection.*

Propose'. See PROFFER and CONTEMPLATE.

Proposi'tion. Thesis, statement. See also PROPOSAL.

Propri'ety. Fitness, suitableness, appropriateness; correctness, decorum.
ANT. *Impropriety, unfitness, inappropriateness; incorrectness, indecency.*

Proscribe'. Outlaw, denounce, banish.
ANT. *Pardon.*

Proscrip'tion. Banishment, outlawry, interdiction.
ANT. *Pardon.*

Pros'ecute. Pursue, continue; charge, indict, arraign.
ANT. *Abandon, desist; defend.*

Pros'pect. Outlook, view, survey, scene; hope, promise.
ANT. *Retrospect.*

Pros'per. Flourish, succeed, thrive.
ANT. *Fail, decline; hinder.*

Prosper'ity. Good fortune, welfare, good luck, success. happiness.
ANT. *Ill-luck, ill-fortune, failure, misery.*

Pros'perous. Fortunate, lucky, successful, flourishing.
ANT. *Unfortunate, unlucky, unsuccessful, depressed.*

Protect'. See PRESERVE.

Protest'. Dissent, remonstrate, repudiate, denounce. See also AFFIRM.
ANT. *Agree, endorse, acquiesce.*

Protract'. See PROLONG.

Protrude'. See PROJECT.

Proud'. Conceited, vain. See also ARROGANT.
ANT. *Modest, humble.*

Prove'. Essay, test, examine; demonstrate, confirm, verify, establish.
ANT. *Disprove, falsify.*

Prov'erb. See ADAGE.

Provide'. See PREPARE.

Prov'ident. Foreseeing, careful, economical, thrifty.
ANT. *Improvident, reckless, unseeing, extravagant.*

Prov'ince. Department, region; function, business.

Provoca'tion. Incitement, annoyance, insult, affront.
ANT. *Appeasement, conciliation.*

Provoke'. See ENRAGE.

Prow'ess. See COURAGE.

Prox'imate. Nearest, closest, next, immediate.
ANT. *Remote, far.*

Proxim'ity. See PROPINQUITY.

Prox'y. Agent, intermediary, substitute, deputy, representative.
ANT. *Self.*

Pru'dence. Sagacity, caution, thoughtfulness, circumspection, judgment.
ANT. *Imprudence, shortsightedness, incautiousness, indiscreetness.*

Pru'dent. Judicious, cautious, discreet; economical, frugal.
ANT. *Imprudent, injudicious, incautious; extravagant.*

Prune'. Cut, clip, trim, lop.

Pub'lic. Popular, general, common, open.
ANT. *Private, personal.*

Pub'lish. See ADVERTISE.

Pu'erile. Childish, boyish, silly, trivial.
ANT. *Manly, sensible.*

Pull'. See DRAW.

Punctil'ious. Particular, precise, scrupulous, nice.
ANT. *Careless, indifferent, unscrupulous.*

Punc'tual. Precise, exact; prompt, in time.
ANT. *Inexact; unpunctual, late, behind time.*

Pun'gent. Sharp, poignant; stinging, acrimonious.
ANT. *Mild, harmless.*

Pun'ish. See CASTIGATE.

Pun'ishment. Correction, chastisement, castigation, penalty.
ANT. *Forgiveness, pardon.*

Pu'ny. Small, weak, insignificant, dwarfish.
ANT. *Big, strong, burly.*

Pu'pil. Scholar, disciple, student, tiro.

ANT. *Master, teacher, tutor.*

Purch'ase. Buy, acquire, procure.

ANT. *Sell, dispose of.*

Pure'. Unmixed, unadulterated; clean, unstained, immaculate; honest, innocent.

ANT. *Impure, tarnished, unclean, stained ; wicked.*

Purge'. See PURIFY.

Pu'rify. Cleanse, clean, purge, clear, clarify.

ANT. *Soil, stain, spot.*

Pu'rity. Cleanness, clearness, genuineness ; honesty, sincerity, chastity.

ANT. *Uncleanness, foulness, cloudiness ; spuriousness ; dishonesty ; unchastity.*

Pur'lieu. See PRECINCT.

Pur'port. See MEANING.

Pur'pose. End, intention, aim, design.

Pursue'. Follow, chase, hunt, track ; practise, continue.

ANT. *Flee, run away, escape.*

Push'. Drive, impel, thrust, press.

ANT. *Pull, draw.*

Pusillan'imous. Chicken-hearted, dastardly, cowardly, timid ; mean.

ANT. *Brave, heroic, daring ; magnanimous.*

Put'. Place, locate, set, deposit.

ANT. *Move, remove.*

Pu'trefy. Rot, decompose, decay.

Pu'trid. Rotten, corrupt, decomposed, stinking.

ANT. *Sound, sanitary, sweet.*

Puz'zle. See BEWILDER.

Q

Quack'. Charlatan, impostor, mountebank, humbug.

ANT. *Professional ; qualified person.*

Quag'mire. See MARSH.

Quail'. Shrink, cower, flinch, tremble.

ANT. *Stand firm, confront.*

Quaint'. Singular, odd, curious, whimsical.

ANT. *Normal, ordinary.*

Quake'. Shake, quiver, quail, tremble, shiver.

ANT. *Be firm, be fearless.*

Qualifica'tion. Fitness, capacity, capability ; modification, exception, restriction.

ANT. *Unfitness, disqualification.*

Qual'ify. Fit, adapt, enable, prepare ; modify, restrict.

ANT. *Unfit, disable, forbid.*

Qual'ity. Property, nature, attribute ; character, kind ; rank, position.

Qualm'. Pang, scruple, nausea.

Quant'ity. Amount, sum, aggregate.

Quar'rel (*n.*). See ALTERCATION.

Quar'rel (*vb.*). Squabble, dispute, disagree, strive.

ANT. *Agree, be friendly.*

Quar'relsome. Irascible, choleric, fiery, contentious, disputatious.

ANT. *Peaceful, placable, affable.*

Quash'. See ANNUL.

Queer'. See ODD.

Quell'. Crush, repress, subdue, calm.

ANT. *Arouse, agitate.*

Quench'. Extinguish, put **out** ; stifle, suppress ; allay.

ANT. *Light, ignite ; arouse ; excite.*

Que'ry (*vb.*). See QUESTION (*vb.*).

Que'ry (*n.*). See QUESTION (*n.*).

Ques'tion (*vb.*). Ask, interrogate, inquire ; controvert, doubt.

    ANT. *Answer, confute.*

Quest'ion (*n.*). Interrogation, inquiry, query ; proposition, subject.

    ANT. *Answer, refutation.*

Quest'ionable. Doubtful, disputable, uncertain, debatable. See also PROBLEMATIC.

    ANT. *Unquestionable, indisputable, certain.*

Quick'. Swift, fast, rapid, lively, adroit. See also AGILE.

    ANT. *Slow, tardy, sluggish, dull.*

Quick'ness. See CELERITY.

Qui'et. Calm, rest, repose, stillness, peace, tranquillity.

    ANT. *Disturbance, agitation, noise, uproar, perturbation.*

Qui'et (*vb.*). See ALLAY.

Qui'et (*adj.*). Calm, still, silent, peaceful, tranquil.

    ANT. *Agitated, perturbed, noisy.*

Quit'. See ABANDON.

Quiv'er. See QUAKE.

Quote'. Cite, adduce, extract, repeat.

R

Rab'ble. See MOB.

Rab'id. Furious, mad, frenzied, frantic.

    ANT. *Sane, gentle, quiet.*

Race'. Lineage, ancestry, line, family ; course, pursuit, match.

Rack'. Torture, twist, agonize, harass.

    ANT. *Alleviate, soothe.*

Ra'cy. Spicy, lively, pungent, piquant, smart.

    ANT. *Dull, flat, uninteresting.*

Ra'diance. Brilliancy, brightness, splendour, lustre.

    ANT. *Dullness, dimness.*

Ra'diant. See BRIGHT.

Rad'ical. Fundamental, organic, entire, thorough.

    ANT. *Superficial ; incomplete, piecemeal.*

Rage'. See ANGER.

Rag'ged. Torn, tattered, rent, jagged.

    ANT. *Even, untorn.*

Raid'. See FORAY.

Rai'ment. Clothing, clothes, garments, vesture, dress, attire.

    ANT. *Nakedness.*

Raise'. Arouse, collect. See also LIFT.

    ANT. *Disperse.*

Rake'. Profligate, debauchee, libertine.

Ra'kish. Dissolute, debauched, licentious.

    ANT. *Sober, modest, orderly.*

Ram'ble. Roam, stray, wander, stroll, saunter.

Ram'bling. Incoherent, desultory, discursive.

    ANT. *Coherent, sensible, concise.*

Ram'pant. Vehement, headstrong, arrant, aggressive.

    ANT. *Calm, inoffensive.*

Ramp'art. Defence, bulwark, bastion, fortification.

Ran'cid. Tainted, sour, musty.

    ANT. *Untainted, sweet.*

Ran'corous. Spiteful, malignant, malevolent, virulent, bitter.

    ANT. *Generous, charitable, kind.*

Ran'cour. See ANGER.

Range'. Row, line ; scope, sphere, compass, extent.

Rank'. Row ; class, degree, station, grade.

Ran'sack. Search, overhaul, explore, rummage, plunder.

Ran'som. See REDEEM.

Rapa'cious. See GRASPING.

Rap'id. Swift, fast, hurried, expeditious.

    ANT. *Slow, tardy.*

Rapid′ity. See CELERITY.

Rap′ine. Plunder, pillage, depredation.

Rap′ture. See BLISS.

Rare′. Thin ; scarce, uncommon, singular, extraordinary.

 ANT. *Thick ; common, frequent, ordinary.*

Ra′rity. Thinness, scarcity, unusualness, infrequency.

 ANT. *Thickness ; frequency, commonness.*

Ras′cal. See CAITIFF.

Rash′. Impetuous, headstrong, imprudent, foolhardy, precipitate, venturesome.

 ANT. *Steady, self-controlled, cautious, prudent.*

Rate′. Appraise, estimate, value ; scold, chide.

Rate′ (*n.*). Standard ; ratio, proportion ; worth, value ; impost, tax.

Rat′ify. See CONFIRM.

Rat′ional. Sane, intelligent, reasonable, intellectual.

 ANT. *Irrational, foolish, unintelligent, unreasonable.*

Rav′age. Pillage, plunder, devastate, despoil, lay waste.

Rav′ish. Violate ; enchant, delight, enrapture.

 ANT. *Disappoint, displease.*

Raze′. Throw down, overthrow, demolish, destroy.

 ANT. *Restore, rebuild.*

Read′iness. See ALACRITY.

Read′y. Prepared, dexterous, apt ; handy ; inclined.

 ANT. *Unready, unprepared, behindhand ; clumsy ; unwilling, disinclined.*

Re′al. Actual, substantial ; true, authentic, genuine.

 ANT. *Apparent, unreal, unsubstantial, false.*

Real′ity. Truth, verity, certainty, genuineness.

 ANT. *Falsehood, unreality.*

Realm′. Kingdom, State ; province, sphere.

Reap′. See ACQUIRE.

Rear′. Bring up, train ; lift, erect.

 ANT. *Destroy, throw down.*

Rea′son. Intellect, understanding, sanity ; cause, motive, ground ; argument, proof.

 ANT. *Insanity ; effect ; disproof.*

Rea′son (*vb.*). Argue, infer, deduce, debate.

Rea′sonable. See RATIONAL.

Rebel′lion. Revolt, mutiny, sedition, rising.

 ANT. *Loyalty, submission.*

Rebuff′. Chide, reprimand, rebuke, check, repulse.

 ANT. *Encourage, approve.*

Rebuke′. See ADMONISH.

Recall′. Call back ; remember ; revoke, cancel.

 ANT. *Forget ; reaffirm.*

Recant′. See ABJURE.

Recapit′ulate. Repeat, enumerate, recite.

Recede′. Retire, withdraw, retreat.

 ANT. *Come forward, advance.*

Receive′. Obtain, take, accept ; welcome, entertain.

 ANT. *Give, bestow ; repel, exclude.*

Re′cent. Fresh, modern, novel, late.

 ANT. *Stale, old, out of date.*

Recip′rocal. Mutual, correlative, interchangeable.

 ANT. *Selfish, individual.*

Reci′tal. See ACCOUNT.

Recite′. Narrate, relate, recount. See also RECAPITULATE.

Reck′less. See RASH and REGARDLESS.

Reck′on. See CALCULATE and ESTIMATE.

Reck′oning. Account, bill, score, calculation.

Reclaim′. Reform ; recapture, recover.

 ANT. *Spoil, corrupt ; renounce.*

Recline′. Lie, lean, rest.

 ANT. *Stand, sit.*

Recogni′tion. Acknowledgment, avowal, admission ; recollection.
ANT. *Disavowal ; forgetfulness, oblivion.*

Rec′ognize. Acknowledge, know again, own, admit.
ANT. *Disavow, forget.*

Recollect′. See RECALL.

Recollect′ion. Memory, remembrance, reminiscence.
ANT. *Forgetfulness, oblivion.*

Recommend′. See COMMEND.

Rec′ompense (*vb.*). See COMPENSATE.

Rec′ompense (*n.*). Reward, requital, compensation, amends, satisfaction.

Rec′oncile. See CONCILIATE.

Rec′ondite. See ABSTRUSE.

Rec′ord (*n.*). Register, memorandum, note ; memorial.

Record ′(*vb.*). Register, note, chronicle.
ANT. *Forget, disregard.*

Recount′. See RECAPITULATE and RECITE.

Recov′er. Regain, retrieve ; recuperate.
ANT. *Lose ; grow worse.*

Rec′reant. Apostate, backsliding. See also COWARD.
ANT. *Believing, faithful.*

Recrea′tion. See ENTERTAINMENT and GAME.

Recruit′. Repair, refresh, renew ; restore, invigorate.
ANT. *Destroy, injure, weaken.*

Rect′ify. Correct, redress, amend.
ANT. *Falsify, corrupt.*

Rect′itude. Honesty, uprightness, integrity, virtue.
ANT. *Dishonesty, vice, turpitude.*

Redeem′. Buy back, repurchase, recover, deliver, ransom. See also COMPENSATE.
ANT. *Retain, detain, hold.*

Red′olent. Fragrant, sweetsmelling, odorous.
ANT. *Mal-odorous, unpleasant, stinking.*

Redress′ (*n.*). See AMENDS.

Redress′ (*vb.*). Repair, amend, rectify, reform.
ANT. *Undo, destroy.*

Reduce′. Shorten, weaken. See also ABATE.
ANT. *Lengthen, strengthen.*

Redund′ant. Exuberant, overflowing, excessive, superfluous.
ANT. *Scanty, deficient, too few.*

Refer′. Deliver ; impute, belong, relate to ; advert.

Referee′. Arbitrator, arbiter, umpire, judge.
ANT. *Litigants, combatants, players.*

Ref′erence. Relation ; hint, appeal.

Refined′. Polished, elegant, courtly, polite.
ANT. *Unrefined, unpolished.*

Reflect′. Mirror ; ponder, consider, meditate, muse.

Reflec′tion. Image ; meditation, consideration, musing ; reproach.
ANT. *Object ; thoughtlessness ; credit.*

Reform′. Remake, remodel. See also REDRESS (*vb.*).
ANT. *Retain, preserve.*

Reforma′tion. Reform, improvement, amendment, correction.
ANT. *Deformation, deterioration.*

Refract′ory. See OBDURATE.

Refrain′. See FORBEAR.

Refresh′. Renew, renovate, revive, cheer, enliven, regale,
ANT. *Exhaust, weary, depress.*

Ref′uge. See HARBOUR.

Reful′gent. See BRIGHT.

Refund′. Repay, restore, reimburse, return.
ANT. *Spend, borrow.*

Ref′use (*n.*). Dregs, lees, dross, grounds, offal.

Refuse′ (*vb.*). Deny, decline, reject, repudiate.
ANT. *Grant, concede, allow, accept.*

Refute'. See CONFUTE.

Regain'. See RECOVER.

Re'gal. Kingly, royal. See also AUGUST.

ANT. *Menial.*

Regale'. Feast, entertain, refresh, gratify.

ANT. *Starve.*

Regard'. Mark, notice, observe ; heed ; esteem ; consider, deem.

ANT. *Disregard, neglect.*

Regard'less. Careless, heedless, indifferent, unmindful.

ANT. *Careful, heedful, mindful.*

Reg'ister. See RECORD.

Regret'. Concern, repentance, sorrow, grief, compunction.

ANT. *Indifference, impenitence.*

Reg'ular. Orderly, methodical, systematic, uniform ; periodic, stated ; ordinary, usual, constant.

ANT. *Irregular, disorderly ; uncertain ; unusual, abnormal.*

Reg'ulate. See ADJUST.

Rehearse'. See RECITE.

Reimburse'. See REFUND.

Rein'. See CHECK.

Reject'. Repel, discard, decline, repudiate.

ANT. *Accept, admit.*

Rejoice'. Exult ; delight. See also CHEER.

ANT. *Weep ; sadden, displease.*

Relate'. Concern. See also RECITE.

Rela'ted. Allied, akin, kindred, cognate.

ANT. *Unrelated, diverse, irrelevant.*

Rela'tion. See REFERENCE and ACCOUNT.

Rela'tions. Relatives, kinsfolk, kinsmen, kindred.

ANT. *Strangers.*

Rel'atives. See RELATIONS.

Relax'. Loosen, slacken, reduce, abate ; unbend.

ANT. *Tighten, increase ; be haughty.*

Release'. See FREE.

Rel'evant. See APPROPRIATE (*adj.*).

Reli'able. See CREDITABLE.

Reli'ance. See CONFIDENCE.

Relief'. Comfort, aid, help, succour, alleviation.

ANT. *Distress, pain.*

Relieve'. See AID.

Relig'ious. Devout, pious, holy, sacred, strict ; monastic.

ANT. *Irreligious, undevout, unholy, profane ; secular.*

Relinqu'ish. See ABANDON.

Rel'ish. Savour, flavour, gusto, appetite.

Rel'ish (*vb.*). Taste, enjoy, like, appreciate.

ANT. *Dislike, disapprove.*

Reluct'ance. See AVERSION.

Reluct'ant. See AVERSE.

Rely'. Depend, confide, trust.

ANT. *Distrust.*

Remain'. Abide, continue. See also LAST.

ANT. *Pass, depart.*

Remaind'er. Balance, residue, leavings, remnants.

Remark'. Notice, heed ; comment, note ; statement.

ANT. *Neglect, disregard ; silence.*

Remark' (*vb.*). Mark, notice, heed, observe ; comment.

ANT. *Overlook, disregard ; be silent.*

Remark'able. See CONSPICUOUS.

Rem'edy. Antidote, cure, medicine, specific ; redress, relief.

ANT. *Disease, malady, sickness.*

Remem'brance. See RECOLLECTION.

Remem'ber. See RECALL.

Remiss'. See REGARDLESS.

Remis'sion. Abatement, relaxation, intermission ; pardon, forgiveness.

ANT. *Increase, augmentation, continuance ; penalty.*

Remit'. Return, send back; relax, abate ; absolve, forgive ; resign.

ANT. *Retain, keep ; increase ; condemn.*

Rem'nant. See REMAINDER.

Remorse'. See REGRET.

Remorseless'. Ruthless, unrelenting, pitiless, cruel, barbarous.

ANT. *Remorseful, pitiful, considerate.*

Remote'. Far, distant, secluded ; alien ; slight.

ANT. *Near ; akin ; considerable.*

Remove'. Move, displace, transfer ; dislodge, take away.

ANT. *Fix, hold, retain.*

Remunera'tion. See RECOMPENSE (*n.*).

Remu'nerate. See COMPENSATE.

Rend'. See SEVER.

Rend'er. Return, restore, pay, give ; translate.

ANT. *Withhold, keep back.*

Ren'egade. See RECREANT.

Renew'. Renovate, repair, resume, revive, restore, repeat.

ANT. *Destroy.*

Renounce'. See ABANDON and REJECT.

Ren'ovate. See RENEW.

Renown'. See FAME.

Renowned'. See CELEBRATED.

Rent'. See BREACH.

Repair'. Mend, patch, restore. See also REDRESS.

ANT. *Break, injure, destroy.*

Repara'tion. See AMENDS.

Repay'. See REFUND.

Repeal'. See ANNUL.

Repeat'. Reiterate, reproduce. See also RECITE.

Repel'. Repulse, withstand, check, resist.

ANT. *Submit, yield.*

Repent'ance. Penitence, remorse, regret, compunction.

ANT. *Impenitence, remorselessness.*

Repine'. Complain, grumble, murmur, grieve, fret.

ANT. *Acquiesce, be patient, submit, smile.*

Replace'. Restore, reinstate ; refund.

ANT. *Remove, take away ; owe.*

Reple'tion. Surfeit, glut, satiety.

ANT. *Lack, scarcity.*

Reply'. Answer, response, rejoinder.

ANT. *Question, letter, challenge.*

Reply' (*vb.*). Answer, rejoin, respond.

ANT. *Question, ask, write letter, challenge.*

Report' (*vb.*). See ADVERTISE.

Report' (*n.*). Announcement, communication, statement ; rumour, tidings ; explosion.

ANT. *Silence.*

Repose'. Rest, sleep, slumber, ease, quiet.

ANT. *Weariness, restlessness, noise.*

Repose' (*vb.*). Rest, sleep, slumber, recline.

ANT. *Be weary, be sleepless, toss.*

Reprehend'. See ADMONISH and REBUFF.

Reprehen'sion. Blame, censure, rebuke, reprimand.

ANT. *Praise, approval.*

Represent'. Exhibit ; stand for. See also PORTRAY.

Representa'tion. Exhibition, show ; personation ; picture, image.

Represent'ative. Agent, deputy, substitute, delegate.

ANT. *Principal, chief, employer.*

Repress'. See CHECK.

Rep'rimand (*vb.*). See ADMONISH and REBUFF.

Rep'rimand (*n.*). See REPREHENSION.

Repri'sal. See RETALIATION.

Reproach' (*vb.*). See ADMONISH and REBUFF.

Reproach' (*n.*). See REPREHENSION.

Rep'robate. See ABANDONED.

Reproof'. See REPREHENSION.

Reprove'. See ADMONISH.

Repu'diate. Renounce, disavow, reject, disown.

ANT. *Avow, admit, own, accept.*

Repug'nance. See REVULSION.

Repug'nant. Distasteful, offensive. See also ADVERSE.

ANT. *Agreeable, pleasant.*

Repul'sive. Repellent, offensive, forbidding, odious, revolting.

ANT. *Attractive, charming, agreeable.*

Re'putable. Estimable. See also CREDITABLE.

ANT. *Worthless.*

Reputa'tion. See CREDIT.

Request' (*n.*). Petition, prayer, entreaty, suit ; demand.

ANT. *Refusal.*

Request' (*vb.*). Ask, desire, petition, solicit, beseech.

ANT. *Refuse, reject.*

Require'. Claim, demand, exact ; need, want.

ANT. *Refuse ; possess.*

Req'uisite. Necessary, needed, needful, indispensable.

ANT. *Unnecessary, needless.*

Requi'tal. Compensation, retribution, satisfaction, remuneration. See also AMENDS.

Requite'. See COMPENSATE.

Rescind'. See ANNUL.

Res'cue. Save, deliver, free, extricate.

ANT. *Destroy, capture.*

Resemb'lance. Likeness, semblance, similarity, image.

ANT. *Unlikeness, dissimilarity.*

Resent'ment. See ANGER.

Reserve' (*vb.*). Keep back, hold, retain, withhold.

ANT. *Give, grant, offer.*

Reserve' (*n.*). Constraint, caution, shyness ; store.

ANT. *Unreserve, openness, frankness.*

Reserved'. Constrained, shy, cautious, cold.

ANT. *Unreserved, unconstrained, frank ; ardent.*

Reside'. Dwell, live, sojourn, inhabit.

Res'idence. Sojourn, inhabitancy, stay ; home, domicile, dwelling, house.

ANT. *Absence.*

Res'idue. See REMNANT.

Resign'. Renounce, give up, surrender, cede, abdicate, quit.

ANT. *Accept, keep, hold.*

Resigna'tion. Surrender, abandonment ; a c q u i e s c e n c e, patience.

ANT. *Capture, tenure ; impatience.*

Resist'. Withstand, oppose, confront, thwart.

ANT. *Attack, coerce, force.*

Resist'ance. Opposition, hindrance, check.

ANT. *Attack, coercion.*

Res'olute. Determined, bold, decided, firm, inflexible, steadfast.

ANT. *Irresolute, undecided, weak, inconstant.*

Resolu'tion. Resolve, determination, courage, steadfastness, firmness ; proposal, motion.

ANT. *Weakness, indecision.*

Resolve'. Analyse, break up ; solve, explain away ; determine, purpose, decide.

ANT. *Blend, fuse ; confuse ; be undecided.*

Resort' (*vb.*). Go, repair, have recourse to, apply.

ANT. *Leave, depart, go away.*

Resort'. Retreat, haunt, refuge.

Resound'. Reverberate, echo, ring, re-echo.

Resource'. Means, expedient, device.

Respect' (*vb.*). Honour, esteem, reverence ; defer to.

ANT. *Dishonour, disregard, treat disrespectfully.*

Respect' (*n.*). Reference, regard ; honour, esteem, deference.

ANT. *Dishonour, irreverence, disrespect.*

Respect'able. See CREDITABLE and REPUTABLE.

Respect'ful. Reverential, deferential, dutiful, submissive.

ANT. *Disrespectful, undutiful.*

Res'pite. Pause, cessation, interval ; reprieve.

ANT. *Continuance, perpetuity.*

Resplend'ent. See BRIGHT.

Respond'. Reply, answer ; correspond, suit.

ANT. *Speak, question, write ; differ.*

Response'. Answer, reply, rejoinder.

ANT. *Speech, question, letter.*

Rest' (*n.*). See REPOSE and RESPITE.

Rest' (*vb.*). Pause, stop, stay, repose, recline, remain.

ANT. *Go on, continue, move, stand.*

Restitu'tion. See AMENDS.

Rest'ive. Impatient, uneasy, restless, obstinate.

ANT. *Patient, submissive.*

Restora'tion. Recovery, reinstatement, renewal, renovation, rebuilding ; reparation, amends.

ANT. *Destruction ; injury.*

Restore'. Repay, return, give back ; rebuild, renew ; reinstate ; heal, cure.

ANT. *Owe, withhold ; destroy ; make worse.*

Restrain'. See CHECK.

Restraint'. Check, hindrance, prevention ; reserve ; confinement.

ANT. *Freedom, licence ; frankness.*

Restrict'. Limit, confine, bound.

ANT. *License, permit.*

Restric'tion. Limitation, confinement.

ANT. *Licence, freedom.*

Result' (*n.*). Effect, consequence, event.

ANT. *Cause, origin.*

Result' (*vb.*). Arise, follow, ensue, end.

ANT. *Originate, cause.*

Resume'. Take back, continue, renew, begin again.

ANT. *Assume, take up, begin.*

Retain'. See RESERVE.

Retal'iate. Revenge, repay, requite.

ANT. *Forgive.*

Retalia'tion. Requital, revenge, reprisal, retribution.

ANT. *Forgiveness, mercy.*

Retard'. Hinder, impede, obstruct, clog, delay.

ANT. *Help, hasten, advance.*

Ret'icent. See RESERVED.

Retire'. Draw back, withdraw, recede, retreat.

ANT. *Advance, go forward, charge.*

Retire'ment. Withdrawal, retreat, seclusion, privacy.

ANT. *Advance, publicity.*

Retract'. Withdraw, take back, revoke. See also ABJURE.

ANT. *Affirm, argue.*

Retreat'. See RETIRE.

Retreat' (*n.*). See RETIREMENT and HARBOUR.

Retrench'. Diminish, cut down, curtail, decrease, lessen.

ANT. *Increase, enlarge.*

Retrench'ment. Diminution, curtailment, reduction, economy.

ANT. *Increase, extension, extravagance.*

Retribu'tion. See RETALIATION.

Retrieve'. See RECOVER.

Ret'rospect. Review, reminiscence, survey.

ANT. *Prospect, anticipation.*

Return'. Revert, come back ; restore, repay, requite.

ANT. *Depart ; refuse, withhold.*

Reveal'. Publish, disclose, open, impart.

ANT. *Conceal, suppress.*

Rev'el. Feast, carouse, riot, luxuriate.

ANT. *Be sober.*

Revenge' (*n.*). Vengeance. See also RETALIATION.

Revenge' (*vb.*). Avenge, requite, retaliate, vindicate.

Revenge'ful. Malicious, spiteful, resentful.

ANT. *Benevolent, kindly, gentle.*

Rev'enue. Receipts, profit, income, proceeds.

ANT. *Outlay.*

Rev'erence. See ADORATION and RESPECT.

Reverse' (*vb.*). Invert, overturn, overthrow ; cancel, repeal.

ANT. *Erect, restore, repair.*

Review' (*vb.*). Reconsider, reexamine, revise, inspect ; criticize.

ANT. *Forecast.*

Review' (*n.*). Re-examination, reconsideration, inspection ; criticism.

ANT. *Forecast.*

Revile'. See ABUSE.

Revise'. See REVIEW and AMELIORATE.

Revive'. Reanimate, renew, quicken, resuscitate ; comfort, invigorate.

ANT. *Depress.*

Revoke'. See REPEAL.

Revolt'. Rebel, mutiny, resist ; nauseate, shock.

ANT. *Be loyal, obey, submit ; please.*

Revolt'ing. See NOXIOUS.

Revolve'. Circulate, twist, gyrate, whirl ; meditate, ponder.

ANT. *Stand firm.*

Revul'sion. Repugnance, abhorrence, loathing.

ANT. *Liking, fondness.*

Reward' (*n.*). Pay, requital, recompense. See also AMENDS.

ANT. *Service.*

Reward' (*vb.*). See COMPENSATE.

Rich'. Opulent, wealthy, affluent ; copious, abundant, plentiful, costly, precious ; fertile.

ANT. *Poor, needy ; scanty, worthless ; barren.*

Rich'es. Affluence, wealth, opulence, abundance.

ANT. *Poverty, need, scarcity.*

Rid'icule. Banter, rally, chaff, deride, mock.

ANT. *Flatter, humour, encourage.*

Ridic'ulous. Laughable, absurd, comic, grotesque, preposterous.

ANT. *Grave, serious, tragic.*

Ri'fle. See RANSACK.

Rift'. See BREACH.

Right' (*adj.*). Straight ; upright ; just, equitable, lawful ; correct, true ; proper, suitable.

ANT. *Crooked ; low ; unjust, inequitable, unlawful ; incorrect, untrue ; improper, unfit, wrong.*

Right' (*n.*). Rectitude, justice ; uprightness ; truth, goodness ; immunity, privilege.

ANT. *Turpitude, injustice, badness ; wrong.*

Right'eous. Just, godly, upright, virtuous, honest.

ANT. *Unjust, ungodly, dishonest.*

Right'eousness. Uprightness, godliness, piety ; equity, honesty.

ANT. *Ungodliness, impiety, injustice, dishonesty.*

Right'ful. Lawful, legitimate, equitable, reasonable.

ANT. *Wrong, unlawful, illegitimate, inequitable, unreasonable.*

Rig'id. Stiff, unyielding, unbending. See also AUSTERE.

ANT. *Yielding.*

Rig'our. Stiffness, rigidness, sternness, austerity ; inclemency.

ANT. *Pliability ; mildness.*

Ri'ot. Uproar, tumult, fray, row, commotion.

ANT. *Calmness, quiet.*

Ripe'. See MATURE.

Rise'. Arise, ascend, get up, grow, increase, enlarge.
ANT. *Fall, descend, decline.*

Rise' (*n.*). Ascent, acclivity, elevation ; source, origin ; augmentation, increase.
ANT. *Fall, decline.*

Ri'sible. See COMIC.

Risk'. See HAZARD.

Ri'val. Competitor, opponent, combatant, antagonist.

Road'. Way, highway, course, path, route.

Roam'. See RAMBLE.

Roar'. Bawl, yell, howl, vociferate.

Rob'. See PLUNDER.

Rob'bery. Spoliation, depredation, plunder, pillage, filching, pilfering, theft, stealing.

Robust'. See H A L E and STRONG.

Robust'ness See HEALTH.

Rogue'. See CAITIFF.

Rogu'ish. Dishonest, cheating, fraudulent, knavish ; frolicsome, waggish.
ANT. *Honest, straight, serious.*

Roll' (*n.*). See CATALOGUE and LIST.

Roll' (*vb.*). Trundle, revolve, rotate, gyrate ; flow.
ANT. *Stand still, be fixed.*

Roman'tic. Legendary, fanciful, quixotic, sentimental.
ANT. *Ordinary, matter-of-fact, practical.*

Room'. Scope, field, space ; chamber, saloon, apartment.

Root'. Cause, origin, source. See also BASE.
ANT. *Top, summit.*

Ro'seate. Rose, red, blushing, blooming.

Rot'ten. See PUTRID.

Rough'. Rugged, coarse ; unfinished ; severe, violent ; harsh, gruff, rude.
ANT. *Smooth, perfect ; mild, gentle.*

Round'. Circular, spherical, globular ; entire, full, complete.

Rouse'. See AROUSE.

Rout'. See OVERTHROW.

Rove'. See RAMBLE.

Roy'al. Kingly, regal, princely. See also AUGUST.
ANT. *Common, humble.*

Route'. See ROAD.

Rub'. Scrape, abrade, grate ; clean, wipe.
ANT. *Stain, defile, corrupt.*

Rub'bish. Débris, litter, refuse ; trash, nonsense.

Ru'bicund. Ruddy, florid, reddish.

Rude'. Rugged, rough ; vulgar, uncouth, churlish, insolent, impudent.
ANT. *Smooth ; finished : civil, polite.*

Rudiment'al. Embryo, rudimentary, primary, elemental.
ANT. *Final, finished.*

Rue'. See MOURN.

Rue'ful. See MOURNFUL.

Ruf'fle. Pucker, wrinkle ; disturb, perturb, agitate ; disarrange.
ANT. *Straighten, calm.*

Rug'ged. See ROUGH.

Ru'in (*n.*). Destruction, downfall, defeat, wreck ; impoverishment.
ANT. *Repair, recovery ; prosperity.*

Ru'in (*vb.*). Destroy, wreck, demolish, overthrow, impoverish.
ANT. *Restore, set up ; enrich.*

Ru'inous. Dilapidated ; injurious, harmful, destructive, pernicious.
ANT. *Whole, sound ; beneficial, useful.*

Rule'. Sway, government, control, reign, authority ; law, canon, precept, standard, guide, principle.
ANT. *Subjection.*

Rule' (*vb.*). Govern, control, direct ; reign ; decide.
ANT. *Obey, be subject ; leave open.*

Ru'minate. See COGITATE.

Ru'mour. Report, hearsay, story, fame, tidings.

ANT. *Fact, truth.*

Run'. Hurry, race, fly, flee, rush, dart, scamper.

ANT. *Stand, wait.*

Rup'ture. Breach, break, disrupture. See also ALTERCATION.

ANT. *Healing, juncture.*

Ruse'. Artifice, dodge, trick, stratagem, wile.

Rush'. Dash, dart, speed, sweep, hurry.

ANT. *Stand still, be stagnant.*

Rust'. Dross, crust, mould, mildew.

Rus'tic. Rural, countrified; simple, rude, clownish.

ANT. *Urban, oppidan : enlightened ; polished.*

Ruth'less. See CRUEL.

S

Sack'. See PILLAGE and PLUNDER.

Sa'cred. Hallowed, consecrated, holy, divine, inviolable.

ANT. *Profane, unconsecrated, unhallowed.*

Sac'rifice. Offering, oblation, immolation, surrender.

Sacrileg'ious. Profane, impious, irreverent, desecrating.

ANT. *Pious, reverent, hallowing.*

Sad'. See MOURNFUL.

Sad'dle. Load, burden, encumber.

ANT. *Unload, disburden.*

Sad'ness. See MISERY.

Safe'. Secure, unharmed, unhurt, trustworthy, sure, certain, reliable.

ANT. *Unsafe, insecure, untrustworthy, unreliable.*

Saga'cious. See ACUTE.

Sage'. See ACUTE.

Saga'city. See PRUDENCE.

Sake'. Purpose, reason, end, regard, account.

Sal'ary. See HIRE.

Sa'lient. See CONSPICUOUS.

Sal'ly. Sortie, digression, frolic, joke, witticism.

Salu'brious. Healthy, wholesome, salutary.

ANT. *Unhealthy, unwholesome.*

Sal'utary. See SALUBRIOUS.

Saluta'tion. Greeting, address, welcome.

ANT. *Farewell, adieu, good-bye.*

Salute'. See GREET.

Same'ness. Identity, uniformity, similarity, monotony.

ANT. *Variety, diversity, dissimilarity.*

Sam'ple. See EXAMPLE.

Sanc'tion. See AUTHORIZE.

Sanc'tion (*n.*). See APPROBATION.

Sane'. Sound, healthy, sober, sensible.

ANT. *Unsound, unhealthy, insane, senseless.*

Sangu'inary. Bloody, bloodthirsty, cruel, savage.

ANT. *Bloodless, harmless, mild.*

Sangu'ine. Red. See also ARDENT.

Sa'pient. See ACUTE.

Sate'. Gorge, glut, satisfy, satiate.

ANT. *Discontent, dissatisfy, disappoint.*

Sa'tiate. See SATE.

Satir'ical. Poignant, pungent, sarcastic, censorious.

ANT. *Genial, kindly, uncritical.*

Satisfac'tion. Contentment, gratification, complacency, payment, discharge. See also AMENDS.

ANT. *Dissatisfaction, discontent.*

Sat'isfy. Convince, assure. See also SATE.

ANT. *Dissatisfy.*

Sau'cy. Impertinent, rude, forward, impudent.

ANT. *Polite, deferential, modest, reserved.*

Saun'ter. See RAMBLE.

Sav'age. See BARBAROUS.

Save'. Preserve, deliver, rescue, reserve, hold, keep, economize, retrench.

ANT. *Destroy, throw away, reject, waste.*

Sa'vour. Taste, relish, odour, smell.

Sa'voury. Tasty, palatable, piquant, nice, agreeable.

ANT. *Unsavoury, tasteless, unpalatable, unpleasant.*

Saw'. See ADAGE.

Say'ing. Remark, statement. See also ADAGE.

Scand'al. Shame, infamy, slander, calumny, obloquy.

ANT. *Credit, praise.*

Scand'alize. Shock, disgust, offend, horrify.

ANT. *Appease.*

Scant'y. Scant, insufficient, short, slender, pinched, meagre.

ANT. *Abundant, plentiful, full.*

Scarce'. See RARE.

Scar'city. See DEARTH.

Scare'. See AFFRIGHT.

Scathe'less. Unharmed, unhurt, uninjured.

ANT. *Wounded, injured, hurt.*

Scat'ter. Strew, sprinkle, disperse, dispel, disseminate, waste.

ANT. *Retain, hold, economize, husband.*

Scene'. See EXHIBITION.

Scent. See PERFUME.

Sched'ule. See LIST.

Scheme'. See DRAFT and PLAN.

Schol'ar. See PUPIL.

Schol'arship. See KNOWLEDGE.

School'. Seminary, academy, gymnasium, sect, class, disciples.

ANT. *Teacher, professor, master.*

Scin'tillate. See CORUSCATE.

Sci'on. Offshoot, slip, branch, offspring, child.

ANT. *Stock, root, family.*

Scoff'. See DERIDE and JEER.

Scold'. Abuse, vituperate, blame, reprimand, chide.

ANT. *Encourage, soothe, praise.*

Scope'. Aim, design, view, drift, range, room, opportunity.

Scorn' (*n.*). See CONTUMELY.

Scorn' (*vb.*). See CONTEMN.

Scorn'ful. See CONTEMPTUOUS.

Scoun'drel. See CAITIFF.

Scourge' (*n.*). Whip, lash, plague, pest.

Scourge' (*vb.*). Whip, lash, punish, plague.

Scout'. Reconnoitre. See also CONTEMN.

Scrag'gy. Rugged, jagged, uneven, lean, emaciated, skinny.

ANT. *Smooth, even, plump, buxom, corpulent.*

Scrap'. See FRAGMENT.

Screen'. Hide, conceal, cover, mask, defend, shelter.

ANT. *Reveal, show, expose.*

Scrimp'. See ABRIDGE.

Scru'ple (*n.*). Doubt, misgiving, perplexity, difficulty.

ANT. *Confidence, assurance.*

Scru'ple. Hesitate, waver, doubt.

ANT. *Be confident.*

Scru'pulous. See CONSCIENTIOUS.

Scru'tinize. Investigate, examine, sift, explore, scan.

ANT. *Ignore, leave.*

Scru'tiny. See EXAMINATION.

Scur'rilous. See VULGAR.

Scurv'y. See CONTEMPTIBLE.

Sear'. Dry, wither, scorch.

ANT. *Revive, water.*

Search' (*n.*). Scrutiny, inquiry, investigation. See also EXAMINATION.

Search' (*vb.*). See SCRUTINIZE.

Sea'son. Period, term, time, juncture, occasion.

Seas'onable. Timely, opportune, fit. See also APPROPRIATE.

ANT. *Untimely, inopportune, unseasonable.*

Seclu'sion. Separation, withdrawal. See also SECRECY.

ANT. *Publicity.*

Sec'ondary. See INFERIOR.

Se'crecy. Concealment, privacy, seclusion.

ANT. *Publicity, openness.*

Se'cret. Concealed, hidden, private, secluded. See also CLANDESTINE.

ANT. *Public, open.*

Sec'ular. Temporal, civil, lay, profane, worldly.

ANT. *Eternal, religious, pious, unworldly.*

Secure'. See SAFE.

Secure' (*vb.*). Guard, protect, fasten, bind, get, obtain, acquire.

ANT. *Leave unguarded, untie, unfasten, loosen ; lose.*

Secu'rity. Guard, protection, shelter, safety, guarantee, pledge, pawn.

ANT. *Insecurity.*

Sedate'. Calm, composed, serene, sober, serious.

ANT. *Perturbed, agitated, excited, foolish.*

Sed'iment. See DREGS.

Sedi'tion. See MUTINY.

Sedi'tious. See MUTINOUS.

Seduce'. See ALLURE.

Seduc'tive. Alluring, enticing, tempting, specious.

ANT. *Repelling, repulsive.*

Sed'ulous. Assiduous, industrious, busy, constant, persevering.

ANT. *Idle, inconstant.*

See'. Behold, view, descry, note, mark, perceive, discern, understand.

Seek'. Search, look for, ask, demand, attempt, endeavour.

Seem'ly. See BECOMING.

Seg'ment. Part, portion, section.

ANT. *Whole.*

Seize'. See CATCH.

Select'. Choose, pick, elect, prefer.

Self'ish. Greedy, self-seeking, mean, mercenary, greedy.

ANT. *Unselfish, unmercenary.*

Sell'. Vend, retail, hawk.

ANT. *Buy, purchase.*

Sem'blance. Resemblance, likeness, form, figure.

ANT. *Unlikeness.*

Sem'inary. See SCHOOL.

Send'. Cast, throw, forward, transmit, despatch.

ANT. *Hold, keep, stay.*

Se'nile. Aged, doting, imbecile.

ANT. *Juvenile, sprightly.*

Senior'ity. Priority, eldership, precedence.

Sensa'tion. Feeling, sense, impression, excitement.

ANT. *Dullness, paralysis.*

Sense'. Feeling, sensation, appreciation, perception, reason, mind, intelligence, meaning, import, purport, signification.

ANT. *Insensitiveness, dullness, stupidity, nonsense.*

Sense'less. See ABSURD.

Sens'ible. Perceptible, tangible ; aware, cognizant, conscious, intelligent, reasonable, wise, sound, judicious.

ANT. *Imperceptible, intangible ; unaware, unconscious, unintelligent, stupid, unsound, injudicious.*

Sens'itive. Susceptible, impressible, delicate, tender.

ANT. *Insusceptible, unimpressible, hard.*

Sens'ual. Carnal, fleshly, animal, voluptuous.

ANT. *Ascetic, spiritual.*

Sen'tence. Doom, decision, judgment, passage, proposition.

Sen'timent. Emotion, sensibility, notion, opinion, thought.

ANT. *Insensibility, belief, certainty.*

Sep'arate. Part, divide, detach, sever, sunder, detach, disjoin.

ANT. *Join, attach, bind.*

Se'quel. See CONSEQUENCE.

Serene'. See BRIGHT and CALM.

Se'ries. Order, row, sequence, line, succession.

ANT. *Confusion, jumble, medley.*

Se'rious. Grave, earnest, sober, thoughtful, momentous, important.

ANT. *Trivial, light-hearted, thoughtless, unimportant.*

Serv'ant. Serf, slave, menial, attendant, helper.

ANT. *Master, lord, superior.*

Serve'. Minister, aid, attend, benefit, forward, satisfy.

ANT. *Rule, govern, hinder.*

Serv'ice. Work, employment, duty, office, advantage, use, respect.

ANT. *Idleness, unemployment, disadvantage, disrespect.*

Ser'viceable. Beneficial, advantageous, profitable.

ANT. *Disadvantageous, unprofitable.*

Serv'ile. Slavish, menial. See also ABJECT.

ANT. *Masterly, lordly.*

Servil'ity. Bondage, slavishness, obsequiousness, meanness.

ANT. *Freedom, liberty, lordliness.*

Serv'itude. Slavery, bondage, thraldom, vassalage.

ANT. *Freedom, liberty.*

Set'. Place, locate, settle, fix, appoint, assign; sink, decline.

ANT. *Remove, disorder; rise.*

Set'tle. Fix, establish, found, colonize, quiet, tranquillize, compose, fall, sink.

ANT. *Disestablish, unfix, intensify.*

Sev'er. See SEPARATE.

Severe'. See AUSTERE.

Sever'ity. Harshness, cruelty, sternness, intensity, violence, strictness, simplicity.

ANT. *Gentleness, mildness, inexactness, ornateness.*

Shack'le. Fetter, chain, impede, hamper, embarrass.

ANT. *Loose, release, aid, ease.*

Shade' (*vb.*). Cloud, dim, obscure, cover, protect.

ANT. *Reveal, illuminate.*

Shadow (*n.*). Shade, darkness, gloom, ghost, spectre, phantom, image.

ANT. *Light, brightness; substance.*

Shake'. Quake, shiver. See also FLUSTER.

Shal'low. Not deep, flimsy, empty, trivial, superficial.

ANT. *Deep, profound, weighty, serious.*

Shame'. Abashment, disgrace, infamy, dishonour.

ANT. *Immodesty, credit, honour.*

Shame'ful. Disgraceful, infamous, discreditable, ignominious.

ANT. *Creditable, honourable.*

Shame'less. Brazen, audacious, impudent, abandoned, indecent, unblushing.

ANT. *Shameful, modest, decent, respectable.*

Shape'. See FORM.

Shape'ly. Graceful, elegant, comely, well-formed.

ANT. *Ungraceful, inelegant, uncomely, ill-formed.*

Share' (*vb.*). See ALLOT.

Share' (*n.*). Lot, portion, part, quota.

ANT. *Whole, entirety.*

Sharp'. See ACUTE and BITTER.

Sheer'. Pure, unmixed, mere, bare, naked.

ANT. *Mixed, impure.*

Shel'ter. See HARBOUR.

Shift'. Change, displace, remove, transfer, veer.

ANT. *Fix, stand still.*

Shine'. Gleam, glare, radiate, glisten, glitter, sparkle.

ANT. *Be dim, be dull.*

Shiv'er. Shatter, break. See also FLUSTER and SHAKE.

ANT. *Mend, repair.*

Shock' (*n.*). Collision, clash, blow, concussion.

Shock' (*vb.*). Stun, astound, appal, terrify, offend.
ANT. *Delight, soothe, appease.*

Shock'ing. Appalling, horrifying, frightful, offensive, disgusting.
ANT. *Soothing, delightful, agreeable.*

Short'. Low, brief, laconic, succinct, abrupt, scanty, destitute.
ANT. *High, long, verbose, abundant, rich.*

Short'en. See ABRIDGE.

Shove'. See PUSH.

Show'. Publish, prove. See also DISPLAY.

Show' (*n.*). See EXHIBITION.

Show'y. See FLASHY.

Shred'. See FRAGMENT.

Shrewd'. See ACUTE.

Shrewd'ness. Cunning, craft, sagacity, intelligence, acumen.
ANT. *Simplicity, artlessness, stupidity.*

Shud'der. See SHIVER.

Shuf'fle. Mix, confuse; quibble, cavil, prevaricate, equivocate.
ANT. *Clear; speak truly, be frank.*

Shun'. See AVOID.

Shut'. Close, fasten, bar; imprison, confine.
ANT. *Open, unbar, unfasten; enlarge, set free.*

Shy'. Bashful, coy, reserved, retiring; suspicious.
ANT. *Audacious, bold, impudent; trusting.*

Sick'. Ill, ailing, weak, indisposed; disgusted.
ANT. *Well, cured, healed, strong; pleased, delighted.*

Sick'ly. Morbid, unhealthy. See also SICK.

Sick'ness. Ailment, illness, disease, malady, disorder.
ANT. *Health, healing, strength.*

Side'. Margin, border, verge, rim; party, cause.
ANT. *Interior.*

Sift'. Bolt. See also CANVASS.

Sight'. Vision, view, seeing, perception. See also EXHIBITION.

Sign'. Mark, token, badge, proof, indication, type, symptom.

Sig'nal. See CONSPICUOUS.

Signif'icant. Indicative, expressive, pregnant; important, weighty.
ANT. *Unexpressive, pointless; unimportant, trivial.*

Sig'nify. Import, indicate, denote, imply, mean; declare.

Si'lence (*n.*). Hush, calm, quiet, stillness.
ANT. *Noise, clamour, babel.*

Si'lence (*vb.*). Hush, calm, quiet; quell, stifle, muzzle.
ANT. *Disturb, arouse.*

Sil'ly. Foolish, stupid, brainless, foolish; absurd, ridiculous.
ANT. *Wise, sensible, intelligent.*

Simil'itude. Similarity, likeness, image; comparison.
ANT. *Dissimilarity.*

Sim'ple. Unmixed, elementary; plain, unadorned; natural, unsophisticated; credulous, silly.
ANT. *Mixed; gaudy, showy; sophisticated; suspicious.*

Sin'. Crime, wrong, evil, trespass, transgression, wickedness.
ANT. *Good, virtue.*

Sincere'. Genuine, true, unvarnished, unaffected, frank, honest, plain.
ANT. *False, untrue; made up; dishonest.*

Sincer'ity. Honesty, frankness, plainness, veracity.
ANT. *Dishonesty, deceit.*

Sing'le. Sole, separate, individual; alone, solitary.
ANT. *Multiple; combined.*

Sing'ular. Sole, individual; exceptional, peculiar, extraordinary; eccentric, odd.
ANT. *Plural; ordinary, commonplace, normal.*

Sin'ister. Evil ; unlucky, inauspicious, unfavourable, ill-omened.
ANT. *Good ; lucky, auspicious, well-omened.*

Sin'uous. Curved, winding, crooked.
ANT. *Straight, direct.*

Situa'tion. Place, position, location ; condition, state, predicament ; office, berth, employment, post.

Size'. See BULK.

Sketch'. Drawing, outline, plot.
ANT. *Picture, painting.*

Skil'ful. See ADROIT.

Skill'. See ABILITY and DEXTERITY.

Skir'mish. See COMBAT.

Slack'. Loose, easy, relaxed. See also INERT.
ANT. *Tight, firm, stiff.*

Slack'en. See ABATE.

Slan'der. See ASPERSE.

Slaugh'ter. Bloodshed. See also CARNAGE.

Slav'ish. See SERVILE.

Slay'. Kill, murder, slaughter, assassinate, destroy.
ANT. *Spare, keep alive.*

Sleek'. Smooth, silken, shiny, glossy.
ANT. *Rough.*

Sleep'y. Somnolent, drowsy, heavy, torpid, lethargic.
ANT. *Wakeful, lively, active.*

Slen'der. Slim, fragile, slight, weak ; slight, inconsiderable, scanty, meagre.
ANT. *Stout, corpulent, strong ; adequate, abundant.*

Slight'. See SLENDER.

Slight' (*vb.*). Disdain, neglect, overlook, scout.
ANT. *Flatter, court, favour.*

Slim'. See SLENDER.

Sling'. Hurl, cast, fling, throw ; hoist, hang.

Slip'pery Smooth ; uncertain, unstable ; treacherous, deceptive, evasive.
ANT. *Rough, steady, honest, straightforward.*

Sloth'. Torpor, inertia, inactivity ; idleness, indolence.
ANT. *Activity, vigour ; industry, sedulity.*

Sloth'ful. See IDLE.

Slov'enly. Untidy, dowdy, slatternly ; slack, disorderly.
ANT. *Tidy, neat ; orderly, careful.*

Slow'. Deliberate, dilatory ; late ; inactive, dull, stupid.
ANT. *Quick, fast, rapid ; in time ; bright, intelligent.*

Slug'gish. See INERT.

Slur'. Stigma, ban, reproach, stain.
ANT. *Credit, praise.*

Sly'. See CRAFTY.

Small'. Little, diminutive, puny ; trivial, petty ; scanty, inadequate ; mean, sordid.
ANT. *Large, big, great ; serious ; adequate, ample ; generous.*

Smart'. Piercing, sharp ; quick, active ; clever, witty ; spruce, dashing.
ANT. *Blunt ; slow dull ; shabby.*

Smear'. Smudge, blot, daub, tarnish.
ANT. *Wipe, polish, clean.*

Smell'. Odour, scent, perfume, fragrance.

Smite'. Strike, beat, hit ; slay, destroy ; chasten, afflict.
ANT. *Spare.*

Smooth'. (*adj.*). Level, even, polished, sleek ; bland, easy, flattering.
ANT. *Rough, uneven, unpolished ; brusque.*

Smoothe (*vb.*). Level, flatten. See also ALLAY.

Smoth'er. Choke, suffocate ; stifle, suppress, conceal.
ANT. *Reveal.*

Snare'. Trap, net, gin, foil, springe, device.

Snatch'. Pluck, pull, seize, catch, grasp.

Sneak'. Slink, skulk ; cringe, fawn, truckle.

Sneer'. See JEER.

Snug'. Close, comfortable, cosy, sheltered.
ANT. *Uncomfortable, unsheltered.*

Soak'. Wet, drench, steep.
ANT. *Dry.*

Soar'. Mount, arise, ascend, fly.
ANT. *Sink, fall, drop.*

So'ber. Moderate, calm, grave, self-possessed ; abstemious.
ANT. *Immoderate, excited ; tipsy, drunk.*

Sobri'ety. Abstemiousness, calmness, gravity, moderation.
ANT. *Intemperance, excitability, extravagance.*

So'ciable. Companionable, affable, friendly, festive, genial.
ANT. *Unsociable, unfriendly, uncompanionable ; gloomy, cheerless.*

So'cial. Gregarious, interdependent ; festive.
ANT. *Anti-social, independent, exclusive.*

Soci'ety. See ASSOCIATION.

Soft'. Plastic, flexible, yielding ; gentle, tender ; foolish, silly ; easy, light.
ANT. *Hard, stubborn, unyielding ; sensible ; difficult, weighty.*

Soil' (*vb.*). Defile, foul, pollute, stain, taint, besmear.
ANT. *Cleanse, purify, wipe.*

So'journ. See DWELL.

Sol'ace. Console, comfort, relieve.
ANT. *Vex, pain, annoy.*

Sole'. Single, individual, one, only, exclusive, solitary.
ANT. *Corporate ; many.*

Sol'emn. Formal, ceremonial, sacred, religious ; serious, grave, impressive.
ANT. *Informal ; profane ; trivial.*

Solem'nity. Ceremony, ceremonial ; sacredness ; seriousness, impressiveness.
ANT. *Profanity ; levity.*

Solic'it. See BESEECH.

Solic'itous. Anxious, apprehensive, desirous, concerned, uneasy.
ANT. *Careless, unconcerned, indifferent.*

Sol'id. Firm, compact, hard, dense, substantial.
ANT. *Liquid, flabby, soft.*

Sol'itary. Lone, lonely ; single, sole ; secluded, sequestered.
ANT. *Companionable, sociable ; associated, combined ; open.*

Sol'itude. Loneliness, seclusion, isolation ; desert.
ANT. *Company, association.*

Solu'tion. Liquefaction, melting ; explanation, resolution, key, answer.
ANT. *Hardening, condensation.*

Solve'. See ELUCIDATE.

Som'bre. Gloomy, dark, dull, dismal, melancholy, funereal.
ANT. *Bright, cheerful, cloudless, gay.*

Song'. Chant, air, ballad, ditty, hymn, lay, strain.

Sono'rous. High-sounding, resounding, resonant, ringing.
ANT. *Low, soft, inaudible.*

Soon'. Early, immediately, shortly, anon.
ANT. *Late, later.*

Soothe'. See ALLAY.

Sooth'sayer. Seer, prophet, foreteller.

Sor'cery. Witchcraft, magic, wizardry, necromancy.

Sord'id. Dirty, foul ; mean, covetous, niggardly.
ANT. *Clean ; generous.*

Sor'row. Grief, affliction, distress ; regret, vexation ; adversity.
ANT. *Joy, happiness, pleasure.*

Sor'ry. Grieved, afflicted, distressed ; regretful ; poor, shabby.
ANT. *Joyous, pleased ; handsome, costly.*

Sort'. See GENUS and KIND.

Sort' (*vb.*). See CLASSIFY.

Soul'. Mind, life, spirit, essence; courage, ardour, animation, vivacity.

ANT. *Body ; dullness, apathy.*

Sound' (*adj.*). Whole, uninjured; hale, healthy, vigorous; reasonable, sane, rational; profound; correct, right.

ANT. *Unsound, damaged ; sick, unhealthy ; irrational, insane ; light ; unorthodox.*

Sour'. Acid, tart, sharp, pungent; crabbed, morose, churlish.

ANT. *Sweet ; joyous, genial.*

Source'. See FOUNT.

Sove'reign. Royal, regal, imperial; chief, paramount; effectual, efficacious.

ANT. *Subject , ineffectual.*

Spa'cious. See AMPLE.

Spare' (*adj.*). Scanty, scarce, stinted; lean, thin, lanky; additional.

ANT. *Ample, abundant ; stout, corpulent.*

Spark'.e. See GLEAM and GLITTER.

Spec'ial. Peculiar, particular, distinctive, individual; extraordinary, exceptional.

ANT. *Ordinary, general.*

Spe'cies. See GENUS.

Specif'ic. Peculiar, particular, especial, characteristic; precise.

ANT. *General, ordinary ; inexact, vague.*

Spec'ify. Mention, designate, particularize, define, state.

ANT. *Leave unsaid.*

Spec'imen. Sample, example, model, proof, illustration.

Spe'cious. Seeming, plausible, fair, showy.

ANT. *Real, genuine ; unattractive.*

Speck'. See BLEMISH.

Spect'acle. See EXHIBITION.

Specta'tor. Onlooker, bystander, witness, observer, beholder.

ANT. *Actor, performer.*

Spect're. See GHOST.

Specula'tion. Thought, contemplation; theory, conjecture.

ANT. *Action ; fact.*

Speech'. Language, tongue, idiom; talk, harangue, address, oration.

ANT. *Silence.*

Speed'. See HASTE.

Speed'y. Quick, nimble, fleet; prompt, early.

ANT. *Slow, tardy, unready.*

Spend'. Expend, disburse; lay out; waste, consume, exhaust; employ, bestow.

ANT. *Save, spare.*

Sphere'. Globe, orb; range, compass; province, office : rank.

Spir'it. Soul, spectre, ghost; courage, temper, animation, enthusiasm; character, intention.

ANT. *Body ; cowardice, timidity ; apathy.*

Spir'ited. See ARDENT and BOLD.

Spi'ritless. See DEJECTED.

Spir'itual. Non-material, ghostly; holy, pure, religious.

ANT. *Material ; irreligious, secular.*

Spite'. See MALICE.

Spleen'. Melancholy, despondency. See also ANGER.

Splend'id. Gorgeous, sumptuous, magnificent. See also BRIGHT.

ANT. *Shabby, cheap, ordinary.*

Split'. See BREAK.

Spoil'. Impair, mar, disfigure; corrupt. See also PLUNDER.

ANT. *Repair, restore.*

Sponta'neous. Voluntary, willing, unconstrained, gratuitous.

ANT. *Involuntary, compulsory.*

Sport'. Play, game, diversion, amusement; mockery.

ANT. *Labour, work, toil.*

Spot'. Locality, place. See also BLEMISH.

111

Spread'. Expand, extend, stretch, dilate ; diffuse, circulate.

ANT. *Contract ; suppress.*

Spright'ly. See ACTIVE.

Spring'. Bound, leap, jump ; arise, proceed, start.

ANT. *Stand still ; cause, originate.*

Sprite'. See GHOST.

Spur'. See AROUSE.

Spu'rious. Illegitimate, counterfeit, sham, adulterate.

ANT. *Genuine, legitimate.*

Spurn'. Kick, repel, despise, contemn, reject.

ANT. *Flatter, approve.*

Squal'id. Dirty, filthy ; poor, mean.

ANT. *Clean, bright, costly.*

Squand'er. Dissipate, waste, consume, lavish.

ANT. *Save, economize, husband.*

Squeam'ish. Fastidious, overnice, punctilious.

ANT. *Indifferent, careless.*

Stab'. Pierce, transfix, wound ; thrust.

Stabil'ity. Firmness, steadiness, durability ; constancy.

ANT. *Instability, unsteadiness, infirmity.*

Sta'ble. Fixed, established, permanent, constant, abiding.

ANT. *Unstable, unsteady, inconstant.*

Stag'ger. Reel, totter, waver ; amaze, astonish.

Stag'nant. Still, motionless, lifeless, torpid.

ANT. *Running, moving, animated.*

Staid'. Sedate, serious, sober, demure.

ANT. *Giddy, trifling.*

Stain'. See BLEMISH.

Stake'. Pale ; risk, hazard, venture ; wager, bet.

ANT. *Shirk, avoid.*

Stale'. Flat, insipid, old, effete ; commonplace trite.

ANT. *Fresh, tasty, new.*

Stal'wart. Sturdy, robust, strong, strapping.

ANT. *Weak, flabby.*

Stamp'. Die, mark, impression ; mould, cast, make, character.

Stand'. Continue, remain, abide; stop, halt, pause.

ANT. *Move, depart.*

Stand'ard. See CRITERION.

Starched'. Stiff, formal, precise.

ANT. *Free, easy, informal.*

Stark'. Sheer, mere, bare, naked.

Start'. Flinch, wince, shrink ; raise ; begin.

Start'le. See AFFRIGHT.

State'. Condition, plight, predicament ; commonwealth ; pomp, parade, ceremonial.

State'ly. See MAJESTIC.

Sta'tion. Situation, position ; office, post ; rank, standing.

Sta'tionary. Immovable, fixed, motionless.

ANT. *Movable.*

Staunch'. Firm, steadfast, constant, resolute.

ANT. *Infirm, unsteady, inconstant.*

Stead'fast. Fixed, established, firm, resolute, unswerving.

ANT. *Unfixed, infirm, irresolute.*

Stead'y. Fixed, firm, regular, constant, staunch.

ANT. *Unfixed, infirm, inconstant, unsteady.*

Steal'. Purloin, filch, embezzle, thieve.

Steep'. See PRECIPITOUS.

Step'. Pace, tread ; grade, degree ; action, measure, proceeding.

Ster'ile. Barren, unfruitful, unproductive.

ANT. *Fruitful, productive, fertile.*

Ster'ling. Genuine, pure, unadulterated, real.

ANT. *Counterfeit, adulterated, unreal, worthless.*

Stern'. See AUSTERE.

Stick'. Cement, attach, fasten ; adhere, cling.

ANT. *Unglue, detach ; fall off.*

Stiff'. Rigid, firm, unbending, inflexible ; pompous, starchy; uneasy, cramped.

ANT. *Lax, weak, yielding ; unceremonious, easy ; flowing.*

Sti'fle. See SMOTHER.

Stig'ma. See BLEMISH.

Still'. Silent, mute, quiet, calm, peaceful ; stagnant.

ANT. *Noisy, disturbed ; flowing, running, fresh.*

Stim'ulate. See AROUSE.

Sting'y. Mean, niggardly, parsimonious, ungenerous, shabby.

ANT. *Generous, lavish, bountiful.*

Stip'ulate. Bargain, agree, contract, engage, provide.

Stir'. Move, raise. See also FLUSTER.

Stock'. Stem, trunk ; post, pillar ; lineage, race, family ; store, provision ; funds, capital.

ANT. *Root, branch.*

Stol'id. Stupid, dull, heavy, obtuse.

ANT. *Lively, alert, quick, intelligent.*

Stoop'. Bend, incline, yield ; condescend.

ANT. *Stand up.*

Stop'. Suppress, end, terminate, close. See also HINDER.

Store'. Supply, hoard, stock, provision, reserve ; storeroom, warehouse.

ANT. *Dearth, lack.*

Storm' (*vb.*). Attack, assault ; rage, fume.

ANT. *Retreat ; be calm.*

Storm' (*n.*). Gale, tempest, hurricane, blast ; attack, assault.

ANT. *Calm ; retreat, retirement.*

Storm'y. Rough, blustering, tempestuous, wild, violent.

ANT. *Calm, mild.*

Sto'ry. Narrative, narration, recital, legend, history, tale ; untruth.

ANT. *Fact, truth.*

Stout'. Strong, lusty, robust, stalwart ; brave, manly ; obese, portly.

ANT. *Thin, lean, weak.*

Straight'. Direct, undeviating ; upright ; right, fair, just.

ANT. *Crooked, deviating ; wicked, dishonest.*

Strain'. Stretch, force, wrench ; filter.

ANT. *Relax.*

Strait'. Difficulty, predicament, hardship.

ANT. *Relief.*

Strange'. Alien, foreign ; odd, eccentric, peculiar, rare, astonishing.

ANT. *Native ; usual, ordinary, regular.*

Stran'ger. Alien, foreigner.

ANT. *Native ; friend.*

Strat'agem. Artifice, device, wile, trick, ruse.

ANT. *Honesty, fair means.*

Stray'. Wander, err, deviate, digress, roam.

ANT. *Stay, continue.*

Stream'. Current, flow, tide, drift.

Strength'. See FORCE.

Strength'en. Harden, fortify, invigorate, reinforce ; confirm, substantiate.

ANT. *Weaken, confute.*

Stren'uous. See ENERGETIC.

Stress'. Strain, force, pressure ; importance ; accent, emphasis.

ANT. *Relief.*

Stretch'. Lengthen, pull out, elongate ; reach, spread.

ANT. *Contract, draw in, shorten.*

Strict'. Exact, severe, rigorous, close, accurate.

ANT. *Inexact, gentle, inaccurate.*

Stric'ture. Criticism, censure, animadversion.

ANT. *Compliment, praise, approval, commendation.*

Strife'. Struggle, contest, dispute, quarrel, bickering.

ANT. *Peace, friendship, amity.*

Strike'. Beat, smite, knock, buffet, hit.

Stri'king. See AMAZING.

String'ent. Astringent, contracting. See also STRICT.

ANT. *Relaxing.*

Strip'. Denude, uncover, bare, divest, despoil.

ANT. *Cover, clothe.*

Strive'. Contend, contest. See also ATTEMPT.

Stroll'. Roam, rove, wander, ramble.

ANT. *Stay, walk quickly.*

Strong'. Robust, vigorous, hardy, firm, powerful; efficient, forcible.

ANT. *Weak, powerless, inefficient.*

Struct'ure. Building, construction, formation; edifice, pile, fabric.

ANT. *Destruction.*

Stub'born. Obstinate, obdurate, headstrong, intractable, unyielding.

ANT. *Yielding, tractable, docile.*

Stub'bornness. See OBDURACY.

Stu'dious. Diligent, attentive, assiduous, contemplative.

ANT. *Idle, inattentive, indifferent.*

Stun'. Stupefy; confuse, bewilder, overpower.

Stupend'ous. See AMAZING.

Stu'pid. See STOLID and STUBBORN.

Stur'dy. See STALWART.

Styl'ish. Modish, fashionable, polished, courtly.

ANT. *Unfashionable, dowdy; unrefined.*

Suav'ity. Gentleness, agreeableness, pleasantness, mildness.

ANT. *Harshness, brusqueness.*

Subdue'. Conquer, overcome, vanquish, tame, crush, subjugate.

ANT. *Yield, suffer.*

Subject'. See SUBDUE.

Sub'ject (*adj.*). Subordinate, tributary, obedient, liable, obnoxious.

ANT. *Superior, governing, immune.*

Sub'ject (*n.*). See MATTER and QUESTION.

Sub'jugate. See SUBDUE.

Sublime'. High, exalted, elevated, majestic, magnificent.

ANT. *Low, depressed, lowly.*

Submerge'. See INUNDATE.

Submiss'ion. Surrender, yielding; obedience, compliance; meekness, patience, endurance.

ANT. *Resistance, impatience.*

Submiss'ive. See DOCILE.

Submit'. Surrender, yield, comply, succumb.

ANT. *Resist, contend, disobey.*

Subord'inate. Subject, inferior, secondary, minor.

ANT *Superior, chief, employer.*

Sub'sequent. Succeeding, following, later, posterior.

ANT. *Preceding, prior, antecedent.*

Subserv'ient. Ancillary, inferior, subject, subordinate.

ANT. *Superior, leading.*

Subside'. Sink, collapse, decline; lessen, lull, abate.

ANT. *Rise; increase, heighten.*

Subsid'iary. See SUBSERVIENT.

Sub'sidy. Aid, help, assistance, tax, tribute.

Subsist'ence. Living, existence, livelihood, victuals.

ANT. *Starvation.*

Sub'stance. Being, essence, reality; pith, meaning; matter, material; wealth, means.

ANT. *Accidents, shadow, unreality; poverty.*

Substanti'al. Subsisting; actual, real; strong, solid, firm, massive.

ANT. *Unreal; weak, soft.*

Sub'stitute. Agent, deputy, representative, proxy.

ANT. *Chief, employer.*

Sub'terfuge. Evasion, excuse, quibble, shuffle, pretext.

ANT. *Confession, admission.*

Subt'le. Nice, delicate; rare, thin; crafty, artful, cunning.

ANT. *Rough, coarse; simple, guileless.*

Subvers'ion (*n.*). Overthrow, ruin, demolition, destruction.

ANT. *Reconstruction, restoration.*

Subvert' (*vb.*). Overthrow, ruin, destroy, demolish.

ANT. *Reconstruct, restore.*

Succeed'. Follow, ensue; thrive. prosper.

ANT. *Precede; fail.*

Success'. Victory, achievement; prosperity, fortune.

ANT. *Failure; ill-fortune.*

Success'ful. Victorious, fortunate, prosperous.

ANT. *Unsuccessful, beaten; poor.*

Success'ion. Order, sequence, series, chain.

ANT. *Disorder.*

Succinct'. See CONCISE.

Suc'cour. See AID.

Succumb'. See SUBMIT.

Sud'den. Unexpected, surprising; abrupt, quick, rapid; hasty.

ANT. *Expected; slow; considered.*

Suf'fer. Undergo, endure, bear, experience; allow, let, permit.

ANT. *Resist; refuse, forbid.*

Suf'fering. Endurance, pain, misery, distress, hardship.

ANT. *Relief, remedy; prosperity.*

Suffici'ency. See PLENTY.

Suf'focate. See SMOTHER.

Suggest'. Hint, allude, intimate; propose.

ANT. *Withdraw.*

Suit' (*n.*). Request, prayer, entreaty, application; courtship; prosecution, case, action; set.

ANT. *Response, favour; defence.*

Suit'able. Apt, appropriate, fitting, convenient. See also BECOMING.

ANT. *Unsuitable, unfitting, inconvenient.*

Sulk'y. See MOROSE.

Sul'len. See MOROSE.

Sul'ly. Stain, defile, tarnish, blemish, spoil.

ANT. *Wipe, clean, polish.*

Sum'. Aggregate, amount, total, whole, substance.

ANT. *Detail, item.*

Sum'mary. See ABRIDGMENT.

Sum'mary. (*adj.*). See CONCISE.

Sum'mit. Top, acme, height, apex, crown, head.

ANT. *Base, bottom, foot.*

Sum'mon. Call, bid, cite, convene.

ANT. *Dismiss, close.*

Sumpt'uous. Costly, expensive, splendid, magnificent, gorgeous.

ANT. *Cheap, inexpensive, simple, plain.*

Sun'der. See SEVER.

Sun'dry. Several, some, divers, various.

ANT. *Many, all.*

Superb'. See GORGEOUS.

Supercil'ious. See ARROGANT.

Superfic'ial. Exterior, outer; shallow, flimsy, imperfect.

ANT. *Interior, inner; deep, thorough.*

Super'fluous. Redundant, excessive; useless, needless, unnecessary.

ANT. *Few, useful, necessary.*

Superintend'. Direct, control, oversee, supervise, manage.

Supe'rior. Higher, upper, excellent ; predominant.
 ANT. *Inferior, lower, worthless ; subject.*

Super'lative. Highest, greatest, supreme.
 ANT. *Lowest, smallest, least.*

Supersede'. Annul ; oust, displace, supplant.

Supervise'. See SUPERINTEND.

Supine'. See INERT and INACTIVE.

Sup'ple. See LIMBER.

Sup'plement. Appendix, addition, continuation, postscript.

Sup'plicate. See BESEECH.

Supplica'tion. Prayer, entreaty, petition, request.
 ANT. *Command, assent.*

Supply'. Provide, minister, give, afford, yield, furnish.
 ANT. *Withhold, withdraw.*

Support' (*n.*). Prop, stay ; aid, help, assistance ; favour, patronage, influence ; sustenance, maintenance.
 ANT. *Hindrance ; opposition ; starvation, penury.*

Support' (*vb.*). Brace, prop, uphold ; aid, help, assist ; patronize, back, further ; maintain, feed.
 ANT. *Let down ; hinder, oppose, discountenance ; starve, neglect.*

Support'er. See FOLLOWER.

Suppose'. Imagine, believe, conceive, conjecture, presume, fancy, deem.
 ANT. *Know.*

Supposi'on. See CONJECTURE.

Supposititi'ous. See COUNTERFEIT.

Suppress'. See CHECK and SMOTHER.

Supreme'. Greatest, highest, superlative, predominant, sovereign, principal, chief.
 ANT. *Lowest, least.*

Sure'. See CERTAIN.

Sure'ty. Safety, security, certainty; bail, pledge, guarantee.
 ANT. *Insecurity, uncertainty.*

Sur'feit. See GLUT.

Sur'ly. See MOROSE.

Surmise'. Suspect, conjecture, presume, suppose.
 ANT. *Know, be sure.*

Surmount'. Surpass, excel. See also SUBDUE.

Surpass'. See EXCEED.

Sur'plus. Excess, overplus, remainder, residue.
 ANT. *Defect, lack.*

Surprise'. Astonish, amaze, startle.

Surpris'ing. See AMAZING.

Surrend'er. Yield. See also ABANDON.

Surreptiti'ous. See CLANDESTINE.

Surround'. See ENCIRCLE.

Survey' (*vb.*). Observe, overlook, view ; superintend ; examine, inspect.
 ANT. *Disregard, neglect.*

Sur'vey (*n.*). Prospect, sight, inspection.

Suscept'ible. Sensitive, impressionable, tender.
 ANT. *Hard, unmoved, unimpressionable.*

Suspect'. Guess, conjecture, surmise ; doubt, mistrust.
 ANT. *Know, be certain.*

Suspend'. Sling, hang ; postpone, stop, discontinue.
 ANT. *Drop, let down ; continue.*

Suspense'. Doubt, mistrust, uncertainty ; intermission, pause.
 ANT. *Certainty ; continuance.*

Suspici'on. Guess, conjecture ; distrust, doubt, jealousy.
 ANT. *Certainty, trust.*

Suspici'ous. Doubtful, questionable ; jealous, mistrusting, distrustful.
 ANT. *Certain, reliable ; trustful.*

Sustain'. See SUPPORT.

Sus'tenance. Subsistence, support, food, maintenance, livelihood.
 ANT. *Starvation, famine, poverty.*

116

Swain'. Peasant, rustic, countryman ; lover.

ANT. *Townsman, citizen.*

Swall'ow. See ABSORB and DEVOUR.

Swamp'. See MARSH.

Swarm'. Crowd, multitude, flock, horde, shoal, host.

Swarth'y. Dark, black, tawny.

ANT. *Fair, blond.*

Sway' *(vb.).* Wield, swing ; influence, bend ; govern, direct, rule.

ANT. *Obey, be subject.*

Sway' *(n.).* Rule, dominion, control, government, empire ; ascendancy.

ANT. *Subjection; inferiority,*

Swear'. See AFFIRM.

Sweet'. Saccharine, sugary ; luscious, fragrant ; delicious, charming ; gentle, mild, winning.

ANT. *Sour ; disagreeable, unpleasant, offensive, harsh, forbidding.*

Swell'. Dilate, distend, expand ; increase, augment ; grow ; heave ; enhance.

ANT. *Diminish, lessen.*

Swerve'. Diverge, deviate ; incline.

ANT. *Keep straight.*

Swift'. Quick, speedy, fast, rapid ; eager, prompt, ready ; instantaneous.

ANT. *Slow, tardy, hesitating.*

Swind'ler. Sharper, cheat, rogue, impostor.

Syb'arite. Glutton, epicure, voluptuary.

ANT. *Ascetic.*

Sy'cophant. Parasite, toady, flatterer, hanger-on.

Syll'abus. See ABRIDGMENT.

Sym'bol. Sign, emblem, figure, type.

Symbol'ical. Typical, representative, emblematic, figurative.

ANT. *Actual.*

Sym'metry. Proportion, harmony, shapeliness.

ANT. *Disproportion, ugliness.*

Sym'pathy. See COMPASSION.

Sym'ptom. Sign, indication, note, mark.

Synon'ymous. Equivalent, similar, identical, interchangeable.

ANT. *Dissimilar, contrary.*

Synops'is. See ABRIDGMENT.

Sys'tem. Body, whole ; method, plan, scheme ; rule, orderliness.

ANT. *Part ; disorder.*

Systemat'ic. Methodical, regular, orderly.

ANT. *Unmethodical, disorderly, irregular.*

T

Ta'ble. Slab, tablet, board ; fare, food ; schedule, list, catalogue.

Tac'it. Implied, implicit, understood ; silent, secret.

ANT. *Explicit, expressed, spoken.*

Tac'iturn. Silent, reserved, close, uncommunicative.

ANT. *Open, unreserved, communicative, chatty.*

Tack'le. Grasp, seize, clutch.

Tact'. Judgment, adroitness, address, ability, dexterity.

ANT. *Awkwardness, stupidity.*

Taint' *(n.).* See BLEMISH.

Taint' *(vb.).* See SOIL and TARNISH.

Tale'. S t o r y, anecdote, fable, legend ; reckoning, account.

ANT. *Fact, truth.*

Tal'ent. See ABILITY.

Talk'. See CONVERSATION.

Talk'ative. Garrulous, loquacious, chatty.

ANT. *Taciturn, silent.*

Tall'. High, lofty, eminent, towering.

ANT. *Low, short.*

Tall'y. Match, correspond, coincide.

ANT. *Clash, conflict, disagree.*

Tame'. Gentle, mild, tractable, domesticated ; dull, spiritless.

ANT. *Savage, wild ; spirited, interesting.*

Tang'ible. Tactile, palpable, material, substantial, solid, real.

ANT. *Impalpable, immaterial, unreal.*

Tant'alize. Vex, irritate, tease, provoke.

ANT. *Soothe, appease.*

Tant'amount. Equivalent, equal.

ANT. *Unequal, non-equivalent.*

Tard'y. Slow, slack, late, dilatory.

ANT. *Quick, ready, smart.*

Tarn'ish. Blemish, stain, taint, spot, sully.

ANT. *Polish, cleanse, brighten.*

Tarr'y. Remain, abide, lodge, dwell ; delay, loiter, linger.

ANT. *Depart, go ; hasten, hurry.*

Tart'. Acid, sharp, sour. See also PUNGENT.

Tart'ness. See ACERBITY.

Task'. Work, labour, toil, occupation ; undertaking ; lesson.

ANT. *Leisure.*

Taste'. Relish, savour, gusto ; refinement ; judgment, discernment.

ANT. *Inelegance, nonperception.*

Tat'tle. See BABBLE.

Taunt'. Jeer, upbraid, flout, revile, deride.

ANT. *Soothe, commend.*

Tax'. Censure, blame, accuse ; assess.

ANT. *Forgive, excuse, defend.*

Teach'. Instruct, inform, educate, preach, advise, guide, counsel.

ANT. *Learn, listen, obey.*

Teach'er. Instructor, educator, master, counsellor, guide.

ANT. *Learner, listener, pupil.*

Tear'. Sever, rend, sunder, lacerate.

ANT. *Join, repair, reunite.*

Tease'. Vex, irritate, annoy, torment, provoke.

ANT. *Please, charm.*

Te'dious. Wearisome, irksome, monotonous ; prosy. long.

ANT. *Agreeable, delightful, lively.*

Teem'ing. Pregnant, fertile, abounding, replete, swarming.

ANT. *Empty, scanty, unproductive.*

Tell'. Count, reckon, enumerate ; state, mention, relate, inform, disclose, intimate, report.

ANT. *Keep silence, withdraw.*

Temer'ity. Rashness, audacity, recklessness, foolhardiness.

ANT. *Caution, timidity.*

Temp'er (*n.*). Mood, disposition, temperament, spirit ; passion, anger.

Temp'er (*vb.*). Modify, qualify, moderate, restrain.

ANT. *Aggravate.*

Temp'erance. Self-control, moderation, soberness, chasteness.

ANT. *Intemperance, licence.*

Temp'erate. Moderate, self-controlled, chaste, calm, mild. dispassionate.

ANT. *Immoderate, uncontrolled, wild.*

Temp'est. See STORM.

Tempest'uous. See BOISTEROUS.

Temp'oral. Mundane, worldly, secular ; fleeting, transitory.

ANT. *Eternal, spiritual.*

Tempt'. See ALLURE.

118

Tenac'ity. Adhesiveness; obstinacy, stubbornness, pertinacity.

ANT. *Looseness ; inertia.*

Tend'. Guard, watch, protect, feed, nurse; incline, lean; conduce, serve.

ANT. *Neglect, desert.*

Tend'ency. Inclination, leaning; drift, bias; likelihood.

Ten'der. Weak, fragile, delicate; compassionate, sympathetic; touching, plaintive, pathetic.

ANT. *Hard, strong ; harsh, unsympathetic ; rough.*

Ten'derness. Delicacy, weakness; soreness; sympathy, kindness, pity, humanity.

ANT. *Strength, vigour ; asperity, harshness.*

Ten'et. Doctrine, belief, principle.

Ten'or. Course, manner, way; drift, purport, meaning, sense.

Term'. Bound, boundary, limit; period, season; word, name, expression.

Term'inate. Bound, limit; end, finish, conclude.

ANT. *Begin, open.*

Terrest'rial. Earthly, sublunary, worldly, mundane.

ANT. *Heavenly, celestial.*

Ter'rible. See DREADFUL.

Ter'rify. See AFFRIGHT.

Ter'ritory. Land, domain, province, country, region.

Ter'ror. See FEAR.

Terse'. See CONCISE.

Test'. Trial, proof, experiment; criterion, standard; ordeal.

ANT. *Licence, immunity.*

Test'ify. Bear witness, depose; protest. See also AFFIRM.

ANT. *Deny ; conceal.*

Test'imony. Witness, deposition, evidence, corroboration, proof, affirmation.

ANT. *Concealment, denial, contradiction.*

Test'y. See CROSS.

Text'ure. Fabric, web; make, tissue, constitution.

Thank'ful. Grateful, obliged, beholden.

ANT. *Unthankful, thankless.*

Theat'rical. Dramatic, histrionic, scenic; artificial, pompous, showy, unreal.

ANT. *Natural, ordinary, sober, real.*

Theme'. Subject, topic, text, thesis, essay.

Theoret'ical. Conjectural, speculative, hypothetical; nonpractical.

ANT. *Practical.*

The'ory. Speculation; hypothesis, conjecture, assumption; system.

ANT. *Practice ; certainty.*

The'sis. Doctrine, position; subject, t e x t ; treatise, essay.

Thick'. Close, dense, solid, compact; muddy, turbid; indistinct.

ANT. *Thin, weak ; clear ; articulate.*

Thin'. Slender, slim, lean, flimsy, fine; diluted.

ANT. *Thick, stout ; coarse ; strong.*

Think'. Deem, esteem, reckon, believe, imagine. See also COGITATE.

Thirst'y. Dry, parched; craving, longing, greedy.

ANT. *Watered, irrigated ; satisfied.*

Thought'. Notion, idea; reflection, cogitation, contemplation, opinion, view, supposition.

ANT. *Action, act, deed.*

Thought'ful. Contemplative, dreamy, reflective; considerate, attentive, careful, circumspect.

ANT. *Practical, active : inconsiderate, heedless.*

Thought'less. Heedless, careless, indifferent, giddy, rash.

ANT. *Thoughtful, careful, considerate ; serious.*

Thral'dom. See THRALL.

Thrall'. Slave, serf, vassal ; serfdom, slavery, thraldom, bondage.

ANT. *Lord, master ; freedom.*

Thrash'. Thresh ; beat, flay, bruise, drub.

Threat'. Menace, denunciation, intimidation.

ANT. *Encouragement.*

Threat'en. Menace, denounce, intimidate ; impend.

ANT. *Encourage.*

Threat'ening. Menacing, intimidating, alarming.

ANT. *Encouraging, cheering.*

Thrift'. See ECONOMY.

Thrift'y. Economical, saving, sparing, provident, prudent.

ANT. *Thriftless, uneconomical, prodigal.*

Thrive'. Prosper, flourish, grow, increase, succeed.

ANT. *Decline, waste, fail.*

Throb'. Beat, pulsate, palpitate.

ANT. *Be steady, be calm.*

Throe'. Pain, anguish, agony, spasm.

ANT. *Comfort, ease.*

Throng'. See MOB.

Throw'. Fling, hurl, cast, project.

ANT. *Catch.*

Thrust'. See PUSH.

Thwart'. Oppose, frustrate, baffle, defeat.

ANT. *Help, further, advance.*

Tide'. Ebb, flow ; current, stream, course.

Ti'dings. See NEWS.

Ti'dy. Neat, clean, trim, spruce, orderly.

ANT. *Untidy, disordered.*

Tie' (*n.*). See LINK.

Tie' (*vb.*). See LINK.

Tight'. Close, fast ; tense, stretched.

ANT. *Loose, slack.*

Till'age. Cultivation, agriculture, husbandry, farming.

ANT. *Neglect.*

Time'. Season, period, term, interval, duration ; age, era, date, period.

ANT. *Eternity.*

Time'ly. See OPPORTUNE.

Tim'id. Timorous, fearful, faint-hearted, afraid ; shy, diffident.

ANT. *Plucky, courageous, brave, confident.*

Tinge' (*n.*). Dye, stain, taint.

Tinge' (*vb.*). Dye, stain, tincture.

ANT. *Cleanse, purify.*

Tint'. Tinge, shade, hue.

Ti'ny. Little, puny, diminutive, wee.

ANT. *Large, big.*

Tip'. Top, end, extremity, point.

ANT. *Bottom, handle.*

Tip'sy. Fuddled, drunk, intoxicated, inebriated.

ANT. *Sober.*

Tire'. Weary, fatigue, harass, bore, jade.

ANT. *Rest, comfort.*

Tire'some. Arduous, exhausting ; wearisome, boring, annoying.

ANT. *Easy, delightful.*

Tiro. See NEOPHYTE.

Ti'tle. Appellation, name, designation ; right, claim.

Toil' (*n.*). Labour, work, exertion, drudgery, task.

ANT. *Rest, repose, idleness.*

Toil' (*vb.*). Labour, work, strive, drudge.

ANT. *Rest, idle.*

To'ken. Sign, symbol ; proof, evidence ; presage.

Tol'erable. Endurable, bearable ; middling, passable.

ANT. *Intolerable ; first rate.*

Tol'erate. Endure, bear, allow, permit.

ANT. *Disallow, discourage.*

Tolera'tion. Endurance ; licence, permission ; liberality.

ANT. *Disfavour, illiberality.*

Toll'. Custom, duty, tax, rate, impost.

Tomb'. Grave, sepulchre, vault, mausoleum.

Tone'. Note ; manner, character, mood, temper.

Top'. Apex, summit, head, crown.

Top'ic. Subject, theme, matter, question.

Tor'ment (*n.*). See ANGUISH.

Torment'. Pain, torture, rack, distress, plague, worry.
ANT. *Ease, comfort ; please.*

Tor'pid. Sluggish, sleepy, apathetic, lethargic, numb.
ANT. *Active, alert, strenuous.*

Torp'or. Numbness, inertness, dullness, sluggishness.
ANT. *Activity, alertness, vigour.*

Tor'rid. Parched, dry, scorched, hot, burning.
ANT. *Moist ; cool.*

Tort'uous. Twisted, winding, circuitous ; crooked, deceitful.
ANT. *Straight, direct, honest.*

Tort'ure (*n.*). See ANGUISH.

Tort'ure (*vb.*). Rack, torment, agonize, distress.
ANT. *Relieve, ease, comfort.*

To'tal. Whole, complete, entire, aggregate.
ANT. *Part, incomplete.*

To'tally. Wholly, entirely, completely, fully, quite.
ANT. *Partly, not at all.*

Tot'ter. Shake, tremble, stagger, reel, oscillate.
ANT. *Stand firm.*

Touch'. Feel, handle ; hit ; affect, move, impress ; concern.

Touch'ing. Affecting, moving, piteous, pathetic.
ANT. *Harsh, unsympathetic.*

Touch'y. Cross, peevish, petulant, irascible.
ANT. *Affable, good-tempered, calm.*

Tough'. Tenacious, strong, enduring ; difficult, hard.
ANT. *Flexible, yielding, easy.*

Tour'. See EXCURSION.

Tow'ering. High, elevated, lofty, surpassing ; extreme.
ANT. *Low, mean.*

Toy' (*n.*). See BAUBLE.

Toy' (*vb.*). Trifle, play, sport, frolic.

Trace'. Track, trail ; sketch, draw, delineate.

Track'. Trail, footprint, footstep, course, path, road.

Tract'. District, region, quarter, plot ; pamphlet, essay.
ANT. *Book, volume.*

Tract'able. See DOCILE.

Trade'. Commerce, traffic ; occupation, vocation, calling.
ANT. *Idleness.*

Trade'. Traffic, exchange, barter, sell.
ANT. *Be idle.*

Traduce'. See ASPERSE.

Traf'fic. Trade, bargain, deal, exchange, commerce.
ANT. *Idleness.*

Trag'edy. See ADVERSITY.

Trag'ic. Calamitous, fatal, shocking, sorrowful, distressing.
ANT. *Comic, cheerful.*

Train' (*n.*). Trail ; retinue, suite ; series, succession ; course, process.

Train' (*vb.*). Drag, haul ; instruct, educate, drill.
ANT. *Neglect.*

Trait'. Feature, characteristic, touch, line.

Trait'or. Betrayer, deceiver.
ANT. *Loyalist.*

Trait'orous. Treacherous, perfidious, false ; treasonable.
ANT. *Loyal, faithful.*

Tram'mel (*n.*). Fetter, clog, impediment, bond, shackle.

Tram'mel (*vb.*). Fetter, confine, impede, hinder.
ANT. *Unfetter, advance, help.*

Tranqu'il. Serene, calm, quiet, peaceful, still, composed.
ANT. *Disturbed, agitated, noisy, boisterous,*

Tranqu'illize. See ALLAY and APPEASE.

Transact'. Conduct, perform, manage, negotiate.

Transact'ion. Affair, completion, performance, management ; process.

Transcend'. Exceed, surpass, excel, eclipse, outdo.

ANT. *Fall short, be outdone.*

Transcend'ent. Exceeding, surpassing, pre-eminent, matchless.

ANT. *Inferior, worthless.*

Transfer'. Transmit, transport ; assign, convey, hand over, deliver.

ANT. *Retain, keep.*

Transfig'ure. See TRANSFORM.

Transform'. Transfigure, change, transmute, metamorphose.

Transgress'. Exceed, trespass ; break, infringe, violate, disobey, sin.

ANT. *Obey, observe, be good.*

Transgress'ion. Infringement ; sin, trespass, offence.

ANT. *Observance ; virtue, goodness.*

Trans'ient. Temporary, fleeting, passing, brief, momentary.

ANT. *Permanent, lasting, durable.*

Trans'itory. See TRANSIENT.

Translate'. Construe ; interpret. See also TRANSPORT.

Transmit'. See TRANSFER.

Transpa'rent. See CLEAR.

Trans'port (*n.*). Conveyance ; rapture, ecstasy, bliss.

ANT. *Calmness, indifference.*

Transport' (*vb.*). Convey, carry, bear ; banish ; enrapture, entrance, ravish, delight.

ANT. *Detain ; restore ; annoy.*

Trap' (*n.*). Gin, snare ; ambush, pitfall.

Trap'. Entrap, ensnare.

Trash'. Rubbish, nonsense, trumpery, stuff, twaddle.

Trav'el. Journey, wandering, tour, voyage, trip, expedition.

Trav'erse. Cross ; obstruct, thwart ; contradict, deny.

ANT. *Advance, further, support ; confirm.*

Treach'erous. See TRAITOROUS.

Treach'ery. Perfidy, disloyalty, treason.

ANT. *Loyalty, faith.*

Trea'son. See TREACHERY.

Trea'sonable. See TRAITOROUS.

Treas'ure (*n.*). Possessions, wealth, riches, store, stock.

ANT. *Trifle ; lack, scarcity.*

Treas'ure (*vb.*). Hoard, save, store ; value, esteem.

ANT. *Squander ; undervalue.*

Treat'. Use, act toward ; feast, entertain ; bargain.

Treat'ise. Essay, disquisition, tractate, dissertation.

Treat'y. See COMPACT.

Tremb'le. See QUAKE.

Tremend'ous. See DREADFUL.

Trem'ulous. Vibratory, shivering, quaking, trembling.

ANT. *Steady, firm.*

Trench'. Infringe, trespass, encroach.

ANT. *Respect, observe.*

Trench'ant. Sharp, cutting, biting, sarcastic, stinging.

ANT. *Mild, gentle, encouraging.*

Trend'. Direction, course, inclination, tendency.

Trepida'tion. Disturbance, agitation, flutter, fright, emotion.

ANT. *Calmness, tranquillity.*

Tres'pass (*vb.*). See TRANSGRESS and TRENCH.

Tres'pass (*n.*). See TRANSGRESSION.

Tri'al. Test, examination ; attempt, endeavour, essay ; temptation ; suffering, grief, hardship ; ordeal, proof.

ANT. *Success, attainment ; comfort, ease.*

Tribe'. Clan, family, race.

Tribula'tion. Trouble, distress, misery, woe, grief.

ANT. *Relief, happiness, joy.*

Trib'ute. See TOLL.

Trick'. Wile, cheat, artifice, slight, antic, freak, vagary.

ANT. *Honesty.*

Tri'fle (*n.*). See BAUBLE.

Tri'fle (*vb.*). Toy, wanton, play, dally.

ANT. *Be serious.*

Tri'fling. See PETTY.

Trim' (*adj.*). See TIDY.

Trim'. Adjust ; dock, curtail ; decorate, embellish.

ANT. *Neglect, leave alone.*

Trip' (*vb.*). Skip, hop ; fall ; stumble ; err.

ANT. *Stand ; be right.*

Trip' (*n.*). Error, blunder, stumble, mistake ; excursion, tour, jaunt.

ANT. *Truth, certainty.*

Trite'. Commonplace, stale, hackneyed, threadbare.

ANT. *New, fresh.*

Tri'umph (*n.*). Victory, achievement, conquest ; exultation, jubilation.

ANT. *Failure ; lamentation.*

Tri'umph (*vb.*). Exult ; prevail, win, succeed.

ANT. *Lament ; fail, be defeated.*

Triumph'ant. Victorious, successful ; exultant, bragging.

ANT. *Unsuccessful, beaten , lamenting.*

Triv'ial. Trifling, petty, common, ordinary, unimportant.

ANT. *Important, uncommon.*

Troop'. Crowd, company, gang, multitude.

Troub'le (*vb.*). See ANNOY.

Troub'le (*n.*). See ADVERSITY.

Troub'lesome. Annoying, vexing, vexatious, irritating ; importunate ; difficult, laborious.

ANT. *Pleasing, comforting ; easy.*

Troub'lous. Tumultuous, disturbed. See also TROUBLESOME.

ANT. *Quiet, calm.*

Tru'ant. Idle, shirking.

ANT. *Industrious, steady.*

Truce'. Armistice ; cessation, pause, intermission.

ANT. *Fighting.*

Truck'. Deal, exchange, barter.

Truck'le. Submit. See also COWER.

Truc'ulent. See FIERCE and FEROCIOUS.

True'. Real, actual, veritable ; honest, veracious, sincere ; accurate, exact ; loyal, constant.

ANT. *Untrue, unreal ; dishonest, unveracious ; false.*

Tru'ism. Platitude, commonplace.

Trump'ery (*n.*). See TRASH.

Trump'ery (*adj.*). Worthless, tawdry, trivial.

ANT. *Valuable, costly, uncommon.*

Trunk'. Stem, stalk, bole, proboscis ; box, chest.

ANT. *Root, branch.*

Trust'. See BELIEF and COMMISSION.

Trust' (*vb.*). Believe, rely on, confide in ; hope, expect.

ANT. *Disbelieve, distrust; doubt.*

Trust'y. Trustworthy, loyal, reliable ; firm, strong.

ANT. *Untrustworthy, disloyal, unreliable ; weak.*

Truth'. Reality, fact, verity ; veracity, honesty, sincerity ; exactness, accuracy.

ANT. *Fiction, unreality mendacity ; inaccuracy.*

Truth'ful. Veracious, accurate, correct, reliable, trustworthy.

ANT. *Unveracious, false, incorrect, unreliable, untrustworthy.*

Try'. See ATTEMPT and ANNOY.

Try'ing. See TROUBLESOME.

Tuft'. Bunch, knot ; crest, plume ; clump.

Tui'tion. Teaching, instruction, education, training, schooling.

ANT. *Neglect.*

Tumb'le. Drop, fall ; toss, heave ; derange, disturb.

ANT. *Stand firm ; arrange.*

Tu'mid. Swollen, distended ; pompous, bombastic, turgid.

ANT. *Contracted ; sober, modest.*

Tu'mult. See AFFRAY.

Tumult'uous. See DISORDERLY.

Tune'. Air, melody, strain ; concord.

ANT. *Discord.*

Turb'id. Thick, muddy, foul, impure.

ANT. *Clear, pure.*

Turb'ulence. Violence, agitation, tumult, rioting, mutiny.

ANT. *Tranquillity, peace, quiet.*

Turb'ulent. See DISORDERLY.

Turg'id. See TUMID.

Tur'moil. Bustle, confusion, hurry. See also AFFRAY.

ANT. *Quiet, peacefulness.*

Turn' (*n.*). Revolution, twist, bend ; change, vicissitude ; action, deed.

Turn' (*vb.*). Revolve, rotate, whirl ; bend, deviate ; alter, change, reverse ; depend on, hinge on.

ANT. *Keep still, straighten.*

Turn'coat. Deserter, renegade, recreant.

Turp'itude. Baseness, depravity, wickedness, vileness.

ANT. *Worthiness, goodness.*

Tu'telage. Guardianship, wardship, protection.

ANT. *Freedom.*

Tu'tor. Guardian ; teacher, instructor, master, preceptor.

ANT. *Pupil, scholar.*

Twig'. Spray, shoot, sprig.

ANT. *Stem, trunk.*

Twine'. Twist, entwine, embrace.

ANT. *Untwist, straighten.*

Twink'le. Glisten, scintillate, sparkle ; blink.

ANT. *Be dull, grow dim ; be still.*

Twist'. Contort, wind, writhe ; distort, wrest.

ANT. *Straighten, untwist.*

Type'. See EMBLEM.

Typ'ical. Emblematic, figurative, symbolical.

ANT. *Actual, real.*

Tyran'nical. See ARBITRARY.

Tyr'anny. Despotism, autocracy ; oppression, cruelty.

ANT. *Constitutionalism ; kindness.*

Tyr'ant. Despot, autocrat ; persecutor, oppressor.

ANT. *Constitutional sovereign ; benefactor.*

Tyr'o. See NEOPHYTE.

U

Ug'ly. Plain, unsightly, hideous, shocking, cross.

ANT. *Beautiful, lovely, attractive ; good-tempered.*

Ult'imate. See FINAL.

Umb'rage. Offence, resentment, displeasure, pique.

ANT. *Toleration, acquiescence.*

Ump'ire. See REFEREE.

Unanim'ity. Accord, concord, agreement, unity.

ANT. *Discord, disagreement.*

Unan'imous. Accordant, concordant, agreeing, harmonious.

ANT. *Discordant, disagreeing.*

Unbri'dled. Violent, uncurbed, unrestrained, licentious.

ANT. *Restrained, mild, orderly.*

Unbro'ken. Continuous, complete, entire, round ; deep, profound, sound.

ANT. *Broken, incomplete ; light.*

Uncert'ain. Ambiguous, doubtful, equivocal ; indistinct ; precarious ; dubious ; irregular ; fitful.

ANT. *Certain, undoubted ; distinct ; safe ; steady, constant.*

Unciv'il. See MOROSE and RUDE.

Unclean'. See FILTHY.

Uncom'mon. See RARE.

Uncom'promising. Stubborn, unyielding, obstinate, inflexible.

ANT. *Yielding, complaisant.*

Uncondit'ional. Unlimited, unqualified, unreserved, absolute.

ANT. *Conditional, restricted, reserved.*

Uncouth'. Strange, odd, clumsy, clownish, ungainly, awkward.

ANT. *Usual ; clever, adroit.*

Undergo'. See BEAR and ENDURE.

Understand'. Perceive, know, comprehend, discern, apprehend.

ANT. *Miss, be ignorant.*

Understand'ing. Intelligence, knowledge, perception ; intellect ; agreement.

ANT. *Misunderstanding.*

Undertake'. Attempt ; embark on, engage in, enter on ; agree, stipulate.

ANT. *Avoid ; disagree.*

Undo'. See ANNUL.

Undoubt'ed. Indisputable, incontestable, unquestionable, indubitable.

ANT *Dubitable, dubious, questionable, disputable.*

Undula'tion. Waving, ripple, fluctuation.

ANT. *Smoothness, stillness.*

Uneas'y. Restless, disturbed, discomposed, unquiet ; awkward, constrained.

ANT. *Easy, calm, comfortable ; natural.*

Une'qualled. See MATCHLESS.

Unexam'pled. See MATCHLESS.

Unfair'. Unjust, wrong.

ANT. *Just, right, fair.*

Unfit'. Unsuitable, inappropriate, unqualified.

ANT. *Fit, suitable, appropriate, qualified.*

Unfold'. Unroll, expand ; disclose, reveal, exhibit.

ANT. *Fold, roll up ; conceal.*

Unfort'unate. Unlucky, unsuccessful, ill-starred, unhappy ; calamitous.

ANT. *Fortunate, lucky, successful, happy.*

Unfound'ed. False, baseless, idle, vain, groundless.

ANT. *True, well-founded.*

Ungain'ly. See AWKWARD and UNCOUTH.

Unhap'piness. Misery, wretchedness, sorrow, misfortune, woe.

ANT. *Joy, pleasure, delight.*

Unhap'py. See MELANCHOLY.

U'niform. Unchanged, unvarying, regular, consistent, undeviating.

ANT. *Variable, irregular, inconstant.*

U'nion. See ALLIANCE.

Unique'. Sole, single, solitary, unmatched.

ANT. *Common, frequent.*

U'nison. Agreement, unanimity, concord.

ANT. *Disagreement, discord.*

Unite'. See LINK.

U'nity. Oneness. See also UNISON.

Univers'al. General, entire, total, whole ; catholic, ecumenical.

ANT. *Particular, individual.*

Unlim'ited. Boundless, infinite, absolute ; undefined.

ANT. *Limited, bounded, definite.*

Unman'ly. Effeminate, womanish ; weak, cowardly.

ANT. *Manly, strong, brave.*

Unnat'ural. Abnormal, irregular ; artificial, forced, strained.

ANT. *Normal, natural, regular.*

Unreas'onable. Irrational, preposterous, immoderate, exorbitant.
ANT. *Rational, reasonable ; cheap.*

Unroll'. See UNFOLD.

Unru'ly. Disorderly, disobedient, insubordinate, refractory, riotous.
ANT. *Orderly, obedient, quiet.*

Unset'tle. Displace, remove ; disturb, upset, disorder.
ANT. *Settle, steady, arrange.*

Unstead'y. Fickle, changeable, unstable, wavering ; reeling.
ANT. *Steady, firm, constant ; sober.*

Untruth'. See FALSEHOOD.

Unu'sual. See RARE.

Unwont'ed. See RARE.

Upbraid'. See BLAME.

Uphold'. See SUPPORT.

Up'right. Perpendicular, vertical, erect ; just, honest, straight, good.
ANT. *Horizontal ; dishonest, crooked, bad.*

Up'rightness. Honesty, virtue, integrity, rectitude.
ANT. *Dishonesty, turpitude.*

Up'roar. Clamour, noise, disturbance, turmoil.
ANT. *Quiet, peace.*

Urban'ity. Civility, politeness, courtesy, affability, suavity.
ANT. *Incivility, rudeness, harshness.*

Urge'. Push, press, drive ; incite, stimulate, instigate ; solicit.
ANT. *Pull, draw ; accede.*

Urg'ent. Instant ; important, earnest, pressing ; importunate.

ANT. *Remote ; unimportant, trivial.*

U'sage. Treatment, handling ; custom, use, practice.

Use' (*n.*). Exercise, employment ; application ; advantage, profit, avail.
ANT. *Misuse, disuse.*

Use' (*vb.*). Employ, handle, exercise, employ, apply ; accustom, habituate.

Use'ful. Profitable, advantageous, beneficial, serviceable.
ANT. *Useless, unprofitable, disadvantageous, harmful.*

Use'fulness. See UTILITY.

U'sual. Customary, wonted, habitual, ordinary, accustomed.
ANT. *Unusual, unwonted, unaccustomed, rare.*

Usurp'. Assume, appropriate.
ANT. *Resign, renounce.*

Util'ity. Usefulness, benefit, advantage, profit.
ANT. *Uselessness, harm, loss.*

Ut'most. Furthest, remotest, extreme, last, greatest.
ANT. *Least, smallest.*

Uto'pian. Ideal, imaginary, visionary, chimerical.
ANT. *Practical, real.*

Ut'ter. Complete, absolute, extreme, thorough, sheer.
ANT. *Incomplete.*

Ut'ter (*vb.*). Speak, pronounce, articulate, express ; issue.
ANT. *Be silent.*

Ut'terly. Entirely, completely, absolutely, altogether.
ANT. *Partly, not at all.*

Ut'terance. Articulation, speech, expression, elocution.
ANT. *Silence, speechlessness.*

V

Va'cant. Empty, void, unoccupied, unfilled ; thoughtless, unemployed.
ANT. *Full, occupied ; busy.*

Vacilla'tion. Hesitation, wavering, fluctuation, inconstancy.
ANT. *Decision, firmness.*

Vag'abond. Tramp, vagrant, rogue, scamp.

Vaga'ry. Fancy, freak, whim, caprice.

Va'grant (*n.*). See VAGABOND.

Va'grant (*adj.*). Wandering, roaming, nomadic, unsettled.

ANT. *Settled, homely.*

Vague'. Uncertain, indefinite, indistinct.

ANT. *Certain, definite, clear.*

Vain'. Empty, worthless, unsatisfying, useless ; conceited, inflated, ostentatious.

ANT. *Useful, effective ; simple, modest.*

Valetudina'rian. Sickly, weakly, delicate.

ANT. *Healthy, strong.*

Val'iant. Valorous, brave, heroic, gallant, redoubtable.

ANT. *Cowardly, unheroic.*

Val'id. Efficient, sound, conclusive, binding, strong.

ANT. *Ineffective, unsound, weak.*

Valid'ity. Efficiency, conclusiveness, authority, cogency.

ANT. *Inefficiency, weakness, unsoundness.*

Val'orous. See VALIANT.

Val'our. See COURAGE.

Val'uable. See COSTLY and ESTIMABLE.

Val'ue (*n.*). Worth, importance ; cost, price.

ANT. *Worthlessness, unimportance.*

Val'ue (*vb.*). Estimate, compute, appraise, esteem, treasure, prize.

ANT. *Ignore, disregard.*

Van'ish. Disappear, pass away, dissolve, fade.

ANT. *Appear.*

Van'ity. Emptiness, unreality, worthlessness ; conceit, egotism.

ANT. *Fullness, reality ; modesty.*

Vanqu'ish. See SUBDUE.

Vap'id. See INSIPID.

Va'pour. Steam, fume, exhalation, mist.

Va'riable. See CHANGEABLE.

Va'riance. Disagreement, quarrelling, dissension, strife.

ANT. *Agreement, peace.*

Varia'tion. Change, mutation, alteration ; diversity, discrepancy.

ANT. *Constancy, unchangeableness ; correctness.*

Vari'ety. Diversity, difference, multiplicity, medley.

ANT. *Uniformity.*

Va'rious. Diverse, several, sundry, manifold.

ANT. *Uniform, single.*

Va'ry. Alter, change, modify, diversify ; disagree, differ.

ANT. *Continue, be fixed.*

Vast'. See COLOSSAL and ILLIMITABLE.

Vaticina'tion. See PROPHECY.

Vaunt'. Boast, brag, triumph.

ANT. *Disclaimer.*

Ve'hemence. Force, violence, might ; passion, ardour.

ANT. *Weakness, coldness, apathy.*

Ve'hement. Violent, passionate, ardent, boisterous.

ANT. *Weak, cold, quiet.*

Veil'. Screen, hide, conceal, cover, mask, disguise, blind.

ANT. *Disclose, uncover, unveil, unmask.*

Veloc'ity. Swiftness, rapidity, celerity, speed.

ANT. *Slowness, tardiness.*

Ve'nal. Mercenary, sordid.

ANT. *Incorruptible.*

Vend'. Sell, retail, hawk.

ANT. *Buy.*

Ven'erable. Reverend, grave, sedate, sage.

ANT. *Trifling, light, foolish.*

Ven'erate. Revere, honour, reverence, adore.

ANT. *Dishonour.*

Venera'tion. Reverence, adoration, dread, awe.

ANT. *Irreverence, disrespect.*

Venge′ance. Revenge, retaliation, retribution.
ANT. *Forgiveness.*

Ve′nial. Pardonable, forgivable, excusable.
ANT. *Unpardonable, inexcusable.*

Ven′om. Poison, virus ; malice, spite, malignity.
ANT. *Antidote ; flattery, praise.*

Ven′omous. Poisonous ; malicious, spiteful, malignant.
ANT. *Harmless : benevolent.*

Ven′omousness. See VIRULENCE.

Vent′ure (*n.*). See ENTERPRISE.

Ven′ture (*vb.*). See ATTEMPT and DARE.

Ven′turesome. Daring, venturous, intrepid, enterprising, presumptuous.
ANT. *Timid, shrinking, unenterprising.*

Vera′cious. See TRUE.

Verac′ity. See TRUTH.

Verbose′. Wordy, prolix, diffuse, long-winded.
ANT. *Terse, laconic.*

Verd′ant. Green, growing, flourishing ; ignorant, raw.
ANT. *Withered, old, declining ; smart, intelligent.*

Ver′dict. Judgment, decision, finding ; answer.
ANT. *Trial.*

Verge′ (*n.*). See EDGE.

Verge′ (*vb.*). Lean, incline, slope, bend.

Ver′ify. Attest, authenticate, confirm, corroborate, substantiate.
ANT. *Disprove, discredit.*

Ver′ily. Truly, really, certainly, positively.
ANT. *Doubtfully.*

Ver′itable. Actual, true, real, genuine, certain.
ANT. *Untrue, spurious.*

Ver′ity. See TRUTH.

Vernac′ular. Native, indigenous.
ANT. *Foreign, exotic.*

Vers′atile. Clever, adaptable, expert ; changeable, unsteady.
ANT. *Awkward, one-sided.*

Versed′. Conversant, acquainted, proficient, skilled, practised.
ANT. *Ignorant, unskilled.*

Vers′ion. Rending, interpretation, translation.
ANT. *Text.*

Vert′ex. See SUMMIT.

Ver′y. True, real, actual ; same.
ANT. *False, untrue, unreal.*

Vest′. Dress, garment, robe, attire, vestment.
ANT. *Nakedness.*

Vest′ige. Footprint, footstep, trace, sign ; remainder, remnant.

Vest′ure. See VEST.

Vex′. See ANNOY.

Vexa′tion. Annoyance, irritation, chagrin, sorrow, disappointment.
ANT. *Satisfaction, pleasure.*

Vexa′tious. Annoying, harassing, irritating, disappointing, distressing.
ANT. *Satisfying, pleasing.*

Vi′brate. Swing, sway, oscillate, undulate.
ANT. *Be steady.*

Vice′. Corruption, defect, fault, blemish ; sin.
ANT. *Virtue, merit.*

Vicin′ity. See NEIGHBOURHOOD.

Vic′ious. Faulty, defective ; corrupt, depraved, immoral, sinful. See also ABANDONED.
ANT. *Perfect, incorrupt, moral.*

Vict′im. Sacrifice ; dupe, martyr, prey.
ANT. *Priest ; sharper.*

Vict′uals. Food, meat, provisions, bread, viands.
ANT. *Starvation.*

Vie′. Contend, contest, strive, compete.
ANT. *Agree, share.*

View′ (*n.*). Sight, survey, prospect, scene, vista ; picture ; design, purpose, intention ; judgment, opinion.

View' (*vb.*). Behold, see, scan, s u r v e y, contemplate ; regard.

Vig'ilant. W a k e f u l, watchful, wary, circumspect, attentive.
   ANT. *Sleepy, careless, inattentive.*

Vig'orous. See ROBUST.

Vig'our. Power, strength, force, energy ; health, robustness.
   ANT. *Weakness, sickness.*

Vile'. Worthless, despicable, wicked, sinful. See also ABJECT.
   ANT. *Worthy, laudable, virtuous.*

Vil'ify. See ASPERSE.

Vill'ain. Scoundrel, rogue, scamp, rascal, miscreant.
   ANT. *Honest fellow.*

Vill'ainous. See BASE.

Vind'icate. Defend, justify, assert, uphold.
   ANT. *Renounce, resign.*

Vindict'ive. Revengeful, unforgiving, spiteful, implacable.
   ANT. *Forgiving, kindly.*

Vi'olate. Ravish, debauch. See also TRANSGRESS.

Vi'olence. Outrage, injury. See also VEHEMENCE.

Vi'olent. See VEHEMENT.

Vir'gin (*adj.*). Chaste, pure, undefiled, maidenly ; new, fresh, untouched.
   ANT. *Sullied, unmaidenly ; old, stale, cultivated.*

Vir'ile. Manly, masculine, vigorous, nervous.
   ANT. *Feminine, unmanly, weak.*

Vir'tue. Worth, value, goodness ; strength, potency, efficacy.
   ANT. *Vice, demerit, defect.*

Vir'tuous. Blameless, honest, just, upright, meritorious.
   ANT. *Blameworthy, dishonest.*

Vir'ulence. Venomousness, poisonousness, rancour. See also ACERBITY.
   ANT. *Harmlessness.*

Vis'ible. Perceptible, discernible. See also APPARENT.
   ANT. *Invisible, imperceptible.*

Vis'ion. Sight, seeing ; apparition, delusion, ghost, phantom, spectre.

Vis'ionary. Imaginative ; romantic ; imaginary, fantastic, ideal, unreal.
   ANT. *Unimaginative, practical, real, possible.*

Vi'tal. Living ; essential, necessary, obligatory, indispensable.
   ANT. *Unessential, unimportant.*

Vit'iate. Impair, corrupt, spoil, taint, contaminate.

Vitu'perate. See ASPERSE.

Vitupera'tion. See ABUSE.

Viva'cious. Animated, brisk, lively, gay, merry.
   ANT. *Dull, depressed.*

Viv'id. Lively ; clear, bright, striking.
   ANT. *Dull, unimpressive.*

Voca'tion. Calling, profession, business, trade, occupation, mission.

Vocif'erate. Shout, bellow, roar, bawl, rant.

Vogue'. Way, fashion, usage.

Void'. Empty, vacant, hollow, unfilled ; null, invalid, nugatory.
   ANT. *Full ; valid.*

Vol'atile. Giddy, flighty. See also VIVACIOUS.

Vol'uble. Glib, fluent, loquacious, garrulous.
   ANT. *Silent ; dumb.*

Vol'ume. Book, work, tome. See also BULK.

Vol'untary. Spontaneous, free ; willing, intended.
   ANT. *Involuntary, unintended.*

Volunteer'. Offer, proffer, propose, tender.
   ANT. *Refuse, withhold.*

Vora'cious. Greedy, ravenous, insatiable.
   ANT. *Satiable.*

Vouch'. Affirm, aver, protest, warrant.
ANT. *Deny.*
Vouchsafe'. Grant, allow, concede, deign.
ANT. *Refuse.*
Vow'. Devote, swear, promise.
ANT. *Repudiate.*

Vulg'ar. General, common; ordinary; rude, coarse, illbred.
ANT. *Particular; polite, refined, well-bred.*
Vul'nerable. Weak, assailable, exposed, tender.
ANT. *Invulnerable, strong, protected.*

W

Wag'. Droll, jester, wit.
ANT. *Dullard.*
Wage' (*vb.*). Bet, lay, stake, wager.
ANT. *Take.*
Wa'ges. Hire, pay, stipend, earnings, salary.
ANT. *Work, labour, employment.*
Wag'gish. Playful, witty, droll, jocular.
ANT. *Dull, stupid.*
Wail'. Lament, bemoan ; weep, moan.
ANT. *Rejoice.*
Wait'. See LAST and REMAIN.
Waive'. See FORGO and ABANDON.
Wake'. Watch; awake; awaken, arouse, excite, provoke.
ANT. *Sleep ; allay.*
Wan'. Pale, pallid, bloodless, ashy.
ANT. *Rubicund, healthy.*
Wand'er. See RAMBLE.
Wand'ering. Rambling, roaming, strolling, discursive ; unconcentrated.
ANT. *Steady ; concentrated, attentive.*
Want' (*n.*). Lack, deficiency, defect, scarcity, need, requirement ; desire, craving ; poverty, indigence.
ANT. *Supply, abundance ; wealth, opulence.*
Want (*vb.*). Lack, require, need ; crave, desire.
ANT. *Have ; dislike.*
Want'on. Sportive, playful,

thoughtless. See also LASCIVIOUS.
ANT. *Serious.*
Ward'. Defend, guard, watch, protect ; repel.
War'fare. War, contest, strife, struggle.
Wa'riness. Caution, circumspection, watchfulness, vigilance.
ANT. *Incaution, carelessness.*
War'like. Military, martial, soldierly, bellicose.
ANT. *Unwarlike, peaceful.*
Warmth'. Glow, ardour, fervour, intensity, vehemence ; animation, cordiality.
ANT. *Coolness, unfriendliness.*
Warn'. Caution, forewarn ; admonish ; notify, inform.
ANT. *Attend, obey.*
Warn'ing. Caution, notification, admonition, notice.
ANT. *Attention, obedience.*
Warp. Bend, twist, distort, bias.
ANT. *Straighten.*
War'rant (*vb.*). Guarantee, certify, vouch, declare ; authorize.
ANT. *Forbid, disallow.*
War'rantable. Justifiable, lawful, proper, defensible.
ANT. *Unjustifiable, unlawful, improper.*
Wa'ry. See CIRCUMSPECT.
Wasp'ish. Irascible, irritable, peevish, snappish.
ANT. *Patient, calm.*
Waste' (*vb.*). Wear, diminish,

squander ; destroy, ruin, devastate ; decline ; decay.

ANT. *Increase ; save, spare ; grow, flourish.*

Waste' (*adj.*). Devastated, desolate, bare.

ANT. *Flourishing, safe, cultivated.*

Waste'. Loss, squandering ; devastation, havoc ; refuse ; desert, desolation.

ANT. *Gain ; economy ; inhabited country.*

Watch'. See WAKE.

Watch'ful. See VIGILANT and CIRCUMSPECT.

Wave' (*n.*). Billow, breaker, surge ; undulation.

Wave'. Undulate, waver ; shake, brandish.

ANT. *Hold still.*

Wa'ver. Flicker, fluctuate, vacillate.

ANT. *Keep firm.*

Way'. Road, path, passage, progress, route, course ; space, distance ; mode, manner, method, means, plan.

Way'ward. See OBSTINATE.

Weak'. See FEEBLE.

Weak'en. Enfeeble, debilitate, enervate, unnerve ; invalidate ; lower, depress.

ANT. *Strengthen ; confirm ; enliven.*

Weak'ening. Depressing, debilitating, lowering.

ANT. *Enlivening, strengthening.*

Weak'ness. Feebleness, debility ; defect, fault.

ANT. *Strength, ability ; merit.*

Weal'. See PROSPERITY.

Wealth. See AFFLUENCE.

Wealth'y. See OPULENT.

Wear'. Bear, carry ; endure, last.

Wear'iness. See FATIGUE.

Wear'isome. Fatiguing, irksome, tedious, annoying, boring, troublesome.

ANT. *Refreshing, enjoyable, restful.*

Wear'y. Fatigued, tired, exhausted, jaded.

ANT. *Refreshed, rested.*

Weave'. Twine, interlace, plait, braid.

Wed'ding. See MARRIAGE.

Ween'. Judge, suppose, imagine, fancy.

ANT. *Know, be sure.*

Weep'. Cry, shed tears, sob, lament, wail.

Weight'. Burden, load, heaviness, pressure ; influence, power ; importance, gravity, moment, consequence.

ANT. *Lightness ; unimportance, triviality.*

Weight'y. Heavy, ponderous ; grave, serious ; important, momentous.

ANT. *Light, trivial, unimportant.*

Wel'come. Agreeable, acceptable, pleasing, pleasant, grateful.

ANT. *Unwelcome, disagreeable, unpleasant.*

Wel'fare. See PROSPERITY.

Wet'. Humid, watery, damp, moist ; rainy.

ANT. *Dry.*

Wheed'le. See CAJOLE.

Whet'. Sharpen ; incite, excite, stimulate.

ANT. *Blunt ; appease, allay.*

Whim'. See CAPRICE.

Whim'sical. Freakish, eccentric, fanciful, capricious.

ANT. *Serious, staid.*

Whirl'. Spin, rotate, twirl, revolve, gyrate.

Whole' (*adj.*). Sound, entire, healthy ; unbroken, unimpaired ; total, aggregate.

ANT. *Part, incomplete, broken, injured.*

Whole' (*n.*). Sum, total, aggregate, gross.

ANT. *Part, net.*

Whole'some. Healthy, salutary, salubrious, good, sound, beneficial.

ANT. *Unwholesome, unhealthy, harmful.*

Whol'ly. Completely, entirely, utterly, altogether.

ANT. *Partly, not at all.*

Wick'ed. Evil, bad, sinful, impious, reprobate, depraved, nefarious.

ANT. *Good, pious, virtuous.*

Wick'edness. Evil, sinfulness, impiety, depravity, corruption, vice.

ANT. *Good, piety, virtue.*

Wide'. Broad, extensive, large. See also AMPLE.

ANT. *Narrow, contracted.*

Wild' (*n.*). See WILDERNESS.

Wild' (*adj.*). Untamed, savage ; rough, rude, violent ; dissipated ; fanciful.

ANT. *Tame, domesticated ; civilized, refined ; gentle.*

Wild'erness. Desert, waste, wild.

ANT. *Inhabited country.*

Wile'. Lure, snare, artifice, guile, cunning.

Wil'ful. See OBSTINATE.

Will'ing. Voluntary, spontaneous, ready ; minded, disposed.

ANT. *Unwilling, involuntary, unready, disinclined.*

Win'. Get, obtain, achieve, earn ; conquer ; attract.

ANT. *Lose, be defeated.*

Win'ning. See ATTRACTIVE.

Wis'dom. Knowledge, learning ; sagacity, prudence, sense, intelligence.

ANT. *Folly, ignorance, imprudence.*

Wise'. Sensible, sage, judicious, prudent, sagacious ; learned ; advisable, reasonable.

ANT. *Foolish, senseless, imprudent ; unadvisable.*

Wish'. Desire, crave, covet, long for.

ANT. *Be content, be satisfied.*

Wist'ful. Pensive, thoughtful, earnest, eager.

ANT. *Cheerful, happy.*

Wit'. Mind, intelligence, intellect, understanding ; pleasantry.

ANT. *Ignorance, stupidity.*

Withdraw'. Remove, retire, retract, recall, revoke.

ANT. *Advance, give.*

Withhold'. Retain, refuse, reserve, forbear.

ANT. *Give, offer.*

Withstand'. See OPPOSE.

Wit'ness (*n.*). Evidence, testimony ; eye-witness, spectator ; deponent.

ANT. *Disproof.*

Wit'ness (*vb.*). Testify, give evidence, attest ; observe, see.

ANT. *Disprove ; miss.*

Wiz'ard. Conjurer, magician, sorcerer.

Woe'. See ADVERSITY.

Woe'ful. Sad, sorrowful, calamitous, lamentable ; paltry.

ANT. *Cheerful, cheering ; excellent.*

Wond'er. Astonishment, surprise, amazement ; marvel, prodigy.

ANT. *Calmness, imperturbability.*

Wond'erful. Astonishing, amazing, marvellous, prodigious, miraculous.

ANT. *Ordinary, commonplace.*

Wond'rous. See WONDERFUL.

Wont'ed. Customary, accustomed, usual, habitual.

ANT. *Unwonted, unusual, unaccustomed, novel.*

Word'. Term, expression, vocable ; tidings, account ; promise ; command, order.

Word'y. See VERBOSE.

Work' (*n.*). Labour, toil, drudgery ; employment, business ; production, manufacture ; book.

ANT. *Idleness, rest, ease.*

Work' (*vb.*). Toil, labour, drudge, strive ; perform, effect, accomplish.

ANT. *Rest, idle, fail.*

Work'man. Worker, labourer, operative, artificer, mechanic, craftsman.

ANT. *Idler, employer.*

Work'manship. Handiwork, artistry.

World'ly. See EARTHLY.

Wor'ry. See ANNOY.

Wor'ship (*n.*). Honour, eminence, respect. See also ADORATION.

ANT. *Disrespect.*

Wor'ship (*vb.*). Honour, respect, revere, reverence ; adore.

ANT. *Despise, contemn.*

Worth' Desert, merit, excellence, goodness, virtue ; value, price, cost.

ANT. *Demerit ; badness.*

Worth'less. Useless, valueless, paltry, frivolous ; depraved, base, vile.

ANT. *Useful, valuable, important ; worthy.*

Worth'y. Deserving, meritorious, laudable, commendable, valuable, estimable, virtuous. See WORTHLESS.

Wrang'le. Squabble, dispute, altercation, contest, brawl.

ANT. *Be friends, agree.*

Wrath'. See ANGER.

Wrath'ful. Angry, irate, incensed, furious, indignant.

ANT. *Gentle, calm.*

Wreck' (*n.*). Perdition, ruin, destruction.

ANT. *Construction, restoration.*

Wreck' (*vb.*). Ruin, destroy ; founder, strand.

ANT. *Construct, restore; float.*

Wrench'. See WRING.

Wrest'. See WRING.

Wrest'le. Struggle, contest, strive.

ANT. *Give in.*

Wretch'. Outcast, pauper ; villain, scoundrel, miscreant, knave.

ANT. *Rich man ; good man.*

Wretch ed. Unfortunate, unhappy, sad, forlorn, depressed, miserable ; vile, worthless, contemptible.

ANT. *Fortunate, happy, glad ; worthy, excellent.*

Wretch'edness. Misery, sorrow, grief, affliction, destitution.

ANT. *Joy, happiness, good fortune.*

Wring'. Twist, torture ; strain, squeeze ; force, extort.

Wrink'le. Fold, plait, crease, corrugation.

ANT. *Smooth surface.*

Wri'ter. Scribe, penman, clerk, author, composer.

Writhe'. Twist, distort, contort, wrest ; wriggle.

ANT. *Straighten.*

Wrong' (*n.*). Iniquity, injustice, unfairness ; sin, trespass ; grievance.

ANT. *Right, justice, goodness.*

Wrong' (*adj.*). Injurious, immoral, iniquitous ; erroneous, incorrect, mistaken ; unfit, improper.

ANT. *Right, fair, moral ; correct ; suitable.*

Wrong'ful. Unjust, unrighteous, unfair, dishonest.

ANT. *Just, righteous, honest.*

Wroth'. See WRATHFUL.

Wry'. Contorted, twisted, crooked, awry.

ANT. *Straight.*

Y

Yearn'. Covet, crave, long for, hanker.

ANT. *Be content, be satisfied.*

Yell'. Shriek, scream, bawl.

ANT. *Be silent.*

Yet'. Besides, notwithstanding, however, still, nevertheless ; hitherto.

Yield'. Give in, concede, relinquish, resign, forgo ; bear, produce, furnish. [*refuse.*

ANT. *Resist, fight, withhold.*

Yield'ing. Submissive, compliant ; pliant, supple.

ANT. *Unsubmissive, stubborn ; stiff, unyielding.*

Yoke'. Link; bondage, slavery, oppression, servitude.
　ANT. *Freedom, liberty.*

Yoke (*vb.*). Join, couple, associate ; harness.
　ANT. *Unyoke, disunite.*

Youth'. Juvenility, adolescence, minority ; boy, lad, stripling.
　ANT. *Age, senility, man.*

Youth'ful.　Juvenile, young, adolescent, puerile.
　ANT. *Old, aged.*

Z

Zeal'.　Passion, earnestness, eagerness, fervour, energy, enthusiasm.
　ANT.　*Apathy, weakness, indifference.*

Zeal'ot.　Enthusiast, bigot, fanatic.
　ANT. *Trifler, sceptic.*

Zeal'ous. Enthusiastic, fervent, eager, energetic, strenuous.

　ANT. *Cold, unimpassioned, weak.*

Zen'ith. Top, apex, summit.
　ANT. *Nadir, base.*

Zest'.　Flavour, gusto, enjoyment, relish, pleasure.
　ANT. *Distaste, dislike.*

Zone'.　Belt, girdle, cincture ; circuit ; clime, region.

MADE IN GREAT BRITAIN AT THE PITMAN PRESS, BATH
C7—(C.6036)

PUBLISHED BY PITMAN

Standard English
Structure and Style.

By EDWARD H. GROUT, B.Sc., A.C.I.I., F.R.Econ.S.

An authoritative and practical guide to the whole subject of the English language, its grammar and use in literature and speech.

Demy 8vo, cloth gilt, 580 pp. **7s. 6d.** net.

Self-Expression in English

By JOHN BENNETT.

A course of practical instruction, with exercises, for all who wish to perfect their knowledge of English.

Crown 8vo, cloth, 78 pp. **2s.**

Short Story Writing and Free-Lance Journalism

By SYDNEY A. MOSELEY.

An illuminating guide for all who wish to write short stories that will sell.

Demy 8vo, cloth gilt, 241 pp. **7s. 6d.** net. Third Edition.

Books : An Introduction to Reading

By WRIGHT WATTS MILLER, B.A., M.Ed., Manchester.

This guide to leisure reading shows how the full beauty and purpose of the world's greatest writings can be readily appreciated.

Large crown 8vo, cloth, 130 pp. **5s.** net.

Punctuation as a Means of Expression
Its Theory and Practice.

By A. E. LOVELL, M.A.

Thought-Expression—Self-expression—Logical and Emotional Meaning—Punctuation in its Meaning and Scope—Aesthetics of Punctuation—Paragraph and Period—Variation from Direct Statement.

In crown 8vo, cloth, 80 pp. **1s.** net.

London : Sir Isaac Pitman & Sons, Ltd Parker Street, Kingsway, W.C.2

PUBLISHED BY PITMAN

Twenty-Four Lessons in Elocution

By JAMES BERNARD.

Contains twenty-four lessons transcribed as actually delivered, dealing with breath control, voice development, analysis of speech sounds, etc. With many quotations from English literature for illustration and practice.

Demy 8vo, cloth gilt, 174 pp. 5s. net.

How to Speak in Public

By C. F. CARR, *Assistant Manager, Southern Newspapers, Ltd.,* and F. E. STEVENS, *Fellow of the Institute of Journalists.* With a Foreword by the late T. P. O'CONNOR.

A book for political speakers, public speakers, debating society members, social speakers, and others.

In crown 8vo, cloth, 128 pp. 3s. 6d. net. Second Edition.

Working the Mind

By JOHN STEEKSMA.

A complete and practical course in thought, mastery, and development. The book has been compiled after a long experience of mental control and creative thinking, and gives by means of the simplest explanations, an all-round grip of thought development methods, and of the mental and material benefits to which organized thought invariably leads.

In demy 8vo, cloth, 156 pp. 5s. net.

An Alphabet of Attributes

By HAROLD DOWNS, with Forewords by H. A. VACHELL and JAMES HYNES.

This is a thought-inspired and thought-inspiring series of essays on twenty-six aspects of human nature, beginning with Adaptability and ending with Zeal. It includes, besides the author's own clear comments, occasional extracts from the works of great writers, which will cause the reader to think and reflect more deeply on his own philosophy of life.

In crown 8vo, cloth gilt, 216 pp. 3s. 6d. net.

London: Sir Isaac Pitman & Sons, Ltd. Parker Street, Kingsway, W.C.2